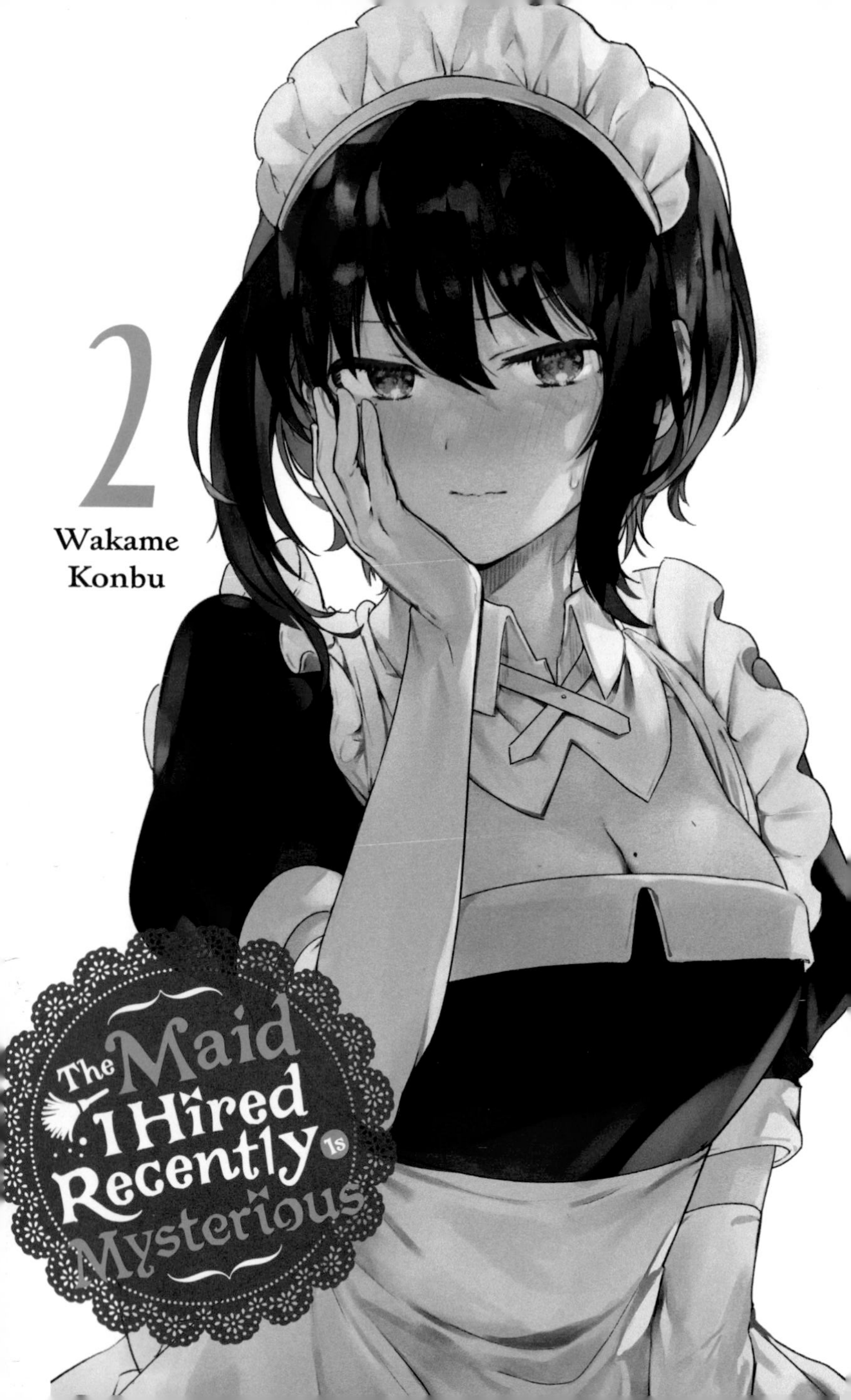
2
Wakame Konbu
The Maid I Hired Recently Is Mysterious

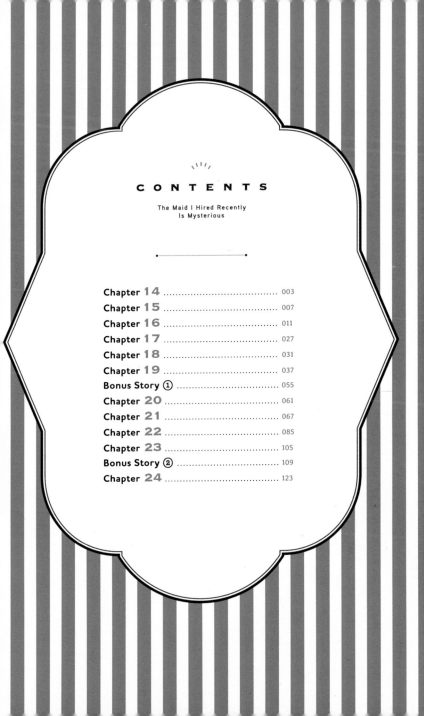

CONTENTS

The Maid I Hired Recently
Is Mysterious

Chapter 14 003
Chapter 15 007
Chapter 16 011
Chapter 17 027
Chapter 18 031
Chapter 19 037
Bonus Story ① 055
Chapter 20 061
Chapter 21 067
Chapter 22 085
Chapter 23 105
Bonus Story ② 109
Chapter 24 123

CHAPTER 14

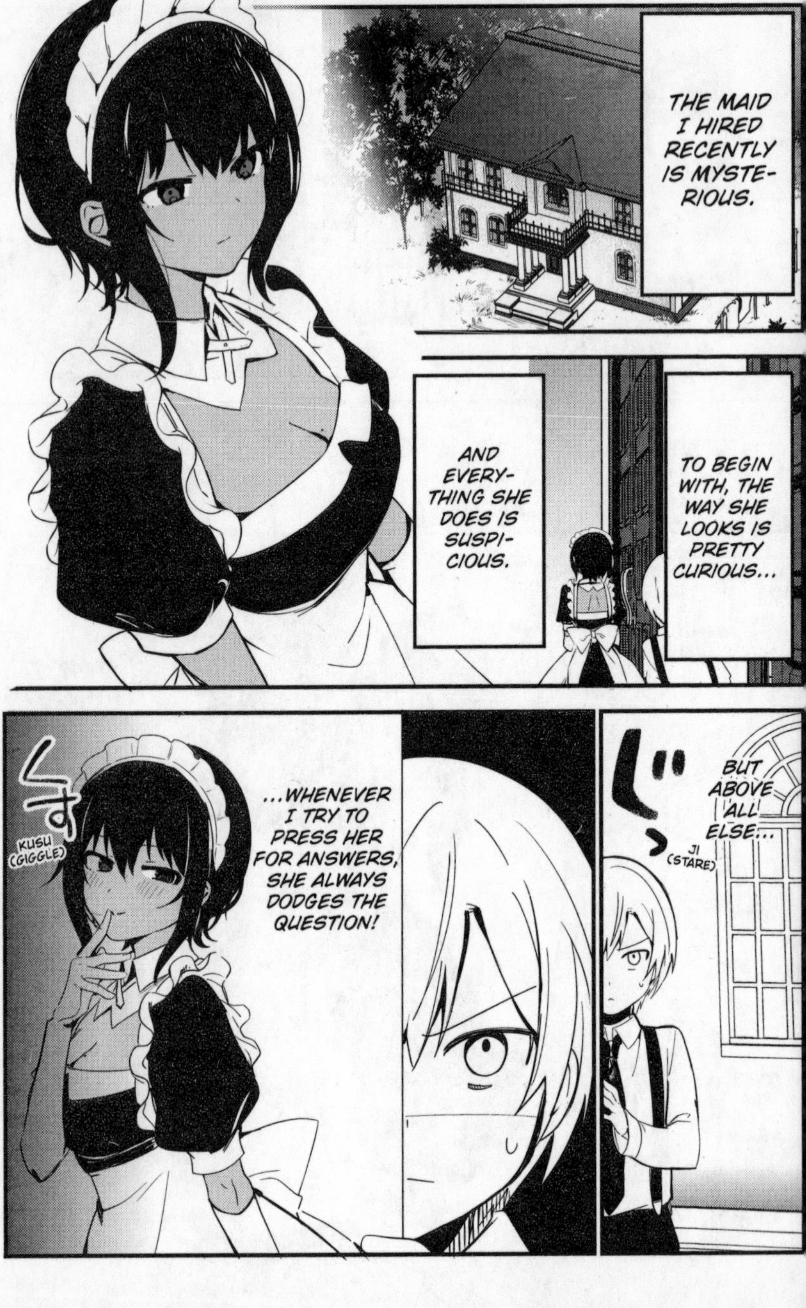
THE MAID I HIRED RECENTLY IS MYSTERIOUS.
TO BEGIN WITH, THE WAY SHE LOOKS IS PRETTY CURIOUS...
AND EVERYTHING SHE DOES IS SUSPICIOUS.
じ
JI (STARE)
BUT ABOVE ALL ELSE...
...WHENEVER I TRY TO PRESS HER FOR ANSWERS, SHE ALWAYS DODGES THE QUESTION!
くす
KUSU (GIGGLE)

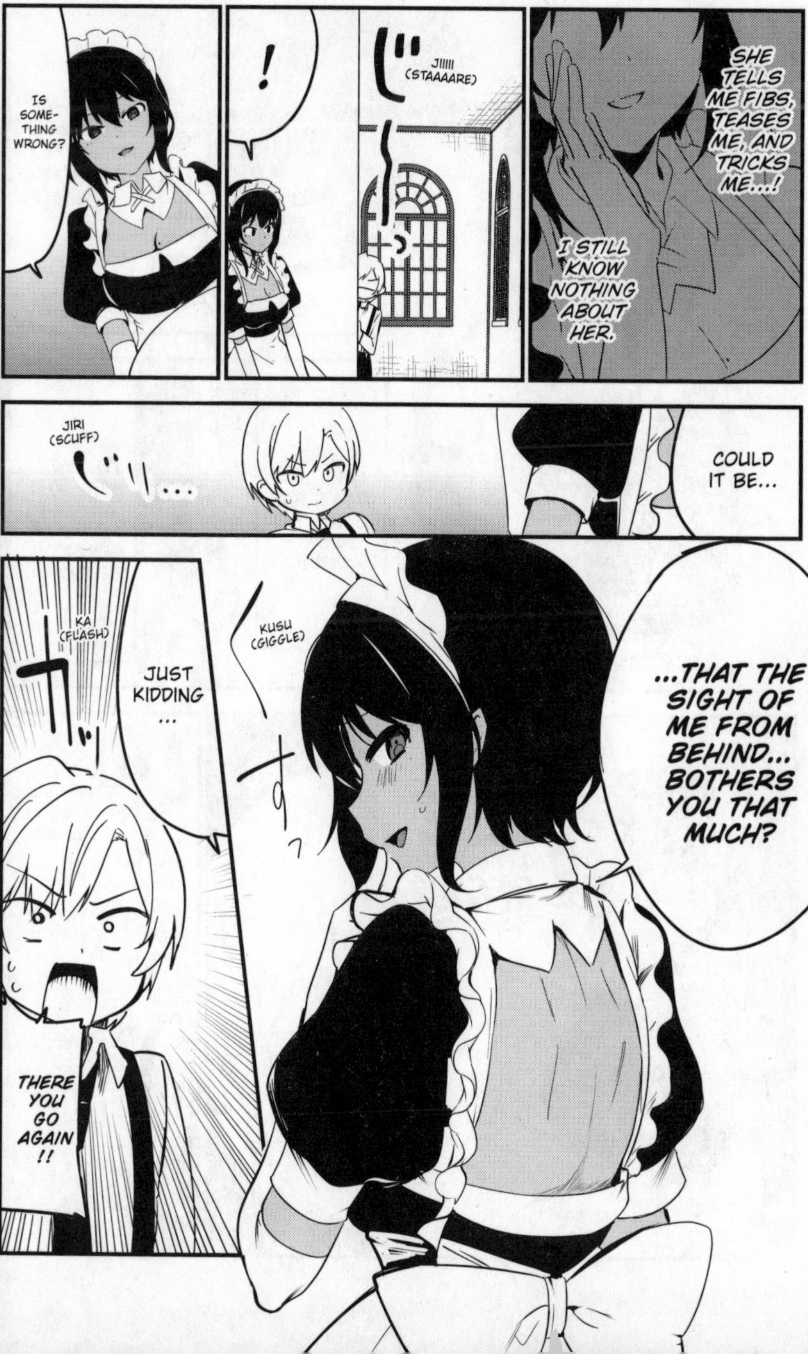
SHE TELLS ME FIBS, TEASES ME, AND TRICKS ME...!
I STILL KNOW NOTHING ABOUT HER.
JIIIII (STAAAARE)
!
IS SOMETHING WRONG?
COULD IT BE...
JIRI (SCUFF)
...THAT THE SIGHT OF ME FROM BEHIND... BOTHERS YOU THAT MUCH?
KUSU (GIGGLE)
JUST KIDDING...
KA (FLASH)
THERE YOU GO AGAIN!!

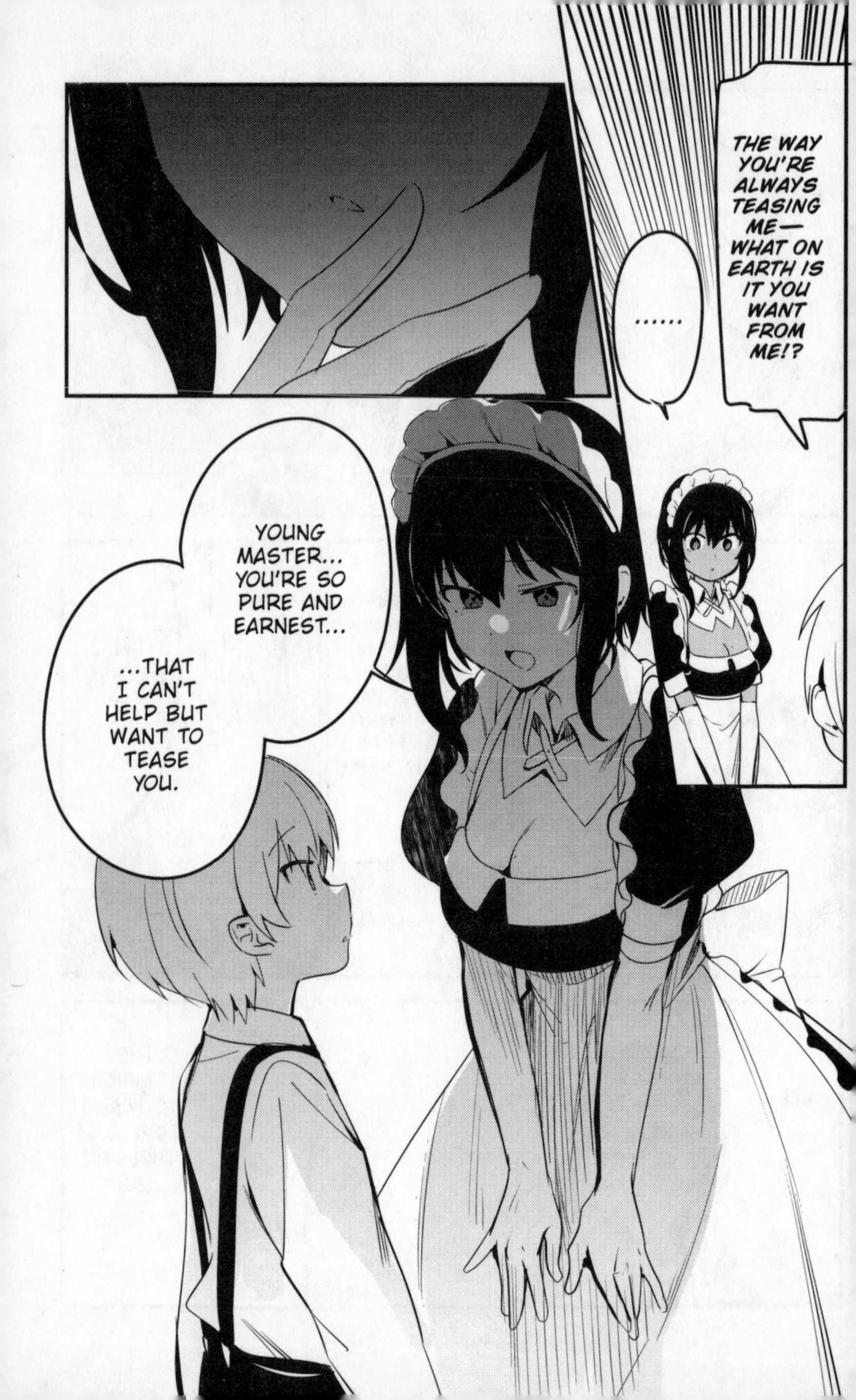
THE WAY YOU'RE ALWAYS TEASING ME— WHAT ON EARTH IS IT YOU WANT FROM ME!?
......
YOUNG MASTER... YOU'RE SO PURE AND EARNEST...
...THAT I CAN'T HELP BUT WANT TO TEASE YOU.

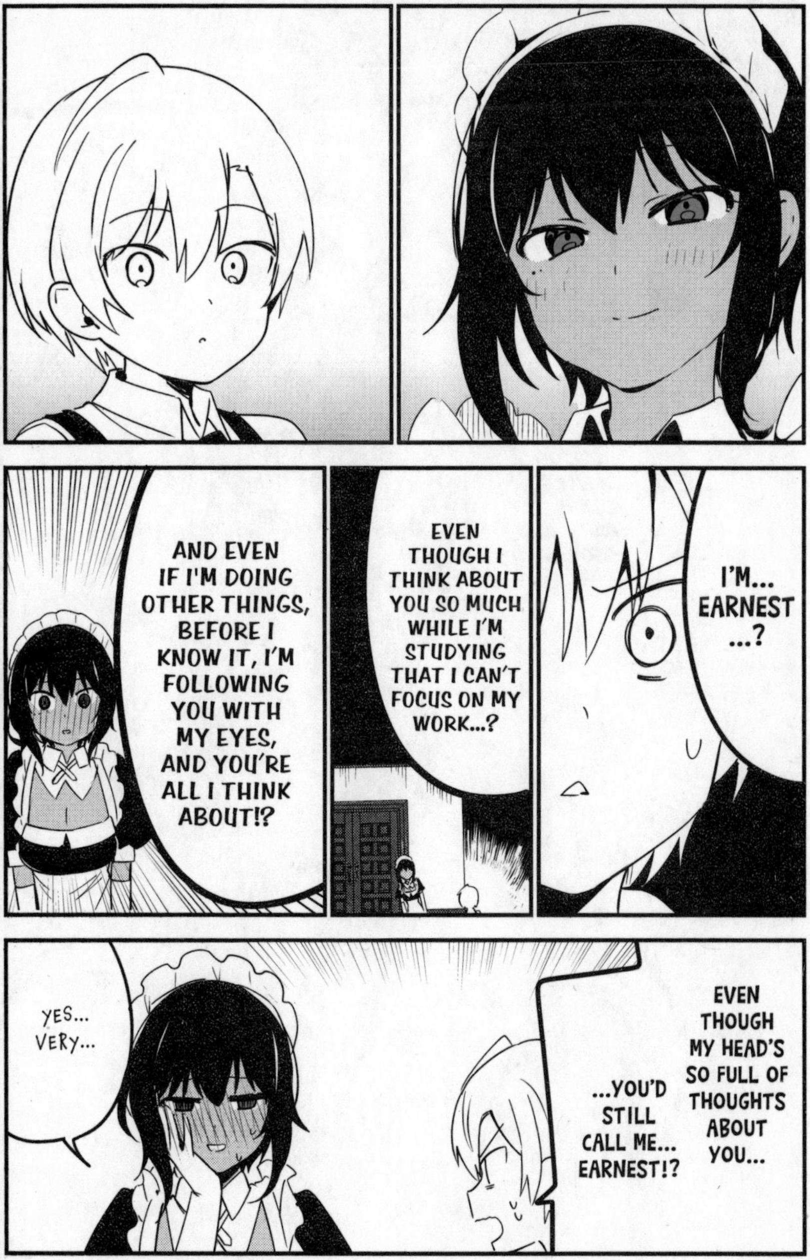
I'M... EARNEST ...?
EVEN THOUGH I THINK ABOUT YOU SO MUCH WHILE I'M STUDYING THAT I CAN'T FOCUS ON MY WORK...?
AND EVEN IF I'M DOING OTHER THINGS, BEFORE I KNOW IT, I'M FOLLOWING YOU WITH MY EYES, AND YOU'RE ALL I THINK ABOUT!?
EVEN THOUGH MY HEAD'S SO FULL OF THOUGHTS ABOUT YOU...
...YOU'D STILL CALL ME... EARNEST!?
YES... VERY...

CHAPTER 15

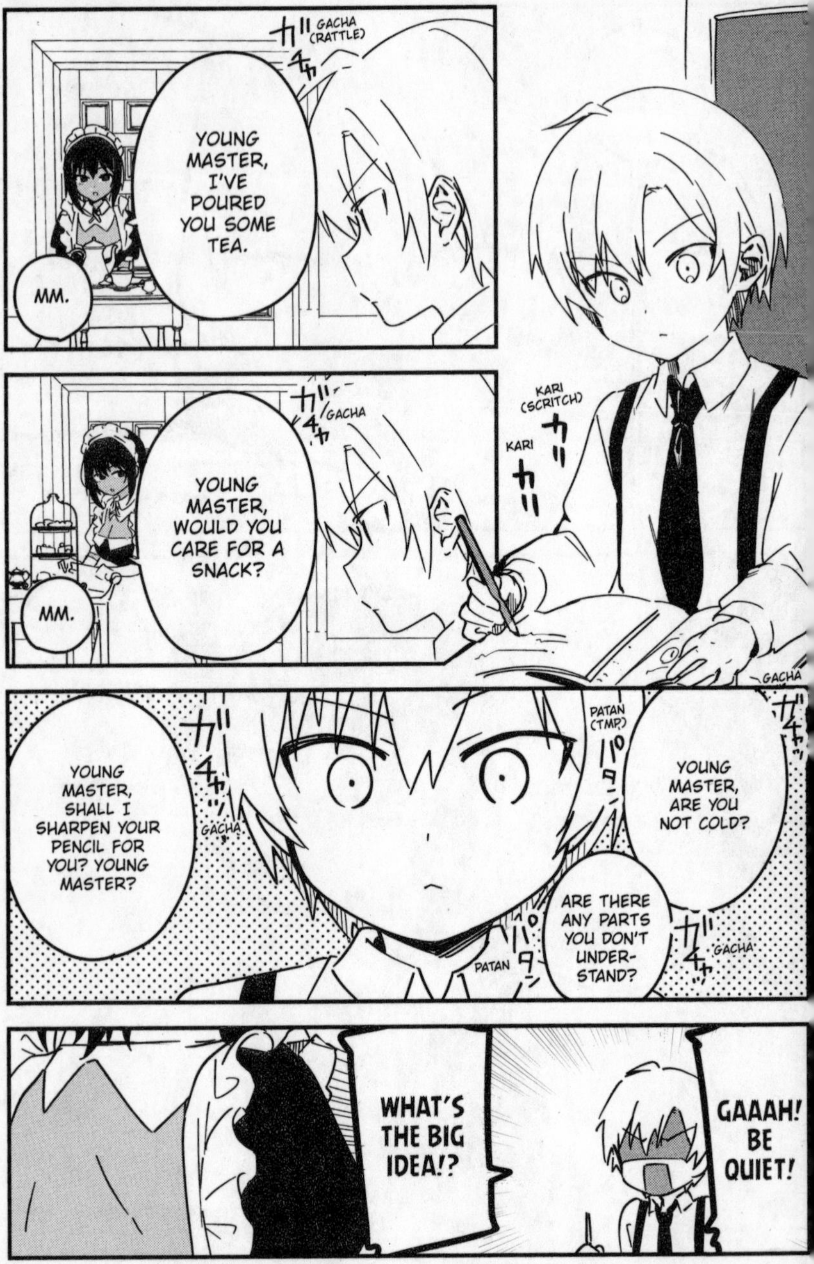
KARI (SCRITCH)
KARI
GACHA (RATTLE)
YOUNG MASTER, I'VE POURED YOU SOME TEA.
MM.
GACHA
YOUNG MASTER, WOULD YOU CARE FOR A SNACK?
MM.
GACHA
YOUNG MASTER, ARE YOU NOT COLD?
PATAN (TMP)
ARE THERE ANY PARTS YOU DON'T UNDER-STAND?
GACHA
PATAN
GACHA
YOUNG MASTER, SHALL I SHARPEN YOUR PENCIL FOR YOU? YOUNG MASTER?
GAAAH! BE QUIET!
WHAT'S THE BIG IDEA!?

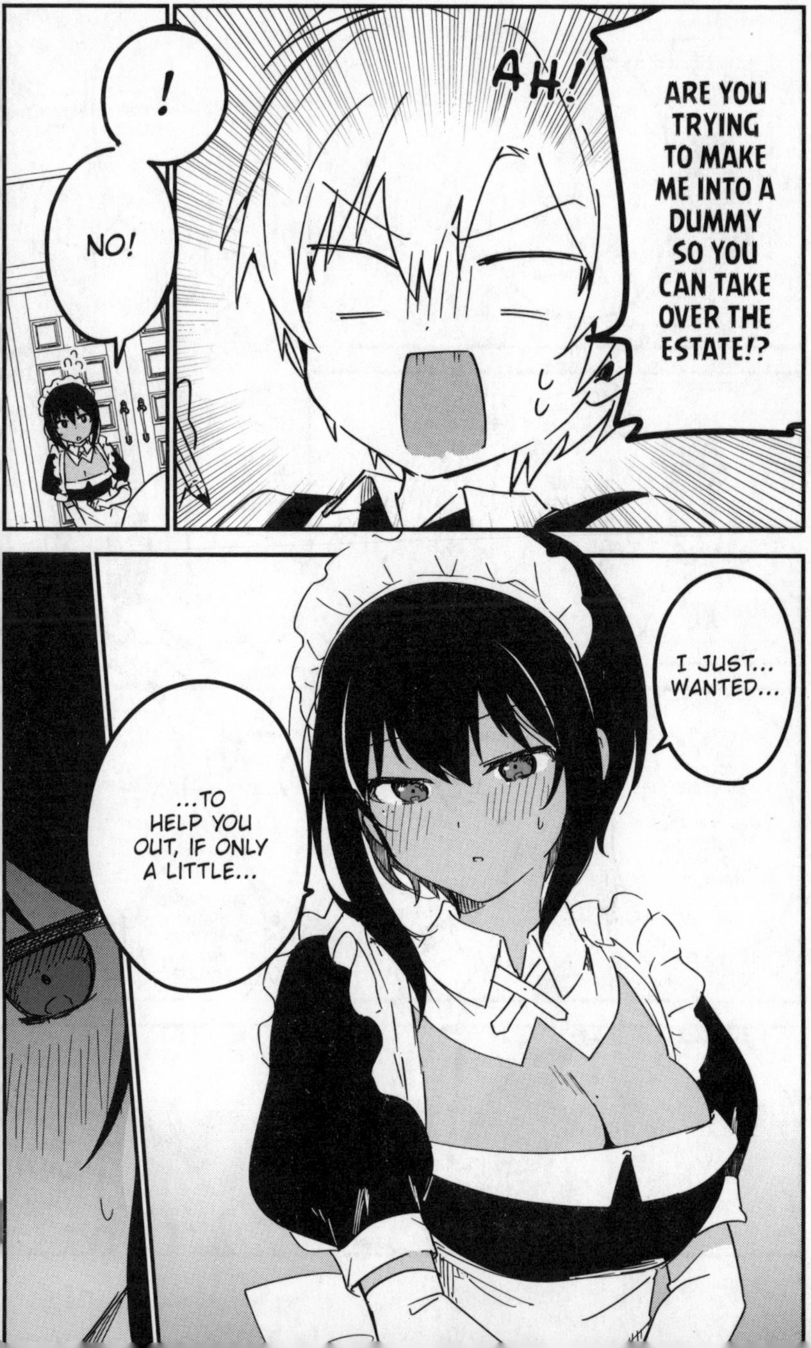
AH!
ARE YOU TRYING TO MAKE ME INTO A DUMMY SO YOU CAN TAKE OVER THE ESTATE!?
!
NO!
I JUST... WANTED...
...TO HELP YOU OUT, IF ONLY A LITTLE...

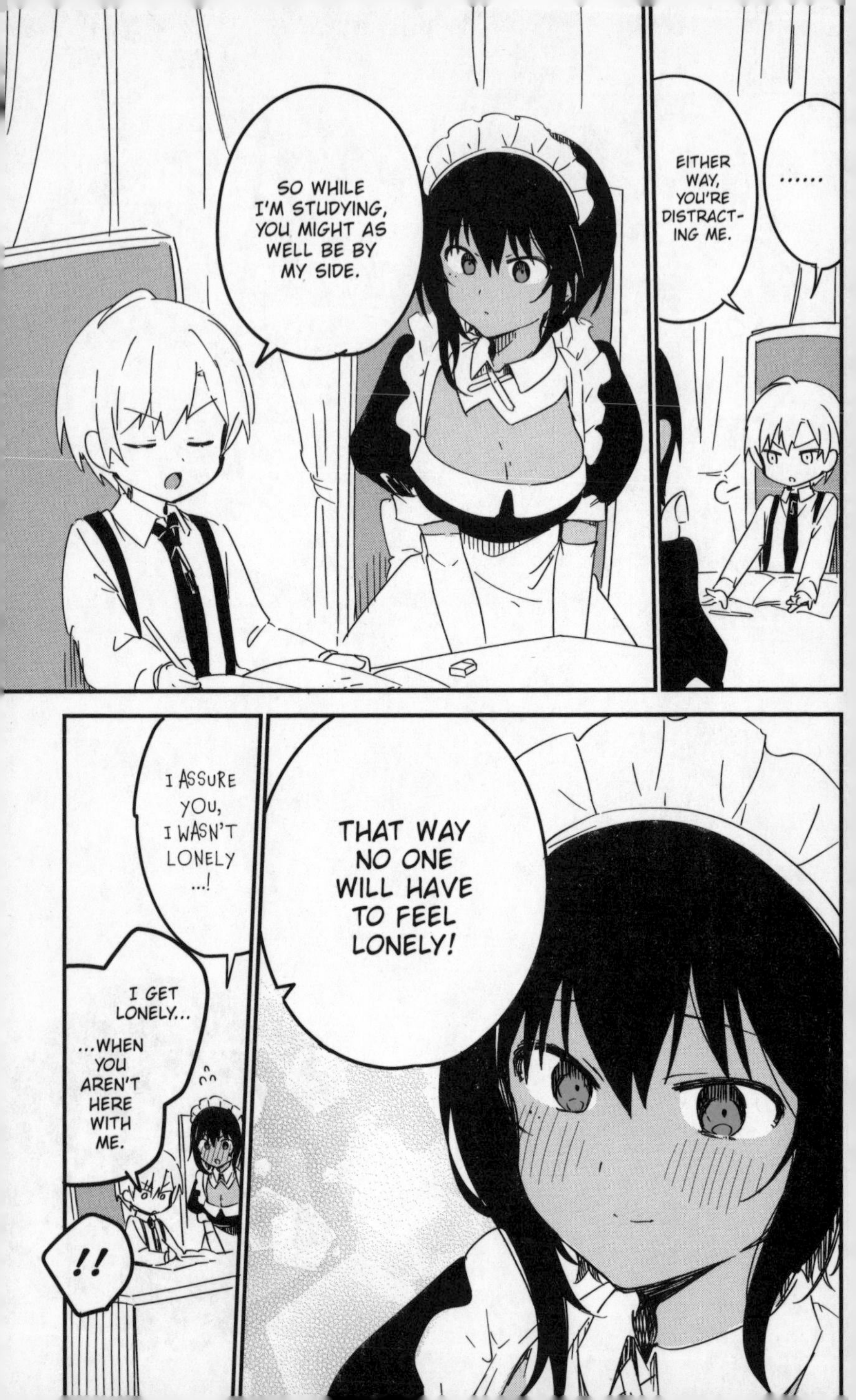
......
EITHER WAY, YOU'RE DISTRACTING ME.
SO WHILE I'M STUDYING, YOU MIGHT AS WELL BE BY MY SIDE.
THAT WAY NO ONE WILL HAVE TO FEEL LONELY!
I ASSURE YOU, I WASN'T LONELY ...!
I GET LONELY...
...WHEN YOU AREN'T HERE WITH ME.
!!

The Maid I Hired Recently Is Mysterious

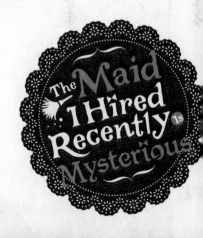

CHAPTER 16

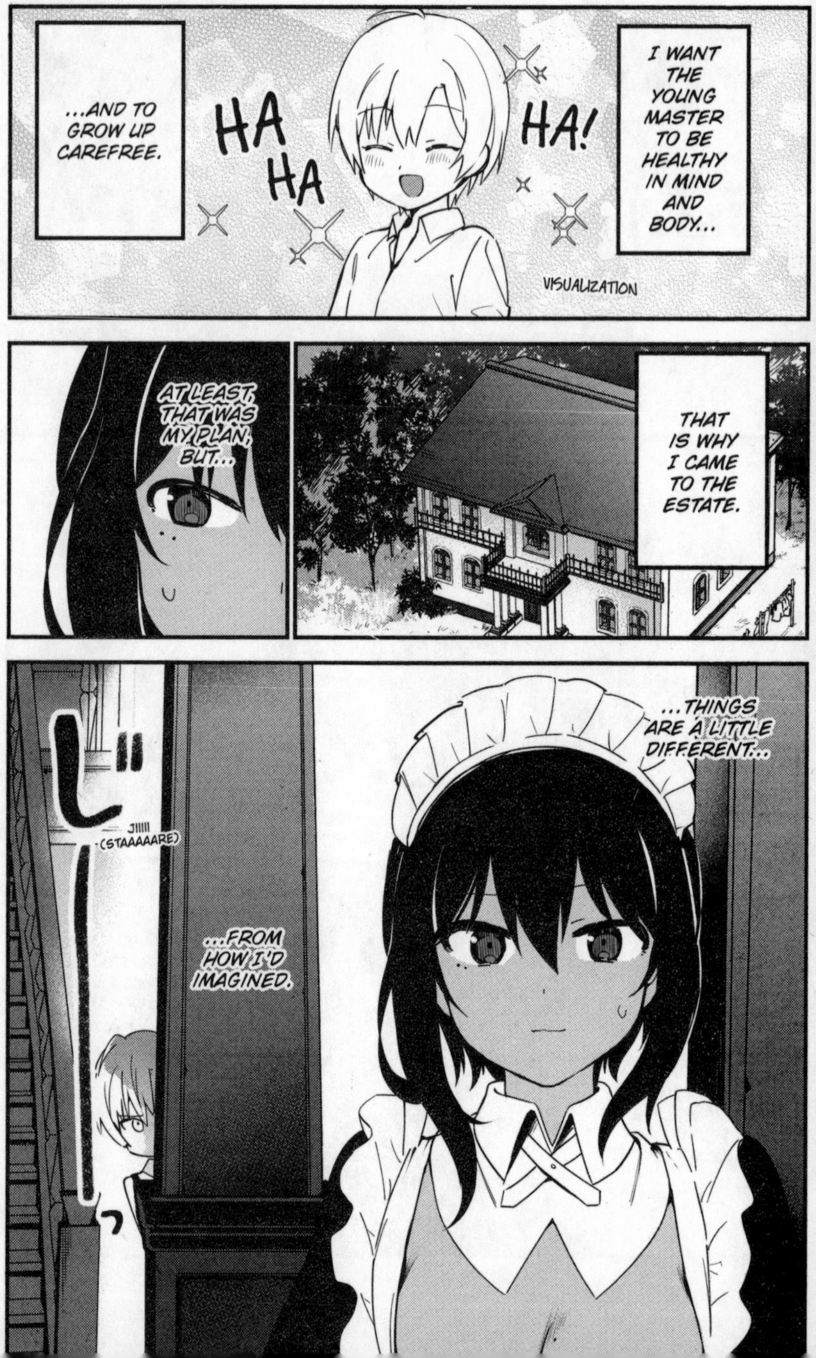
I WANT THE YOUNG MASTER TO BE HEALTHY IN MIND AND BODY...
HA HA HA!
...AND TO GROW UP CAREFREE.
VISUALIZATION
THAT IS WHY I CAME TO THE ESTATE.
AT LEAST, THAT WAS MY PLAN, BUT...
...THINGS ARE A LITTLE DIFFERENT...
...FROM HOW I'D IMAGINED.
じーっ
JIIIII (STAAAAARE)

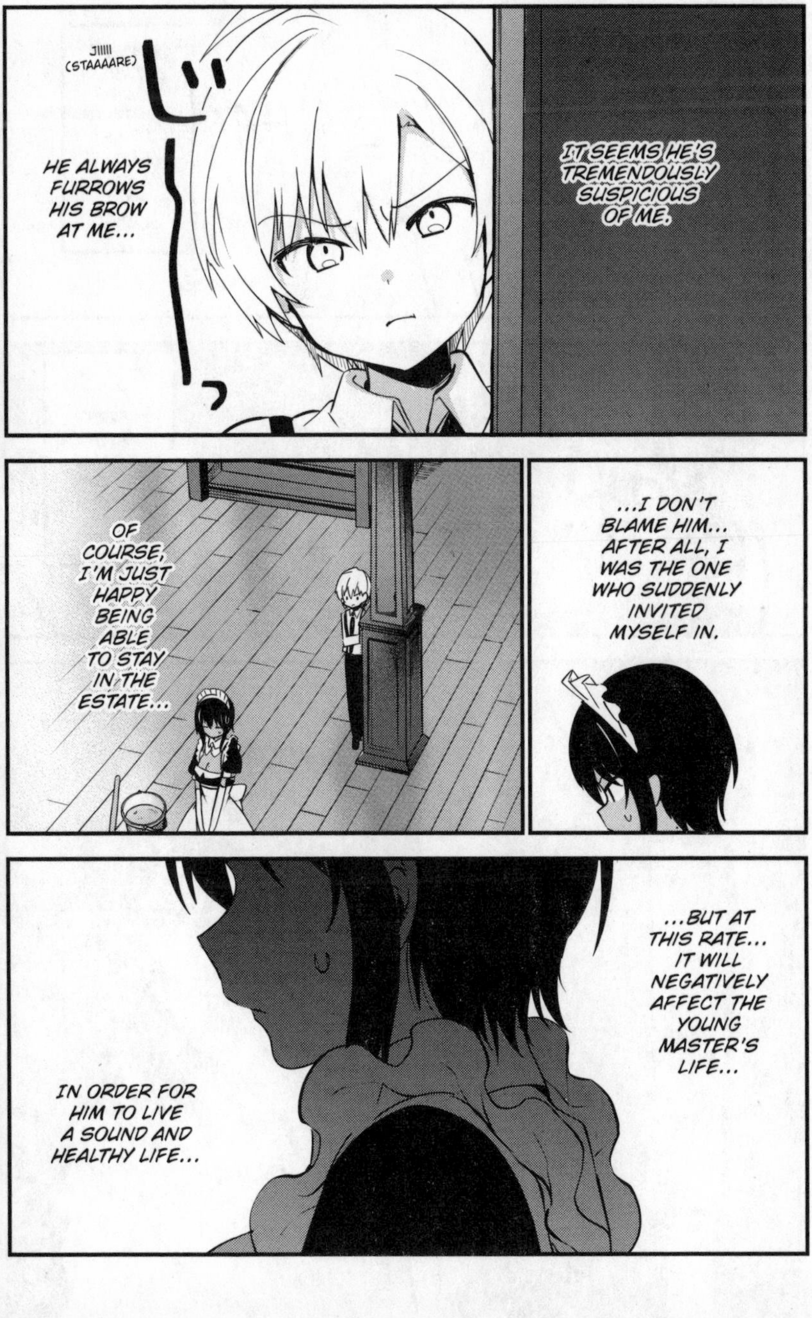
JIIIII (STAAAARE)
HE ALWAYS FURROWS HIS BROW AT ME...
IT SEEMS HE'S TREMENDOUSLY SUSPICIOUS OF ME.
...I DON'T BLAME HIM... AFTER ALL, I WAS THE ONE WHO SUDDENLY INVITED MYSELF IN.
OF COURSE, I'M JUST HAPPY BEING ABLE TO STAY IN THE ESTATE...
...BUT AT THIS RATE... IT WILL NEGATIVELY AFFECT THE YOUNG MASTER'S LIFE...
IN ORDER FOR HIM TO LIVE A SOUND AND HEALTHY LIFE...

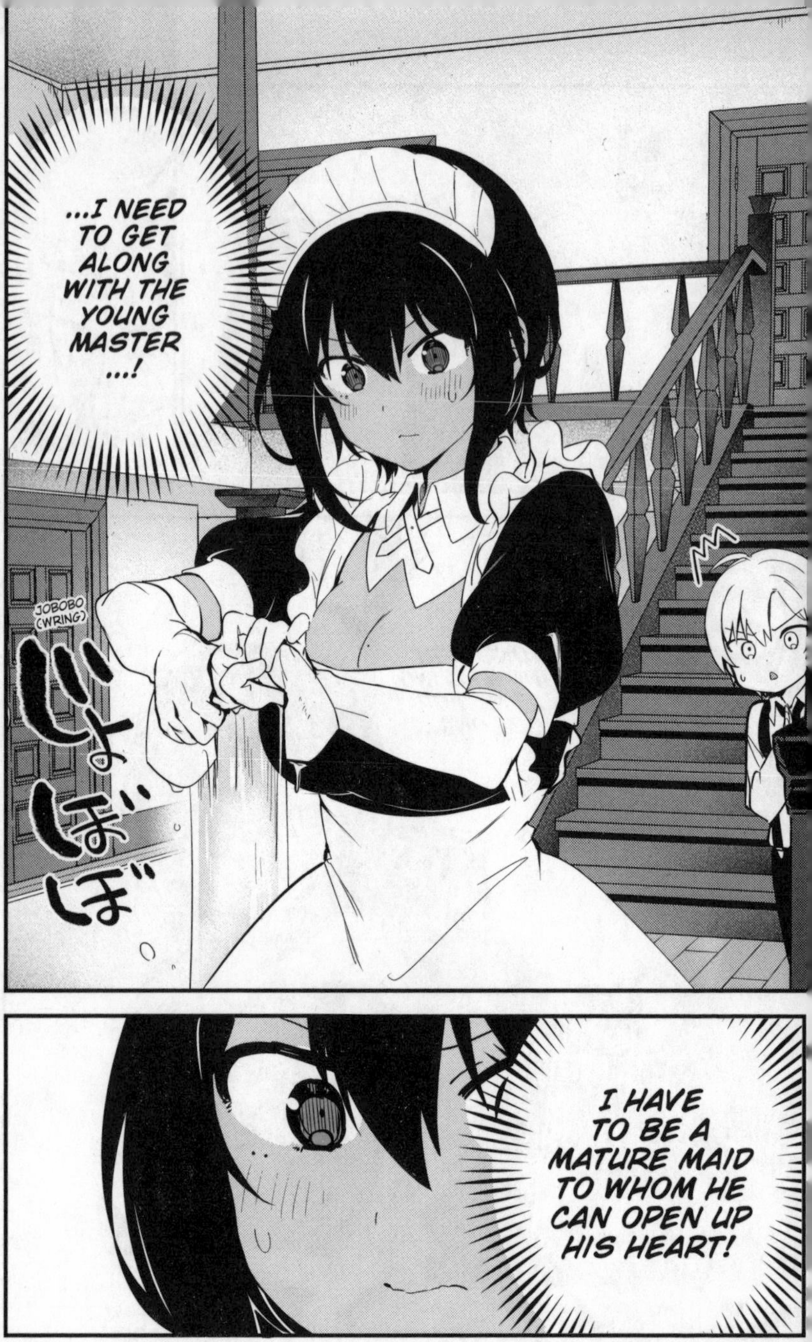
...I NEED TO GET ALONG WITH THE YOUNG MASTER ...!
JOBOBO (WRING)
じょぼぼぼ
I HAVE TO BE A MATURE MAID TO WHOM HE CAN OPEN UP HIS HEART!

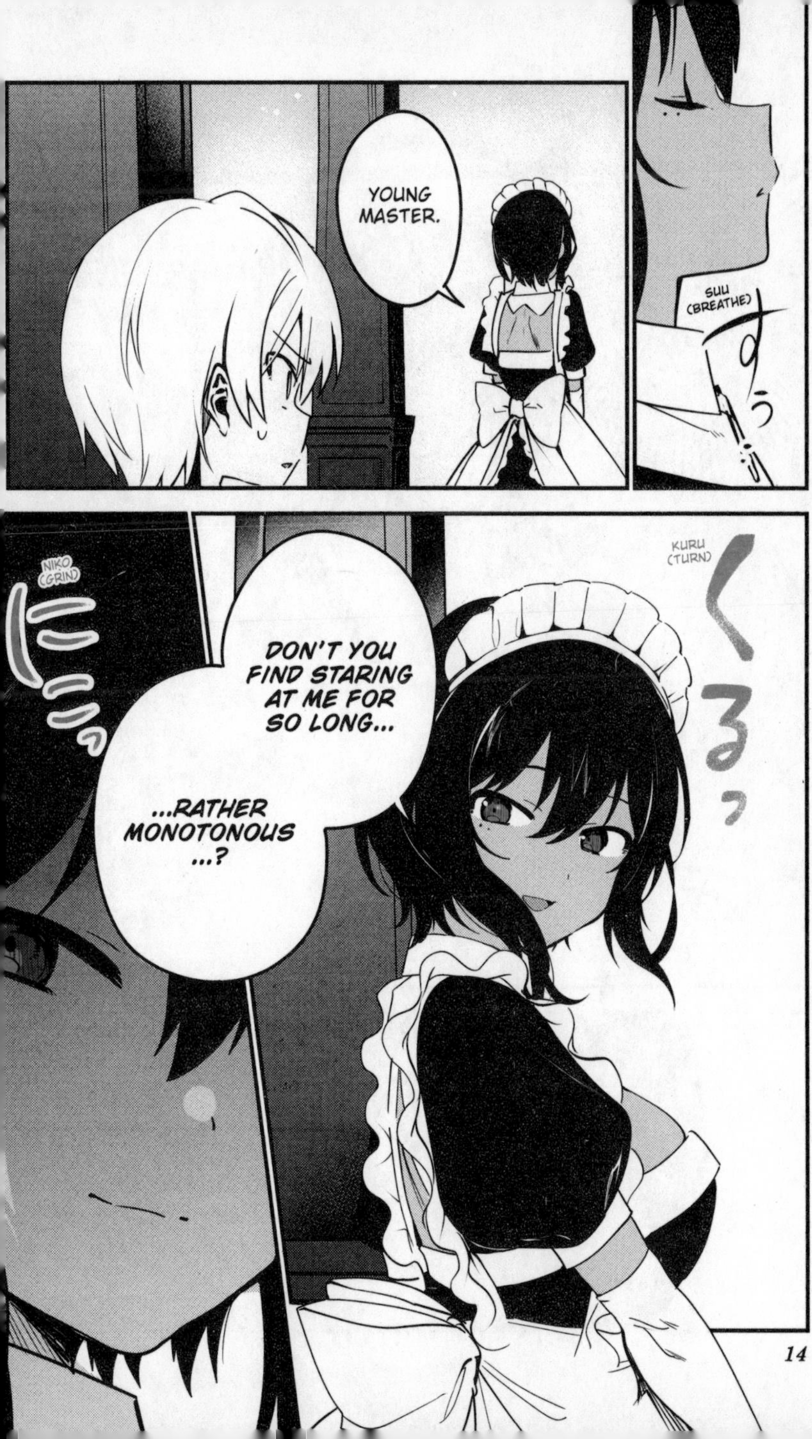
SUU (BREATHE)
YOUNG MASTER.
KURU (TURN)
DON'T YOU FIND STARING AT ME FOR SO LONG...
...RATHER MONOTONOUS ...?
NIKO (GRIN)

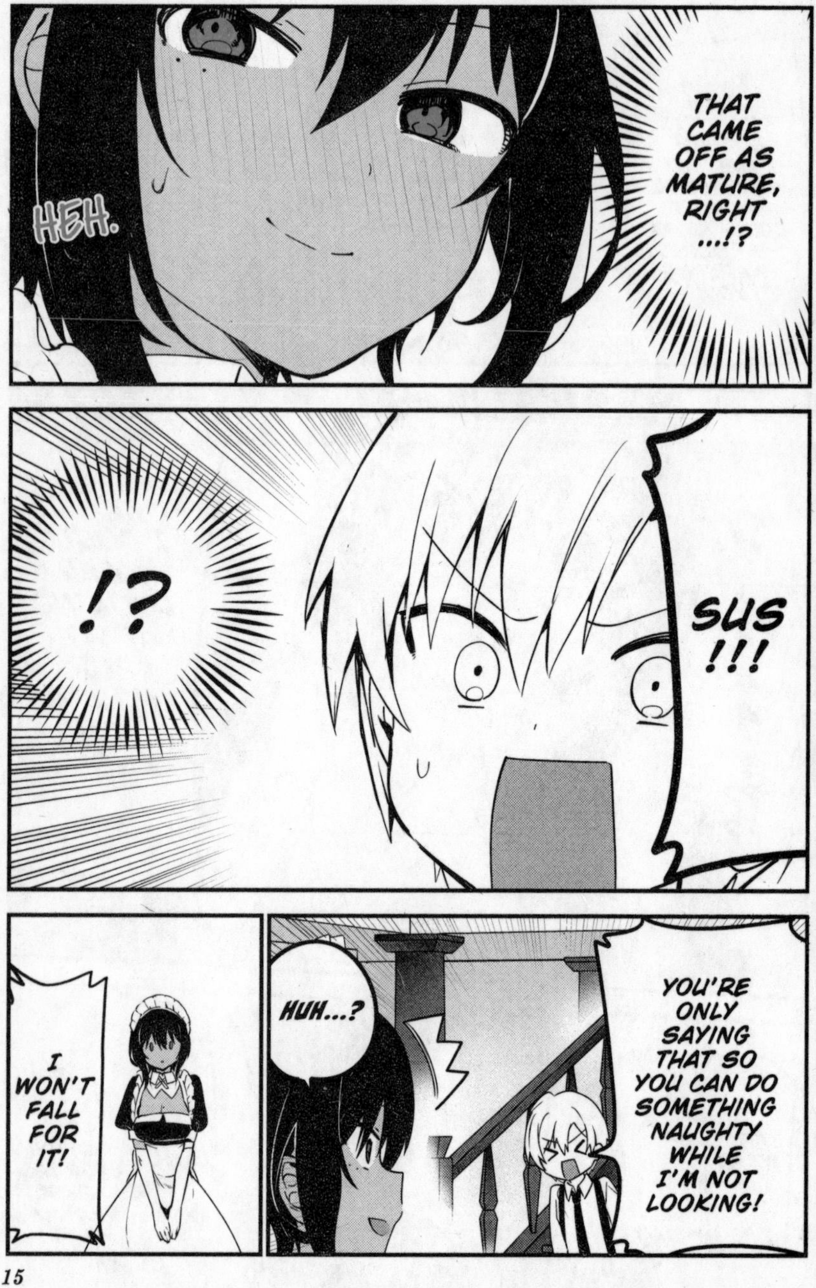
THAT CAME OFF AS MATURE, RIGHT ...!?
HEH.
SUS !!!
!?
YOU'RE ONLY SAYING THAT SO YOU CAN DO SOMETHING NAUGHTY WHILE I'M NOT LOOKING!
HUH...?
I WON'T FALL FOR IT!

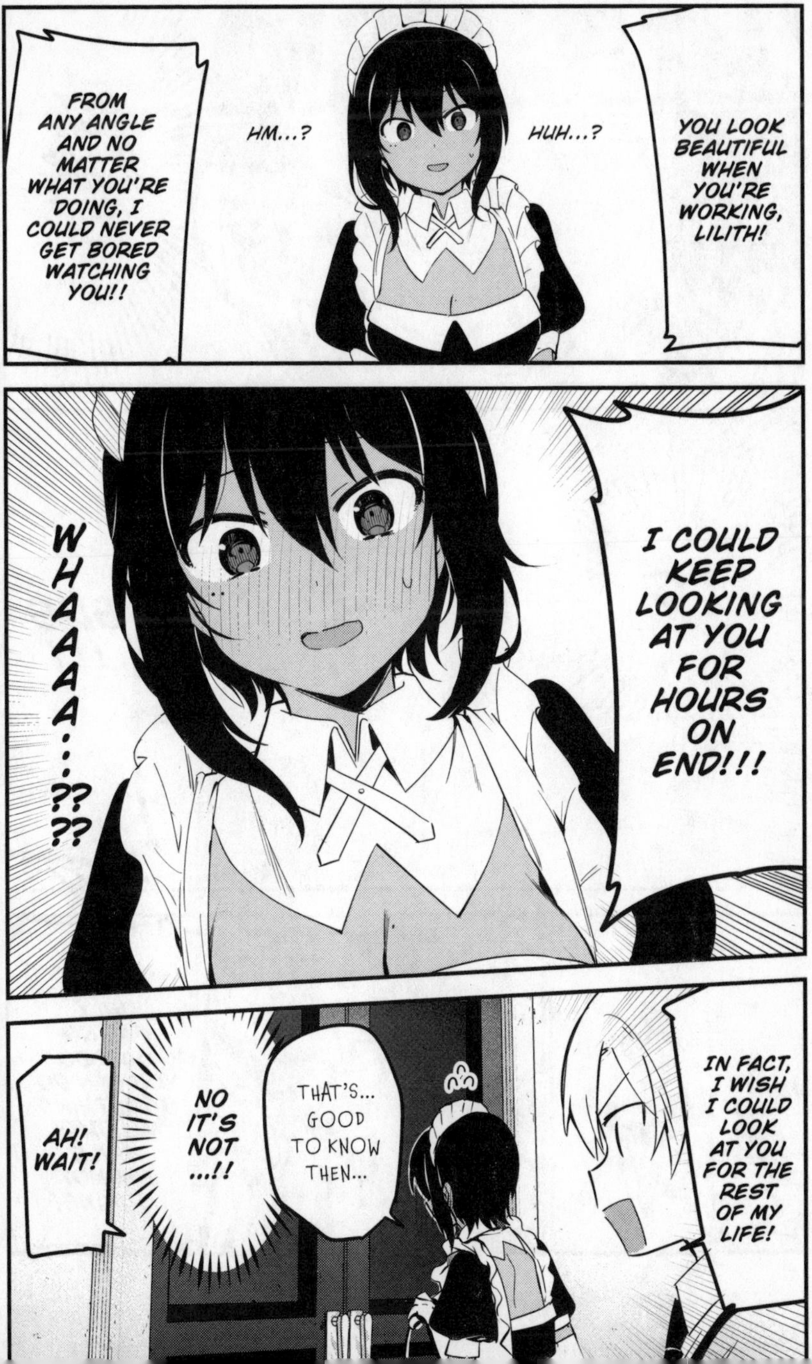
YOU LOOK BEAUTIFUL WHEN YOU'RE WORKING, LILITH!
HUH...?
HM...?
FROM ANY ANGLE AND NO MATTER WHAT YOU'RE DOING, I COULD NEVER GET BORED WATCHING YOU!!
I COULD KEEP LOOKING AT YOU FOR HOURS ON END!!!
WHAAAAA...????
IN FACT, I WISH I COULD LOOK AT YOU FOR THE REST OF MY LIFE!
THAT'S... GOOD TO KNOW THEN...
NO IT'S NOT ...!!
AH! WAIT!

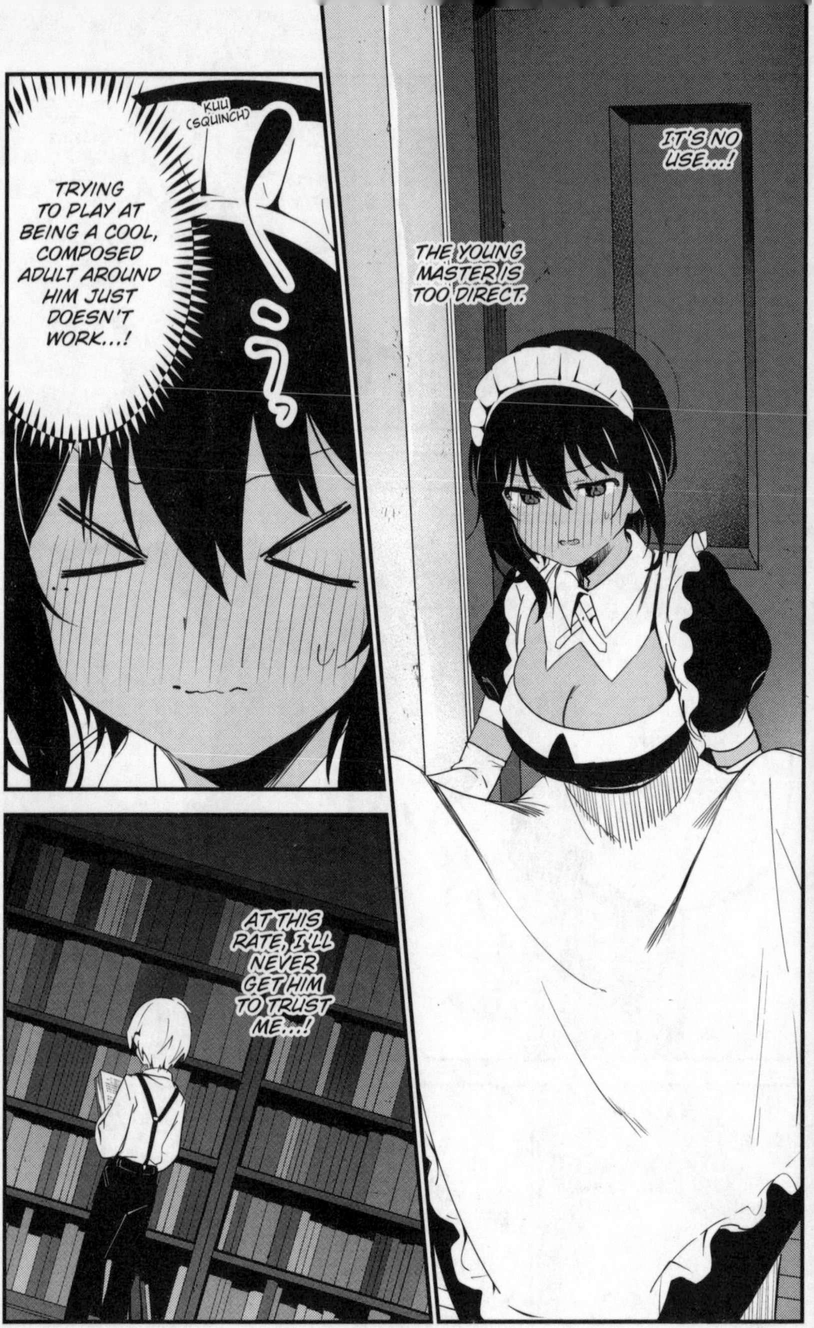
IT'S NO USE...!
THE YOUNG MASTER IS TOO DIRECT.
KUU (SQUINCH)
TRYING TO PLAY AT BEING A COOL, COMPOSED ADULT AROUND HIM JUST DOESN'T WORK...!
AT THIS RATE, I'LL NEVER GET HIM TO TRUST ME...!

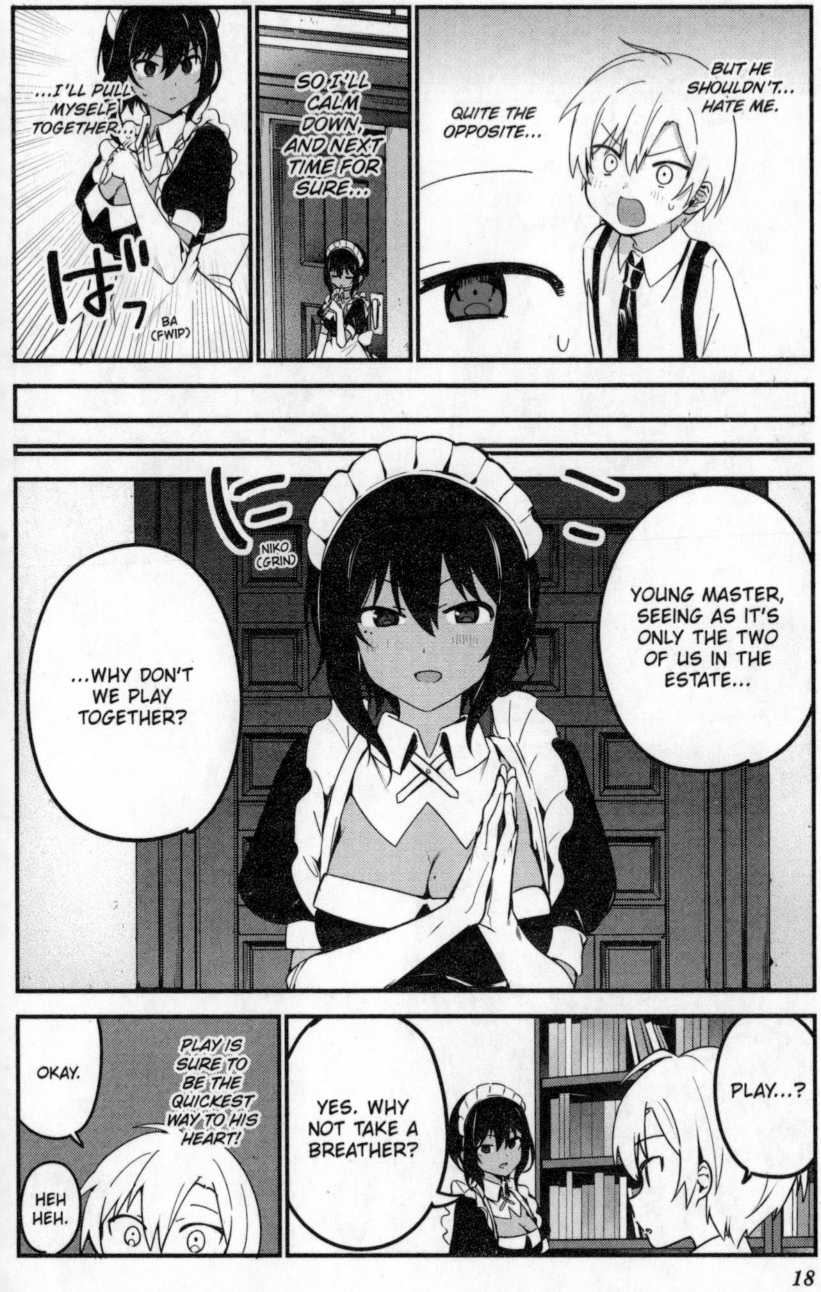
BUT HE SHOULDN'T... HATE ME.
QUITE THE OPPOSITE...
SO I'LL CALM DOWN, AND NEXT TIME FOR SURE...
...I'LL PULL MYSELF TOGETHER...
BA (FWIP)
YOUNG MASTER, SEEING AS IT'S ONLY THE TWO OF US IN THE ESTATE...
NIKO (GRIN)
...WHY DON'T WE PLAY TOGETHER?
PLAY...?
YES. WHY NOT TAKE A BREATHER?
PLAY IS SURE TO BE THE QUICKEST WAY TO HIS HEART!
OKAY.
HEH HEH.

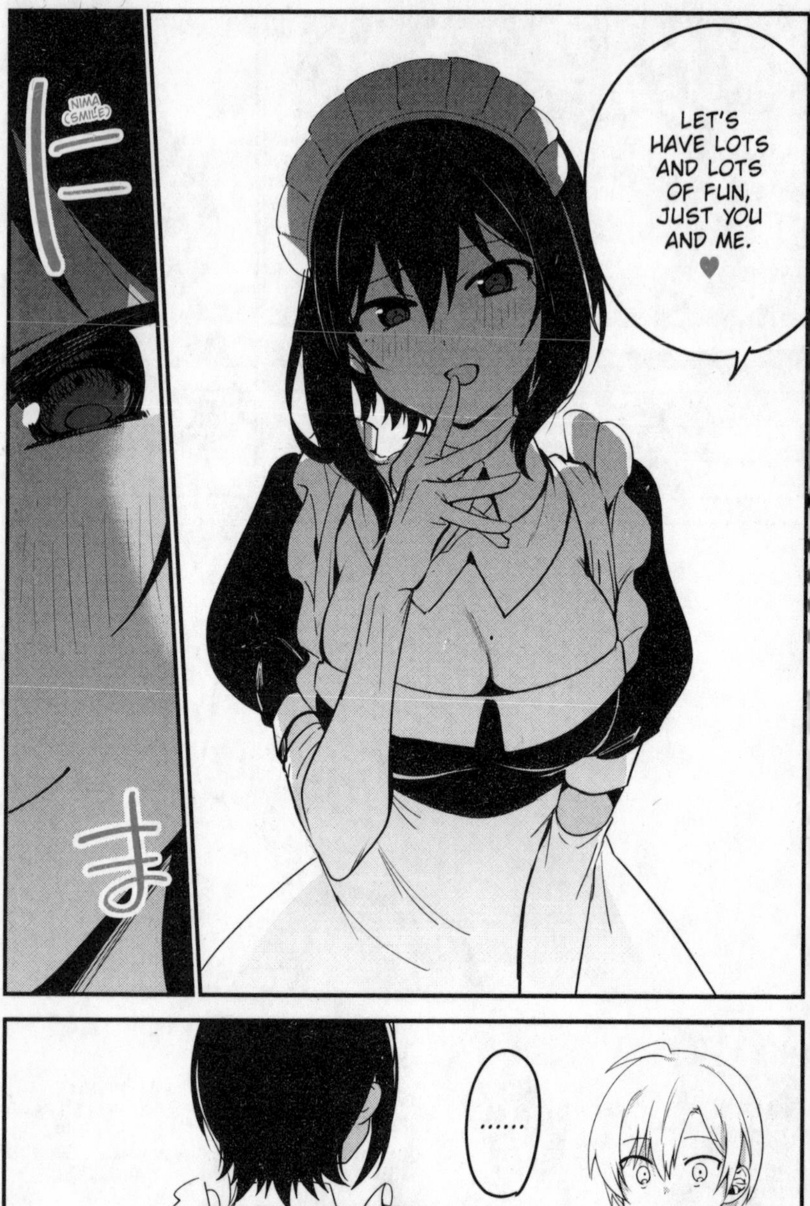
LET'S HAVE LOTS AND LOTS OF FUN, JUST YOU AND ME. ♥
NIMA (SMILE)
......

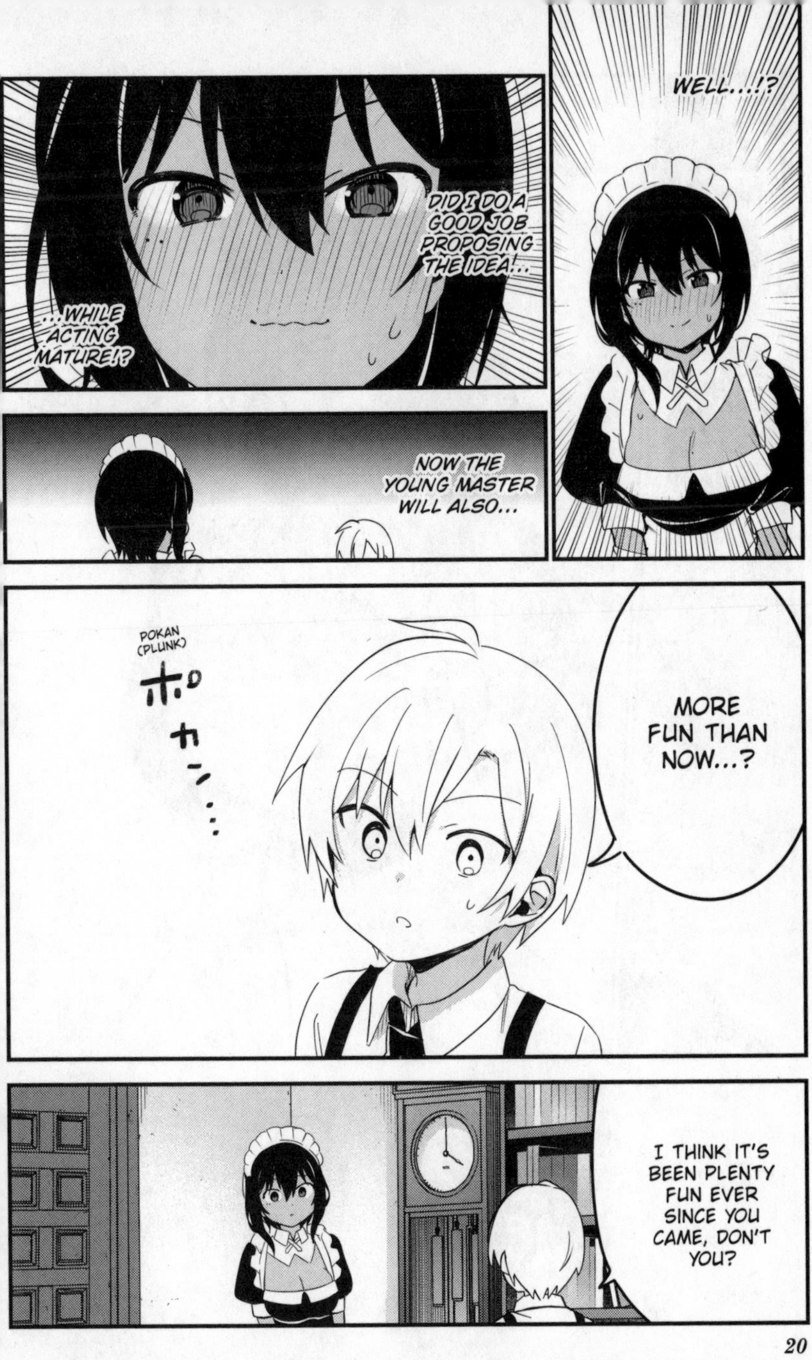
WELL...!?
DID I DO A GOOD JOB PROPOSING THE IDEA!...
...WHILE ACTING MATURE!?
NOW THE YOUNG MASTER WILL ALSO...
MORE FUN THAN NOW...?
POKAN (PLUNK)
ポカン...
I THINK IT'S BEEN PLENTY FUN EVER SINCE YOU CAME, DON'T YOU?

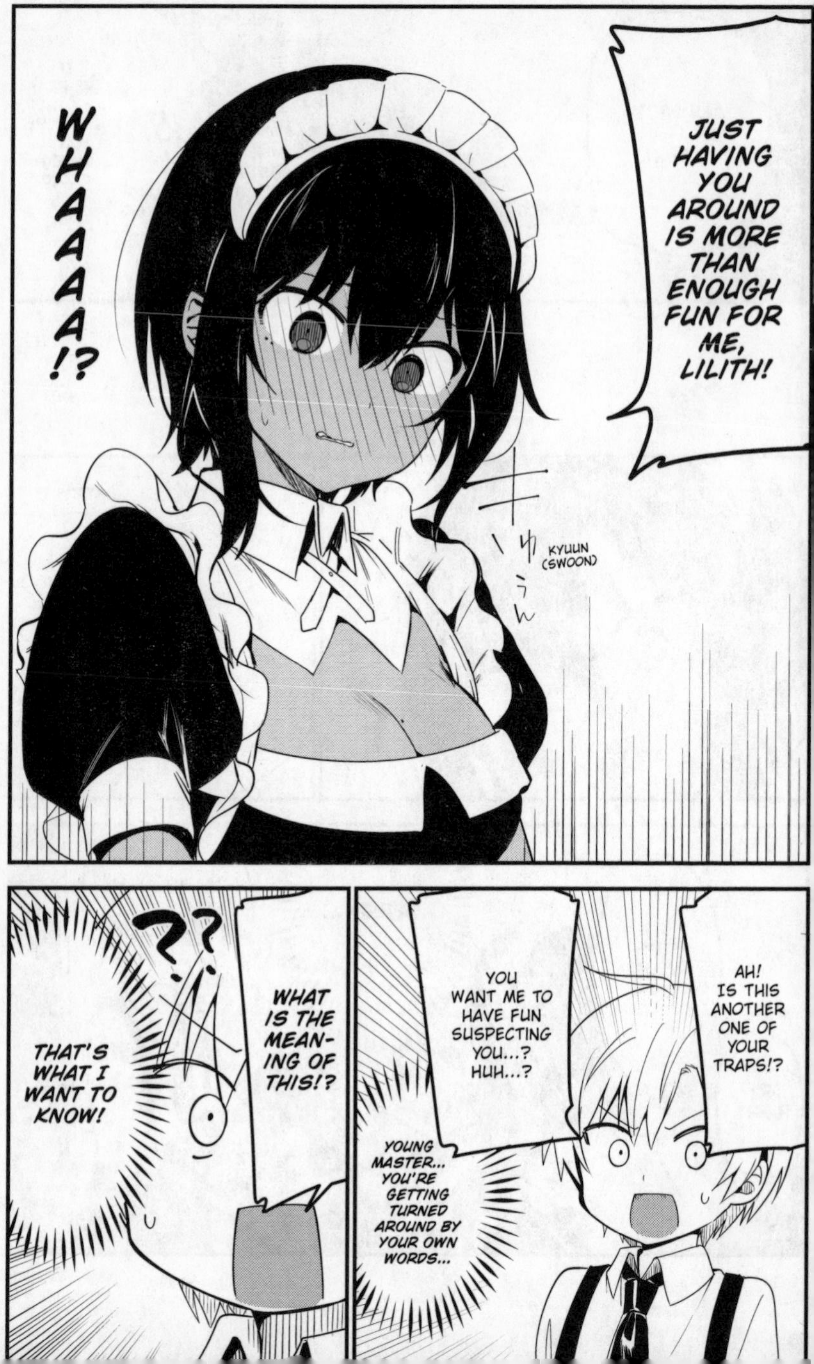
JUST HAVING YOU AROUND IS MORE THAN ENOUGH FUN FOR ME, LILITH!
KYUUN (SWOON)
WHAAAAA!?
AH! IS THIS ANOTHER ONE OF YOUR TRAPS!?
YOU WANT ME TO HAVE FUN SUSPECTING YOU...? HUH...?
YOUNG MASTER... YOU'RE GETTING TURNED AROUND BY YOUR OWN WORDS...
WHAT IS THE MEANING OF THIS!?
??
THAT'S WHAT I WANT TO KNOW!

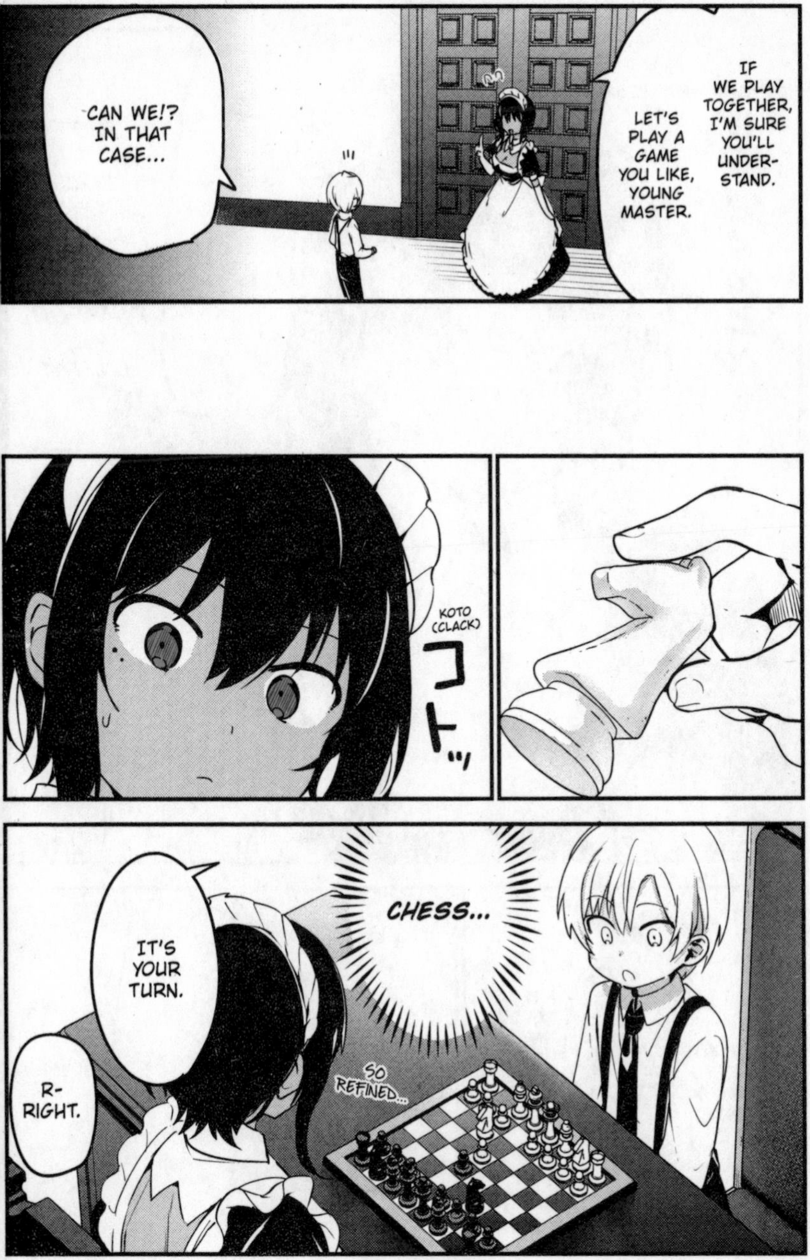
IF WE PLAY TOGETHER, I'M SURE YOU'LL UNDERSTAND.
LET'S PLAY A GAME YOU LIKE, YOUNG MASTER.
CAN WE!? IN THAT CASE...
KOTO (CLACK)
コトッ
CHESS...
IT'S YOUR TURN.
SO REFINED...
R-RIGHT.

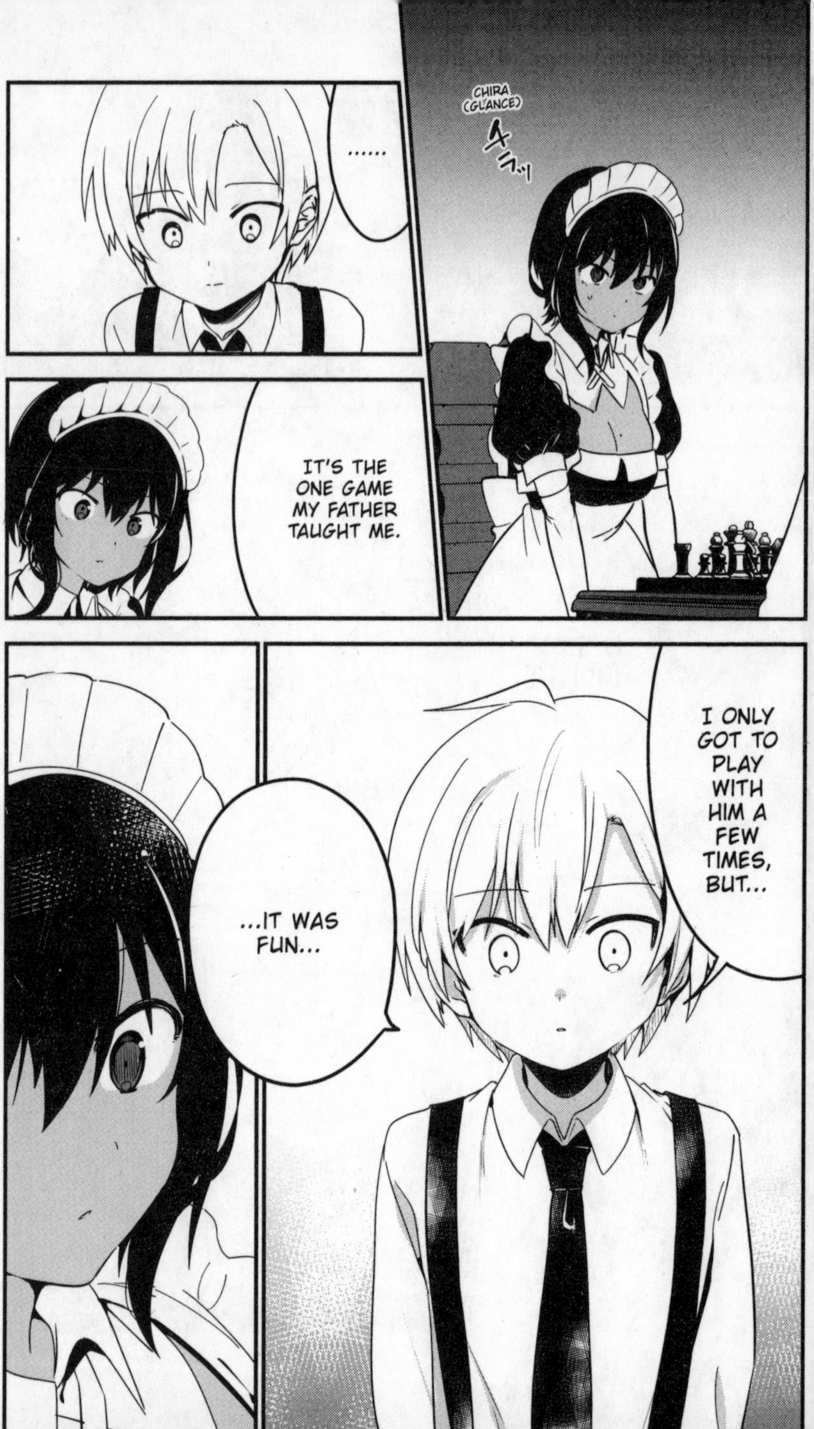

CHIRA (GLANCE)
......
IT'S THE ONE GAME MY FATHER TAUGHT ME.
I ONLY GOT TO PLAY WITH HIM A FEW TIMES, BUT...
...IT WAS FUN...

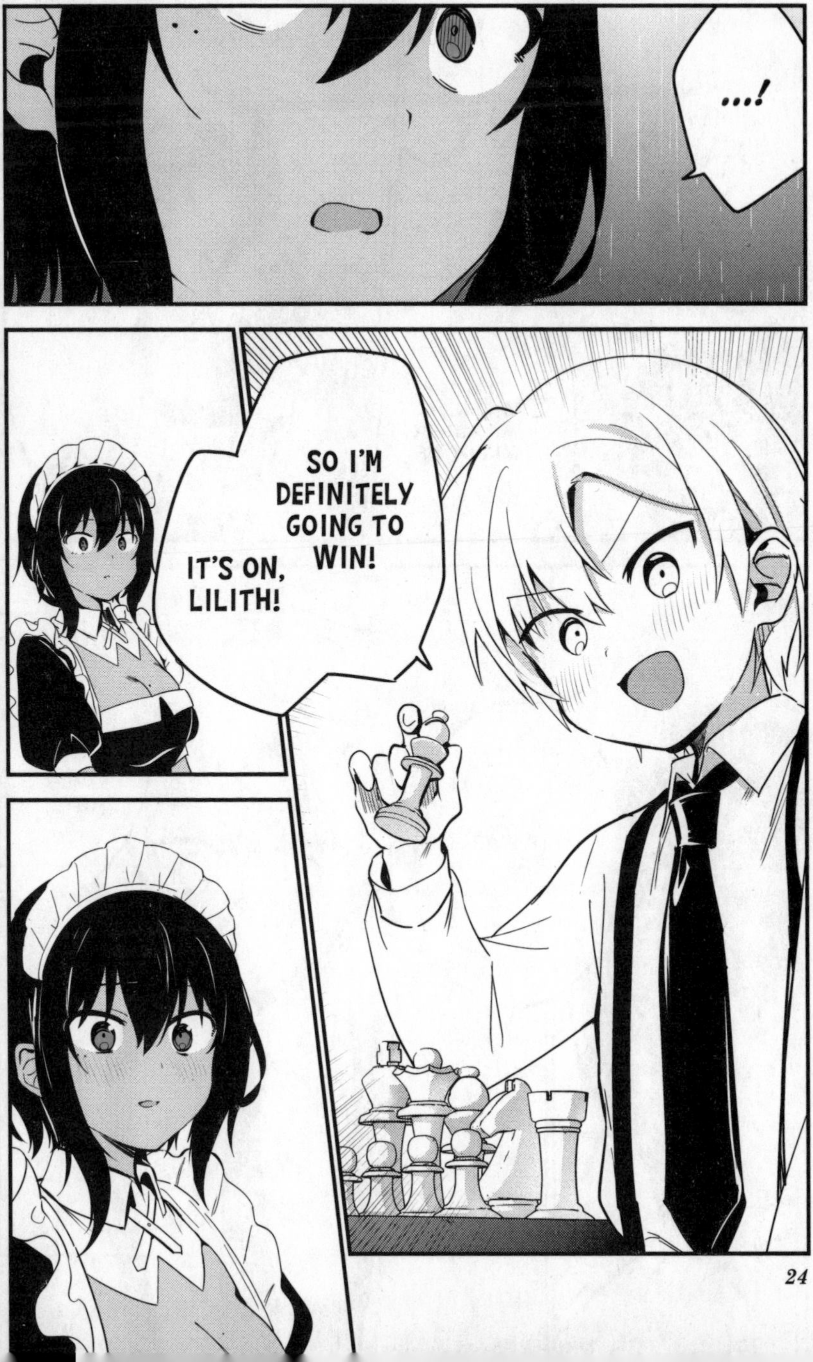
...!
SO I'M DEFINITELY GOING TO WIN!
IT'S ON, LILITH!

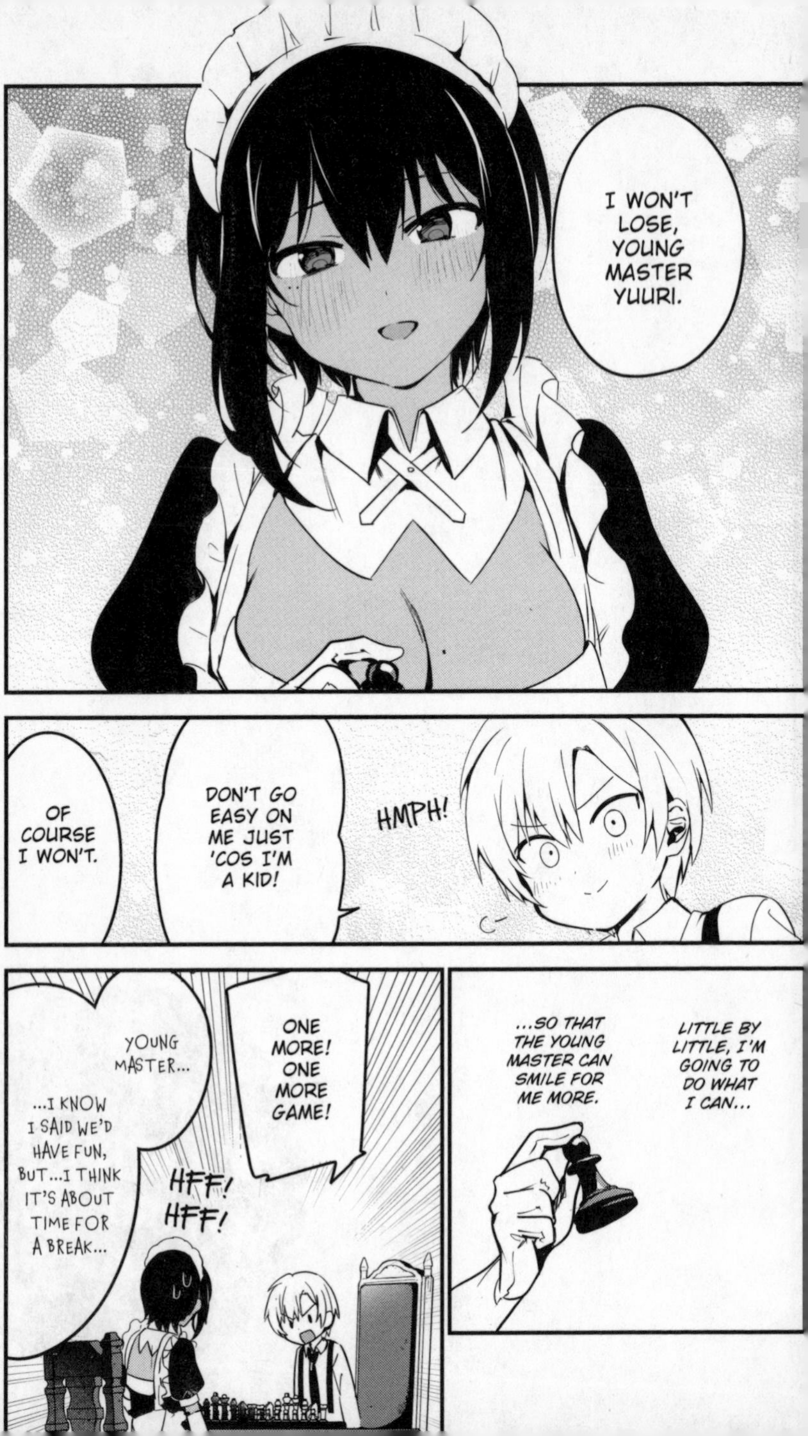
I WON'T LOSE, YOUNG MASTER YUURI.
HMPH!
DON'T GO EASY ON ME JUST 'COS I'M A KID!
OF COURSE I WON'T.
LITTLE BY LITTLE, I'M GOING TO DO WHAT I CAN...
...SO THAT THE YOUNG MASTER CAN SMILE FOR ME MORE.
ONE MORE! ONE MORE GAME!
HFF! HFF!
YOUNG MASTER...
...I KNOW I SAID WE'D HAVE FUN, BUT...I THINK IT'S ABOUT TIME FOR A BREAK...

The Maid I Hired Recently Is Mysterious

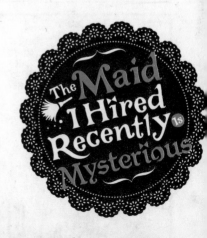

CHAPTER 17

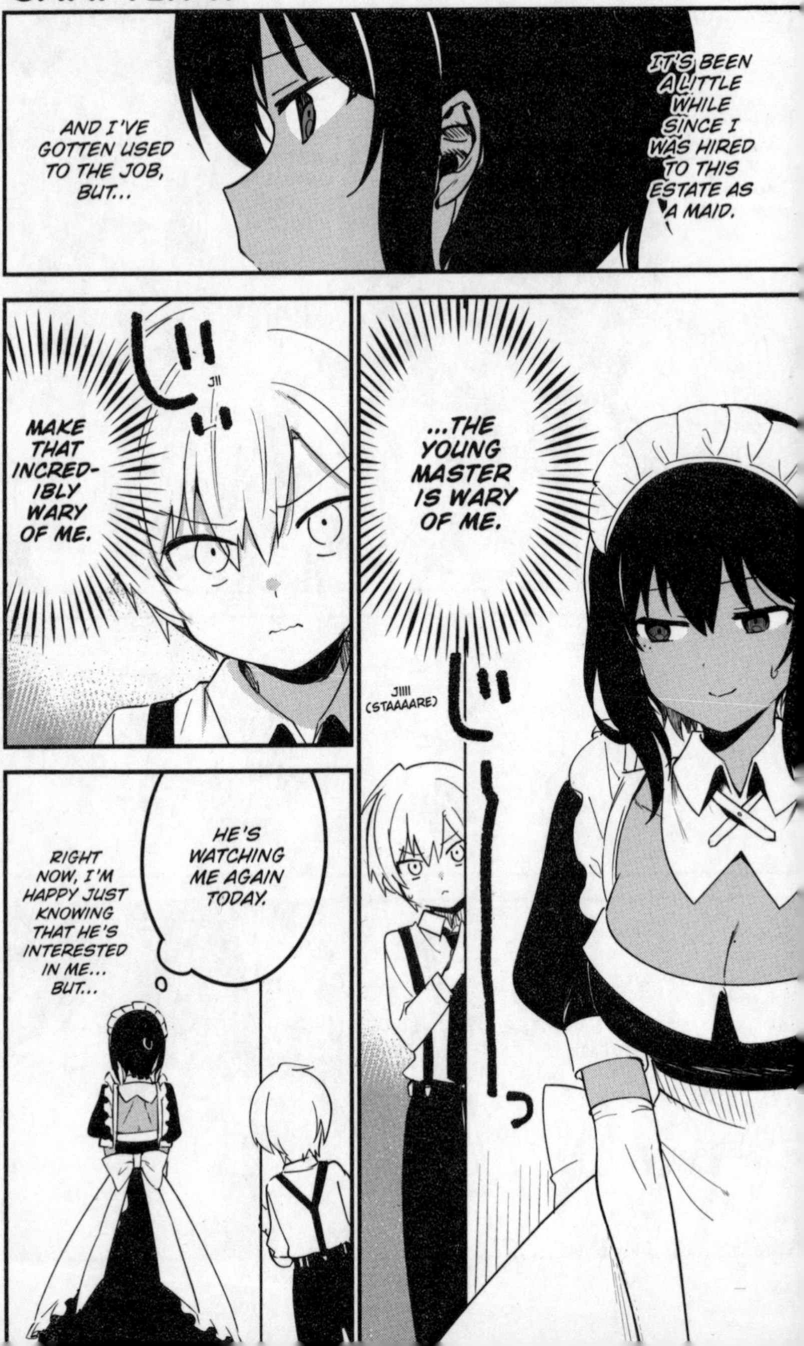
IT'S BEEN A LITTLE WHILE SINCE I WAS HIRED TO THIS ESTATE AS A MAID.
AND I'VE GOTTEN USED TO THE JOB, BUT...
...THE YOUNG MASTER IS WARY OF ME.
JIIII (STAAAARE)
MAKE THAT INCRED-IBLY WARY OF ME.
JII
HE'S WATCHING ME AGAIN TODAY.
RIGHT NOW, I'M HAPPY JUST KNOWING THAT HE'S INTERESTED IN ME... BUT...

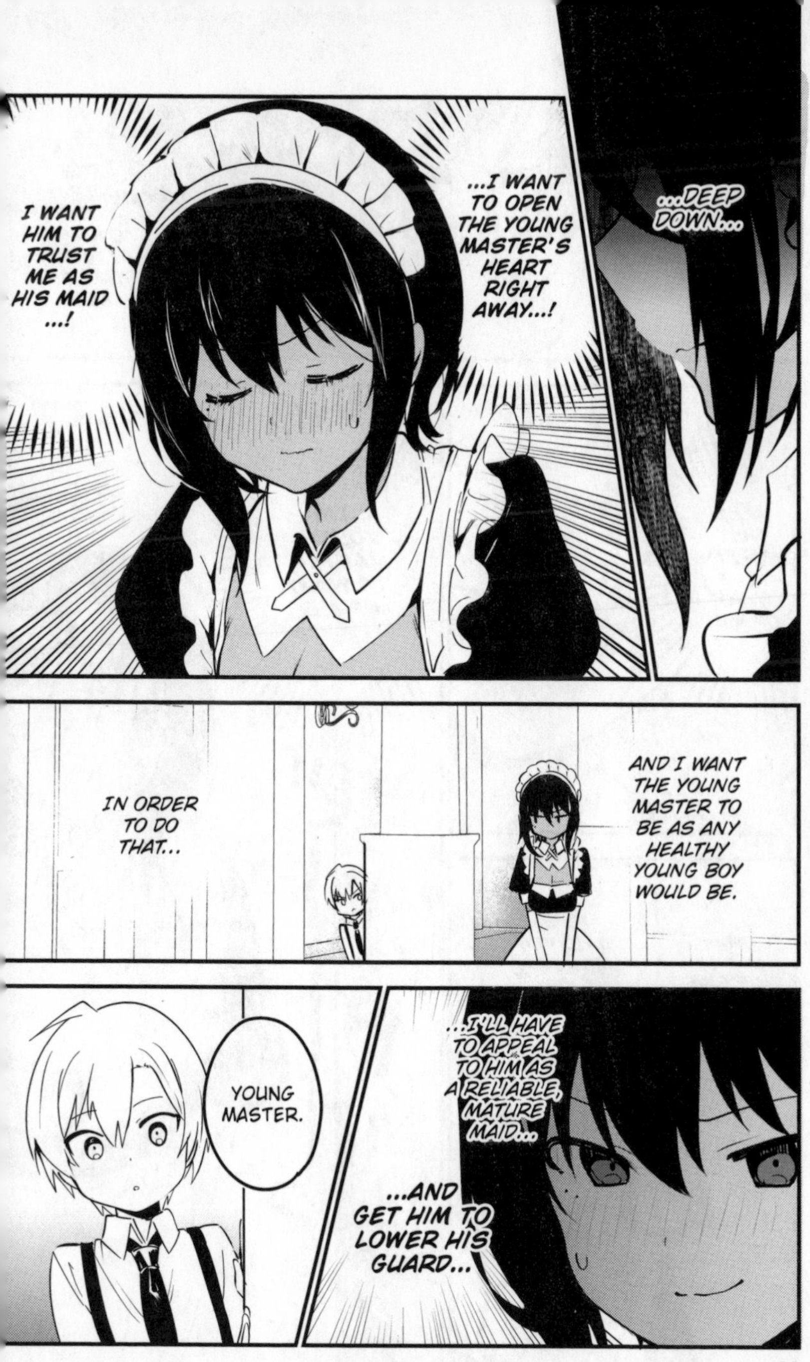
...DEEP DOWN...
...I WANT TO OPEN THE YOUNG MASTER'S HEART RIGHT AWAY...!
I WANT HIM TO TRUST ME AS HIS MAID ...!
AND I WANT THE YOUNG MASTER TO BE AS ANY HEALTHY YOUNG BOY WOULD BE.
IN ORDER TO DO THAT...
...I'LL HAVE TO APPEAL TO HIM AS A RELIABLE, MATURE MAID...
...AND GET HIM TO LOWER HIS GUARD...
YOUNG MASTER.

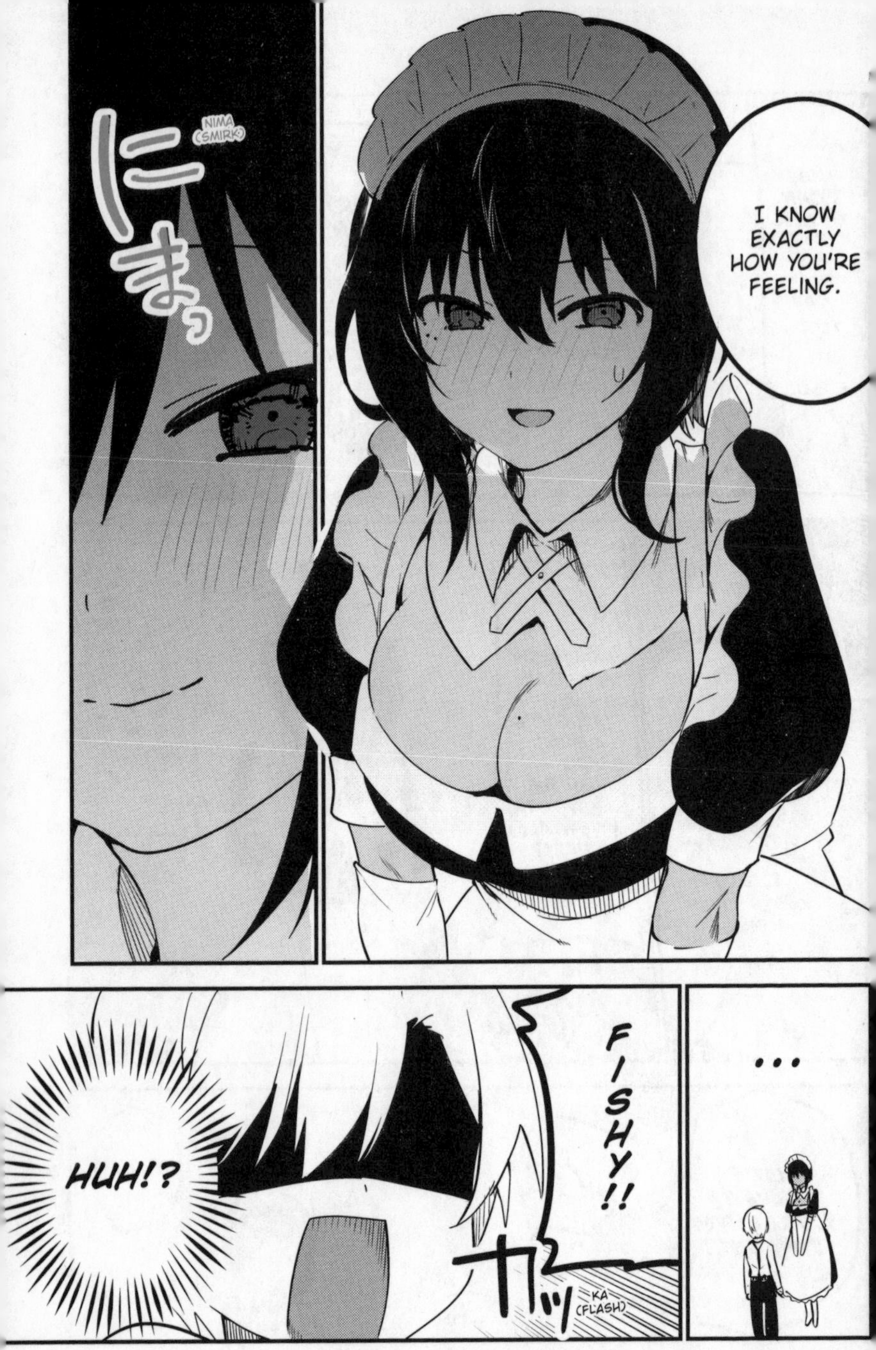
I KNOW EXACTLY HOW YOU'RE FEELING.
にまっ
NIMA (SMIRK)
...
FISHY!!
HUH!?
カッ
KA (FLASH)

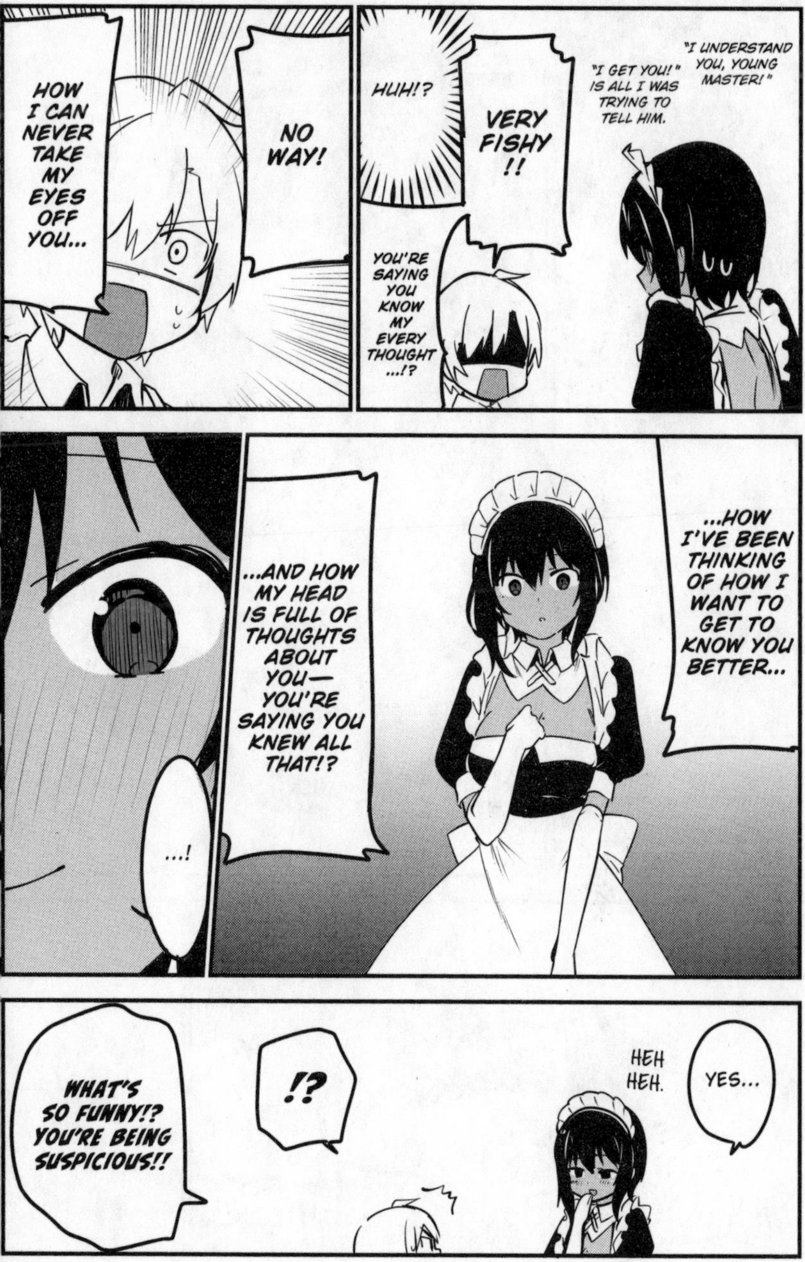
"I UNDERSTAND YOU, YOUNG MASTER!"
"I GET YOU!" IS ALL I WAS TRYING TO TELL HIM.
VERY FISHY!!
HUH!?
YOU'RE SAYING YOU KNOW MY EVERY THOUGHT...!?
NO WAY!
HOW I CAN NEVER TAKE MY EYES OFF YOU...
...HOW I'VE BEEN THINKING OF HOW I WANT TO GET TO KNOW YOU BETTER...
...AND HOW MY HEAD IS FULL OF THOUGHTS ABOUT YOU—YOU'RE SAYING YOU KNEW ALL THAT!?
...!
YES...
HEH HEH.
!?
WHAT'S SO FUNNY!? YOU'RE BEING SUSPICIOUS!!

CHAPTER 18

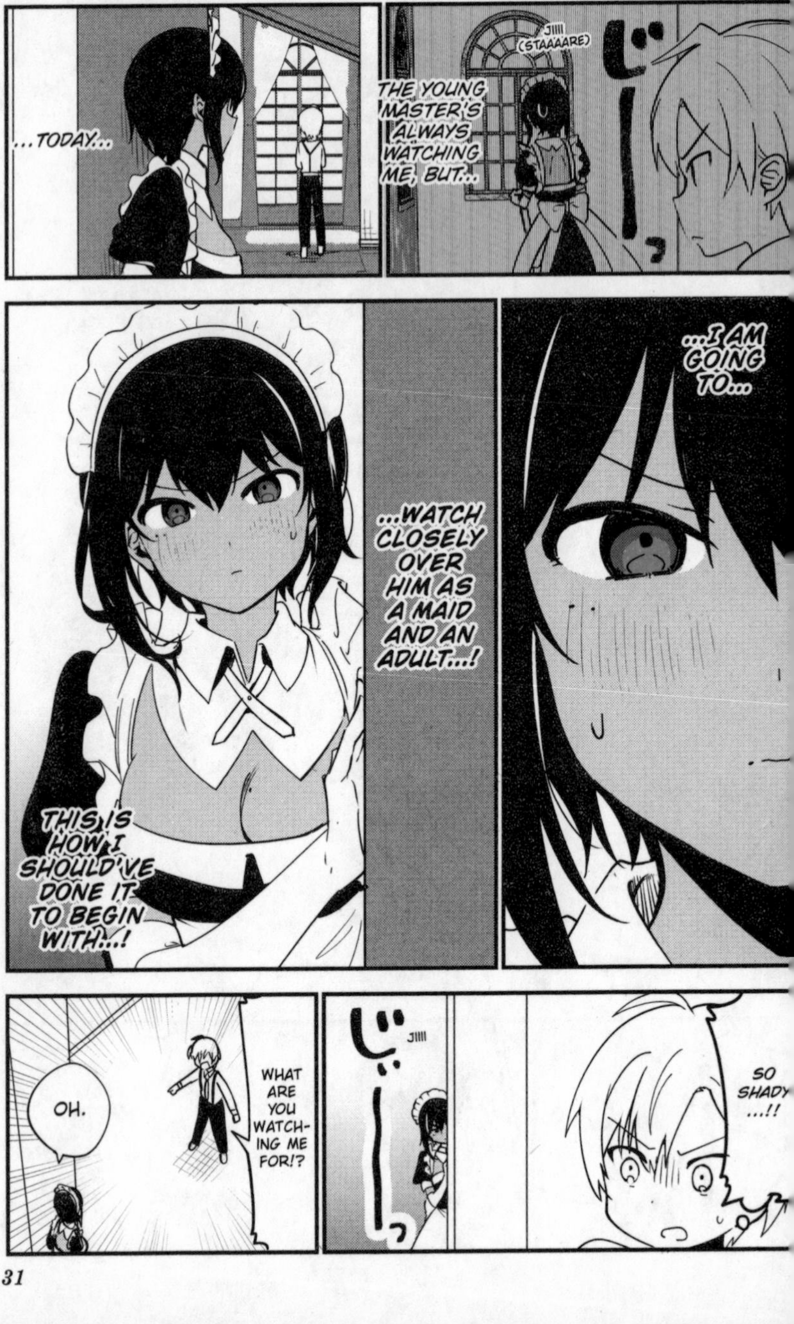
じーっ
JIIII (STAAAARE)
THE YOUNG MASTER'S ALWAYS WATCHING ME, BUT...
...TODAY...
...I AM GOING TO...
...WATCH CLOSELY OVER HIM AS A MAID AND AN ADULT...!
THIS IS HOW I SHOULD'VE DONE IT TO BEGIN WITH...!
SO SHADY ...!!
じーっ
JIIII
WHAT ARE YOU WATCHING ME FOR!?
OH.

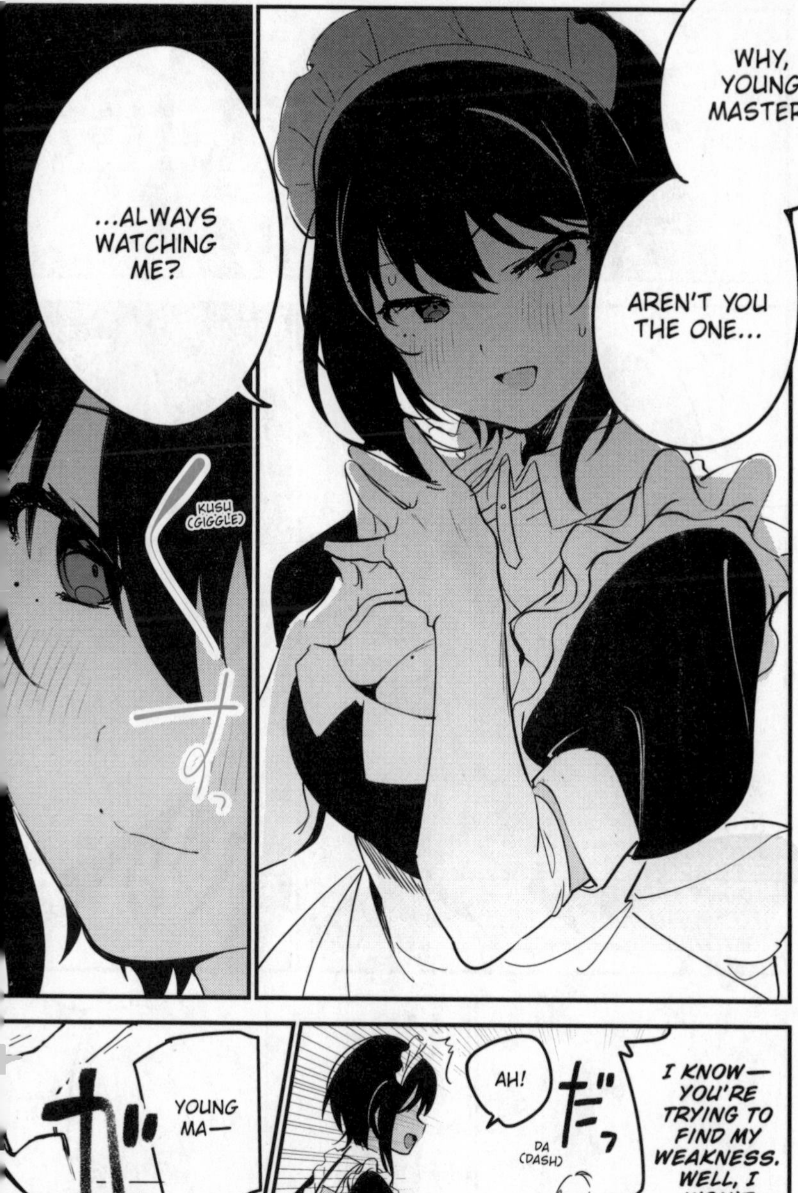
WHY, YOUNG MASTER.
AREN'T YOU THE ONE...
...ALWAYS WATCHING ME?
KUSU (GIGGLE)
I KNOW—YOU'RE TRYING TO FIND MY WEAKNESS. WELL, I WON'T HAVE IT!
DA (DASH)
AH!
YOUNG MA—
GA (TRIP)

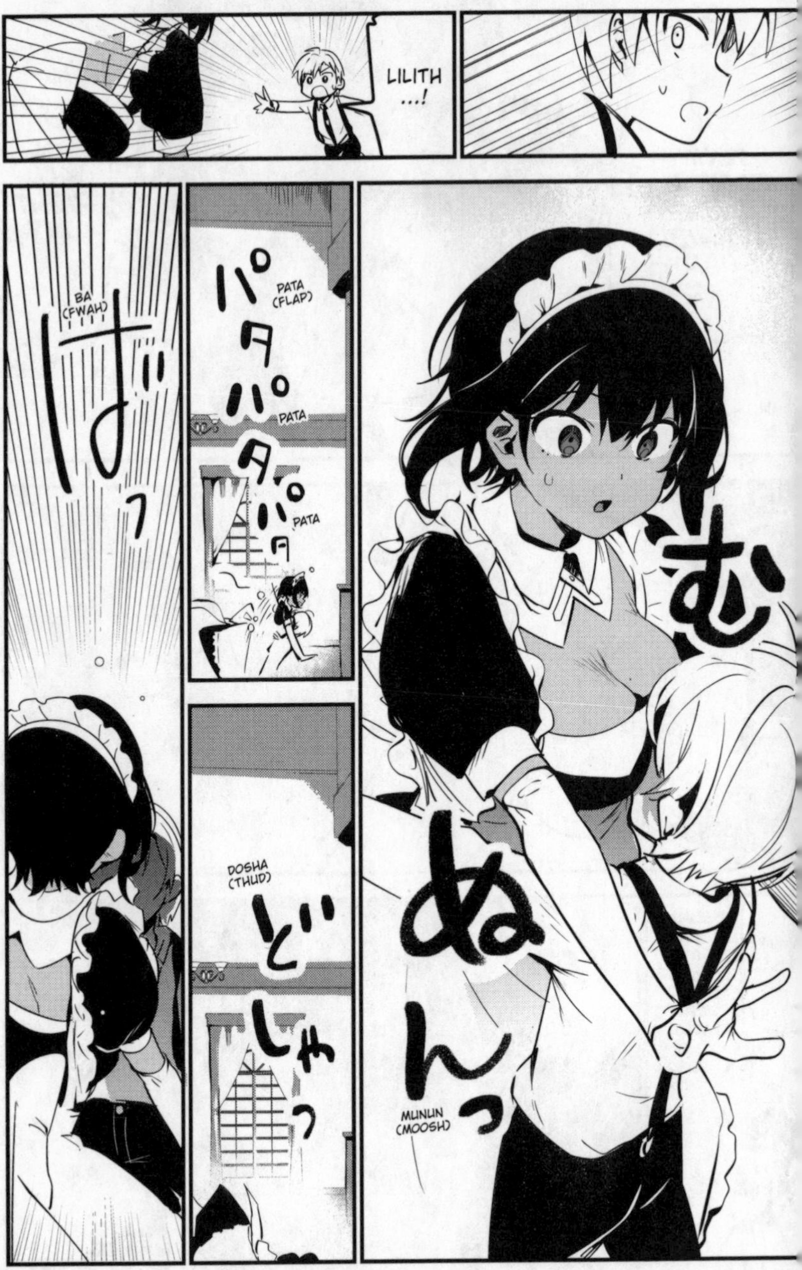
LILITH ...!
むぬんっ
MUNUN (MOOSH)
パタパタパタ
PATA (FLAP)
PATA
PATA
どしゃっ
DOSHA (THUD)
ばっ
BA (FWAH)

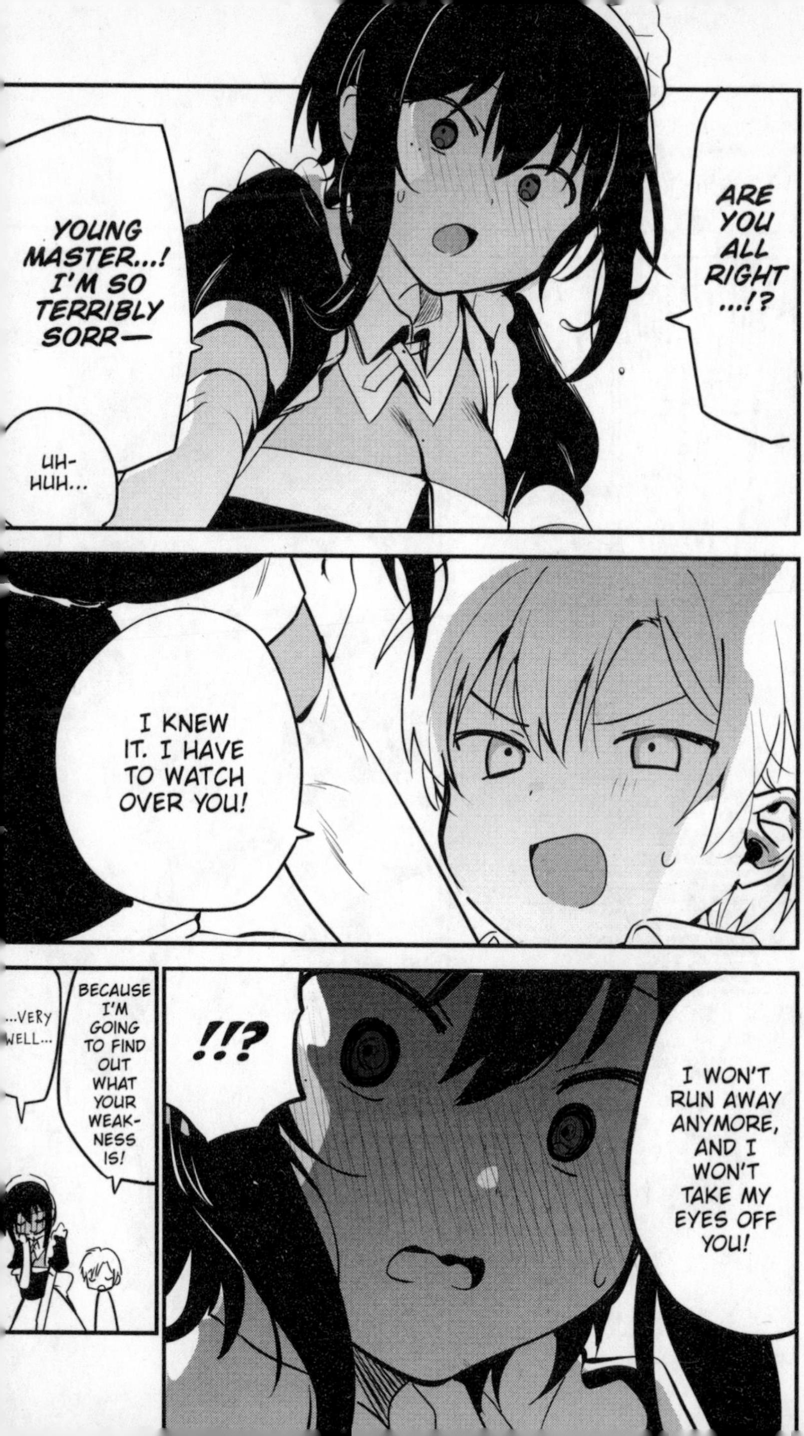
ARE YOU ALL RIGHT ...!?
YOUNG MASTER...! I'M SO TERRIBLY SORR—
UH-HUH...
I KNEW IT. I HAVE TO WATCH OVER YOU!
I WON'T RUN AWAY ANYMORE, AND I WON'T TAKE MY EYES OFF YOU!
!!?
BECAUSE I'M GOING TO FIND OUT WHAT YOUR WEAK-NESS IS!
...VERY WELL...

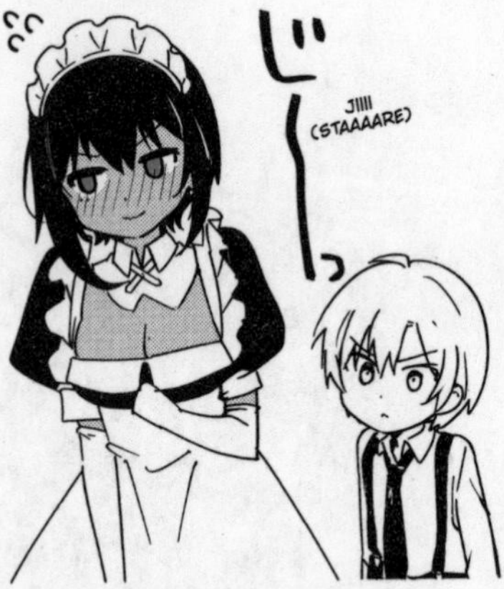
JIIII
(STAAAARE)

The Maid I Hired Recently Is Mysterious

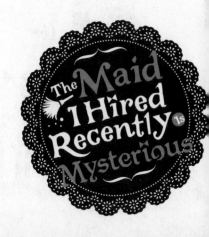

CHAPTER 19

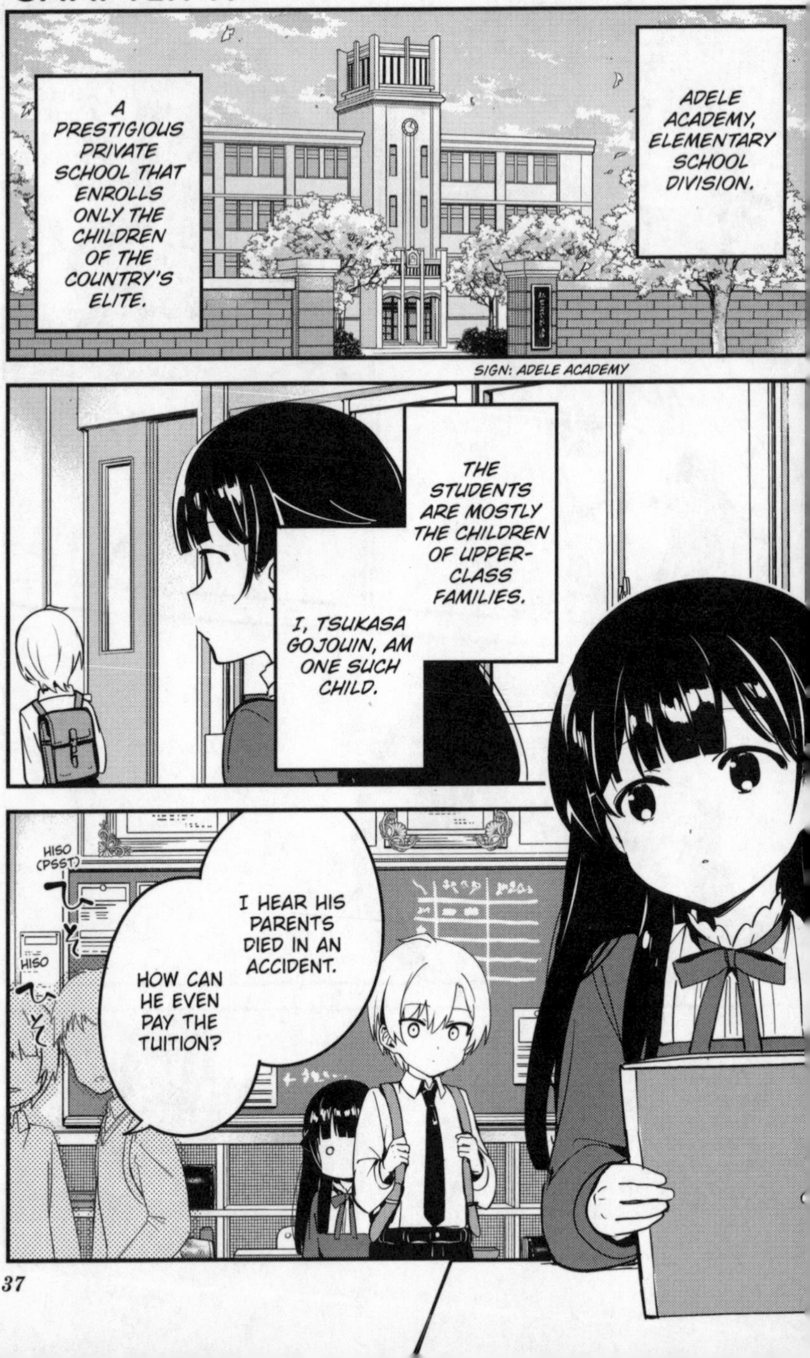
ADELE ACADEMY, ELEMENTARY SCHOOL DIVISION.
A PRESTIGIOUS PRIVATE SCHOOL THAT ENROLLS ONLY THE CHILDREN OF THE COUNTRY'S ELITE.
SIGN: ADELE ACADEMY
THE STUDENTS ARE MOSTLY THE CHILDREN OF UPPER-CLASS FAMILIES.
I, TSUKASA GOJOUIN, AM ONE SUCH CHILD.
I HEAR HIS PARENTS DIED IN AN ACCIDENT.
HOW CAN HE EVEN PAY THE TUITION?
HISO (PSST)
HISO

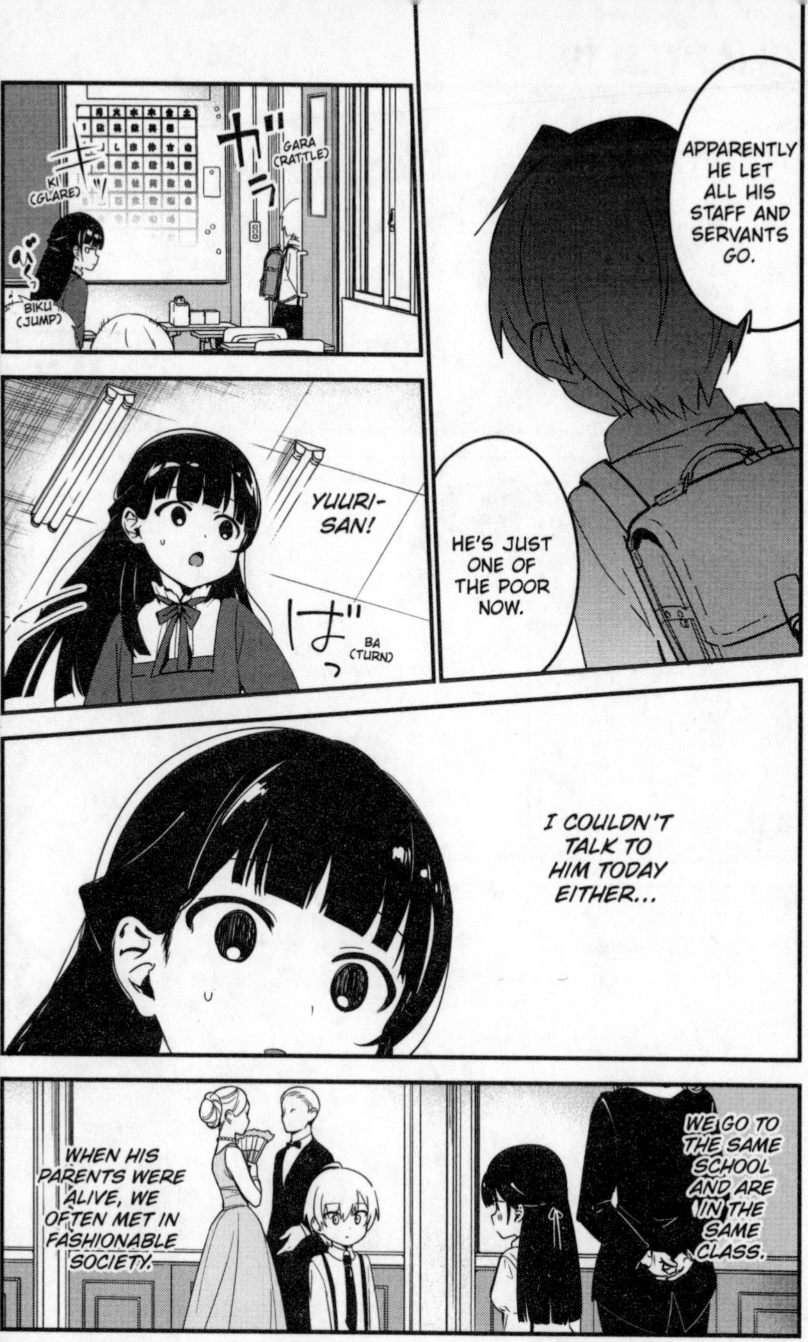
APPARENTLY HE LET ALL HIS STAFF AND SERVANTS GO.
HE'S JUST ONE OF THE POOR NOW.
GARA (RATTLE)
KI (GLARE)
BIKU (JUMP)
YUURI-SAN!
BA (TURN)
I COULDN'T TALK TO HIM TODAY EITHER...
WE GO TO THE SAME SCHOOL AND ARE IN THE SAME CLASS.
WHEN HIS PARENTS WERE ALIVE, WE OFTEN MET IN FASHIONABLE SOCIETY.

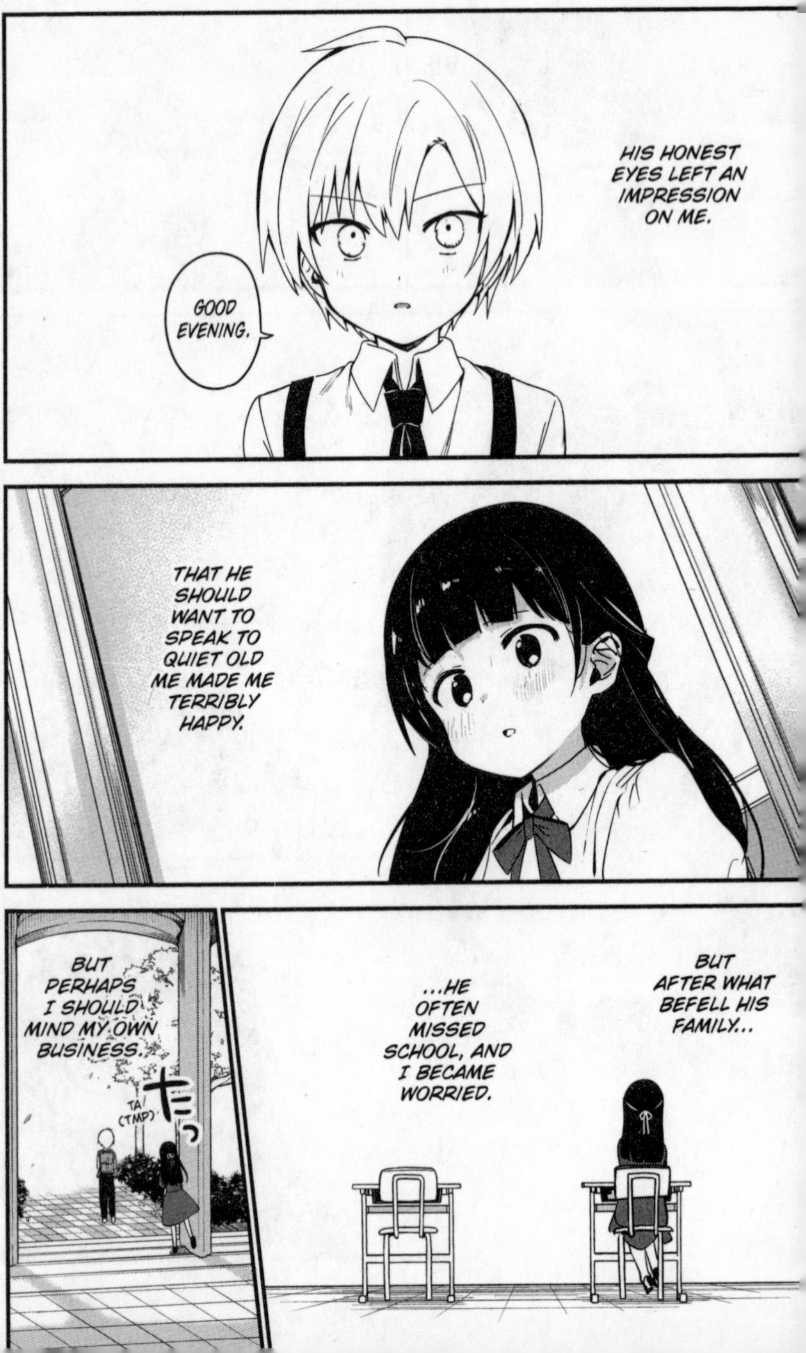
HIS HONEST EYES LEFT AN IMPRESSION ON ME.
GOOD EVENING.
THAT HE SHOULD WANT TO SPEAK TO QUIET OLD ME MADE ME TERRIBLY HAPPY.
BUT AFTER WHAT BEFELL HIS FAMILY...
...HE OFTEN MISSED SCHOOL, AND I BECAME WORRIED.
BUT PERHAPS I SHOULD MIND MY OWN BUSINESS.
TA (TMP)

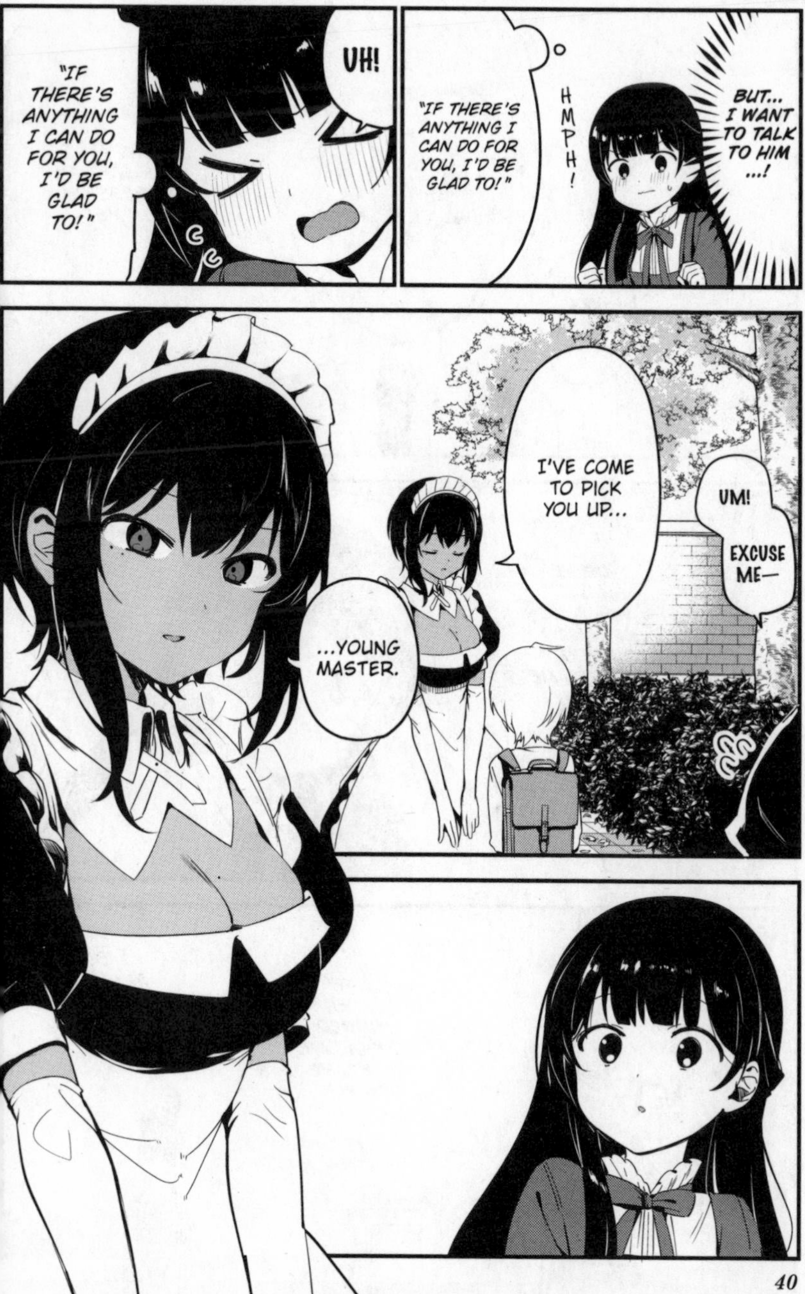
BUT... I WANT TO TALK TO HIM ...!
HMPH!
"IF THERE'S ANYTHING I CAN DO FOR YOU, I'D BE GLAD TO!"
UH!
"IF THERE'S ANYTHING I CAN DO FOR YOU, I'D BE GLAD TO!"
UM!
EXCUSE ME—
I'VE COME TO PICK YOU UP...
...YOUNG MASTER.

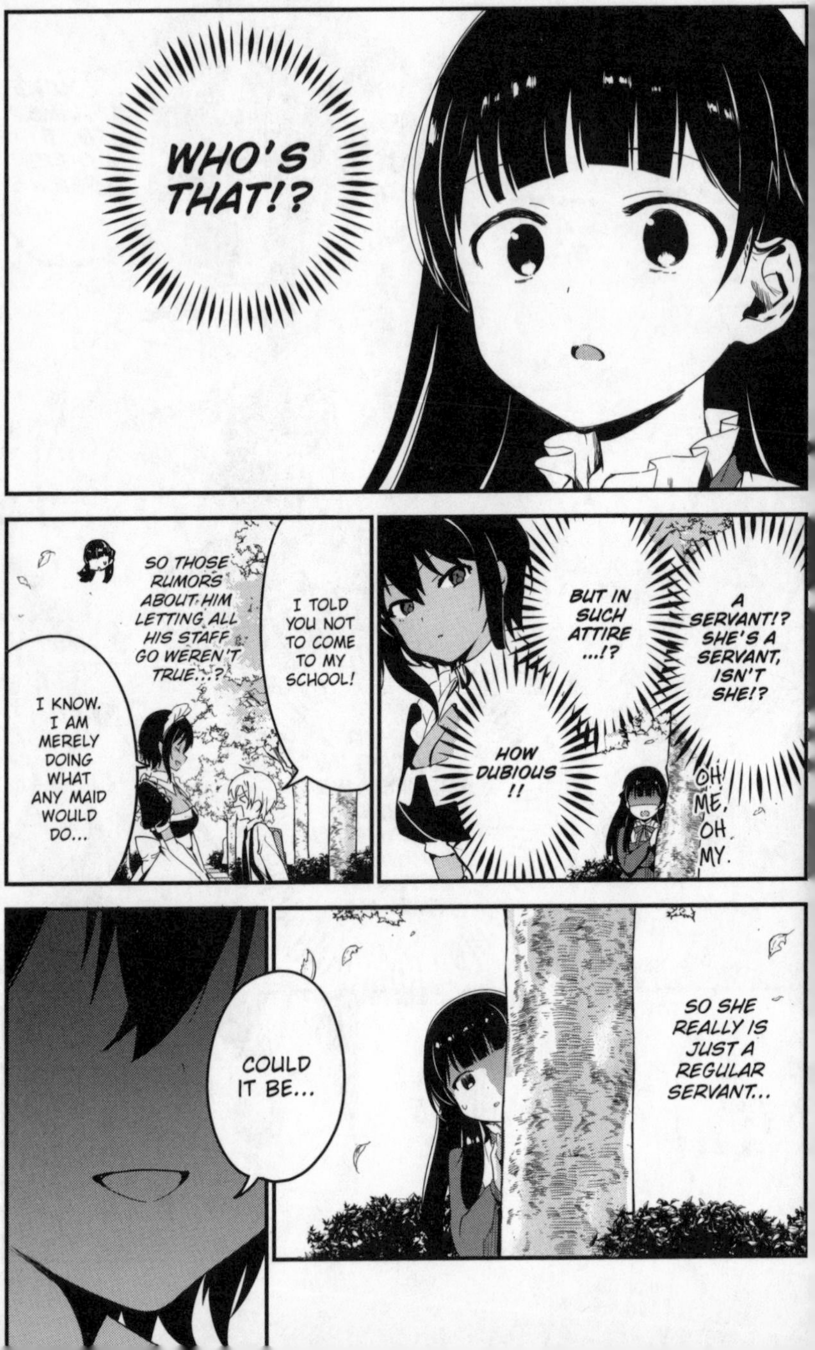
WHO'S THAT!?
A SERVANT!? SHE'S A SERVANT, ISN'T SHE!?
BUT IN SUCH ATTIRE ...!?
HOW DUBIOUS !!
OH ME, OH MY.
I TOLD YOU NOT TO COME TO MY SCHOOL!
SO THOSE RUMORS ABOUT HIM LETTING ALL HIS STAFF GO WEREN'T TRUE...?
I KNOW. I AM MERELY DOING WHAT ANY MAID WOULD DO...
SO SHE REALLY IS JUST A REGULAR SERVANT...
COULD IT BE...

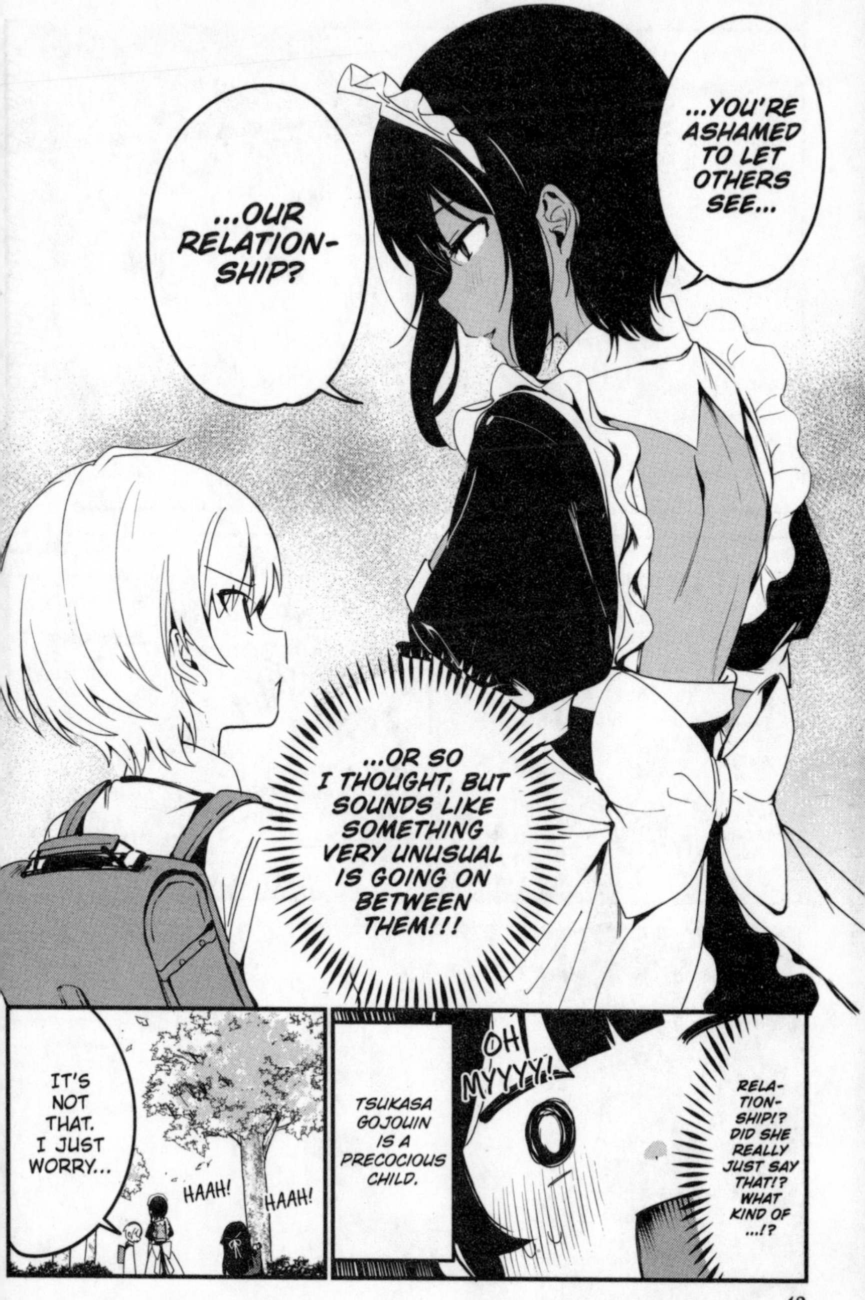
...YOU'RE ASHAMED TO LET OTHERS SEE...
...OUR RELATION-SHIP?
...OR SO I THOUGHT, BUT SOUNDS LIKE SOMETHING VERY UNUSUAL IS GOING ON BETWEEN THEM!!!
OH MYYYY!
RELA-TION-SHIP!? DID SHE REALLY JUST SAY THAT!? WHAT KIND OF ...!?
TSUKASA GOJOUIN IS A PRECOCIOUS CHILD.
IT'S NOT THAT. I JUST WORRY...
HAAH!
HAAH!

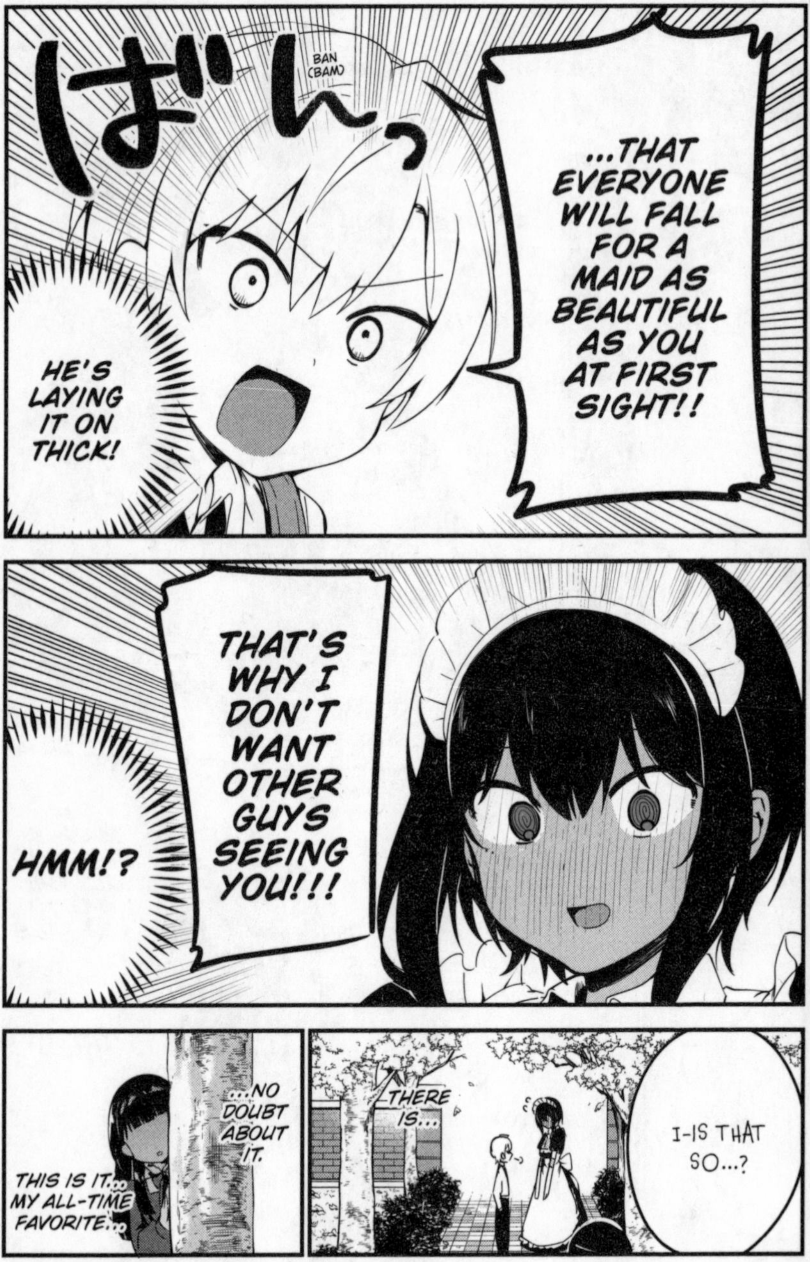
...THAT EVERYONE WILL FALL FOR A MAID AS BEAUTIFUL AS YOU AT FIRST SIGHT!!
ばんっ
BAN (BAM)
HE'S LAYING IT ON THICK!
THAT'S WHY I DON'T WANT OTHER GUYS SEEING YOU!!!
HMM!?
I-IS THAT SO...?
THERE IS...
...NO DOUBT ABOUT IT.
THIS IS IT... MY ALL-TIME FAVORITE...

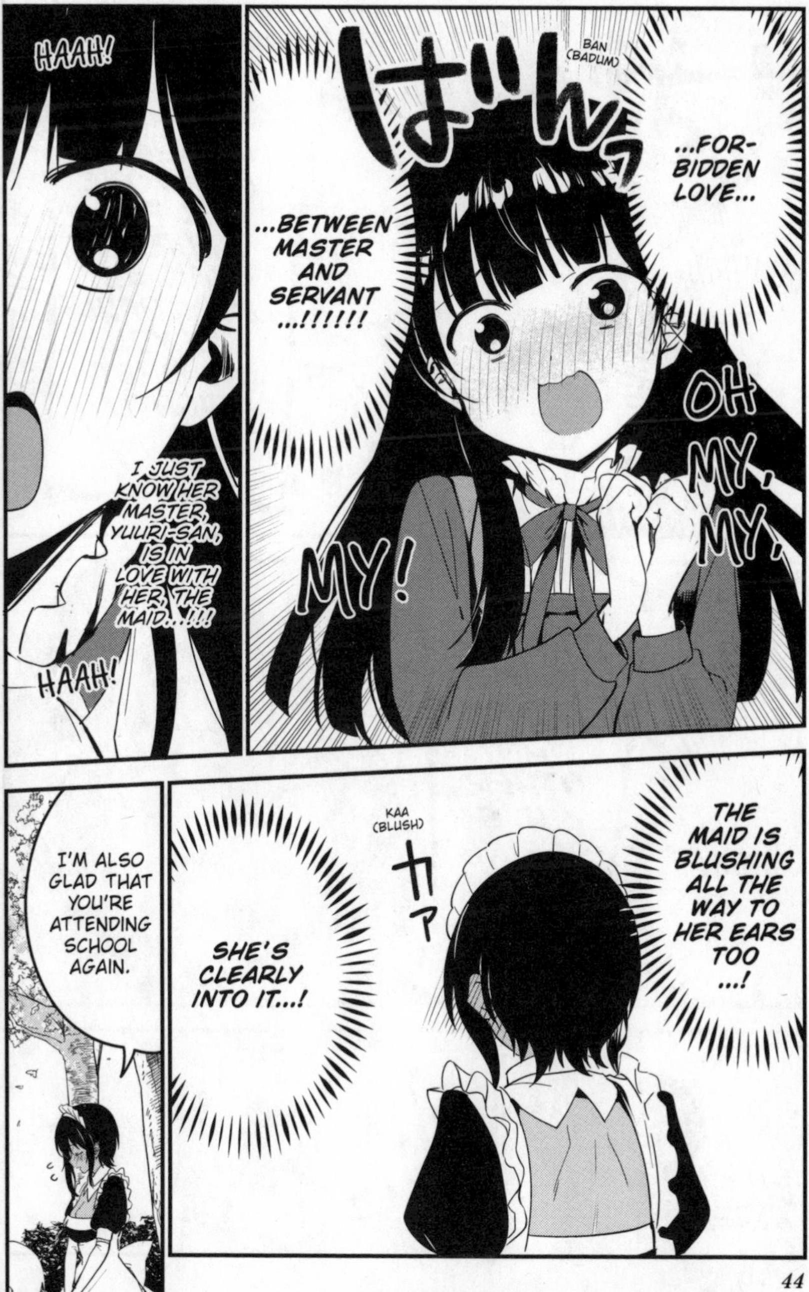
ばんっ
BAN (BADUM)
...FOR-BIDDEN LOVE...
...BETWEEN MASTER AND SERVANT ...!!!!!!
OH MY, MY, MY,
MY!
HAAH!
I JUST KNOW HER MASTER, YUURI-SAN, IS IN LOVE WITH HER, THE MAID...!!!
HAAH!
THE MAID IS BLUSHING ALL THE WAY TO HER EARS TOO ...!
カァ
KAA (BLUSH)
SHE'S CLEARLY INTO IT...!
I'M ALSO GLAD THAT YOU'RE ATTENDING SCHOOL AGAIN.

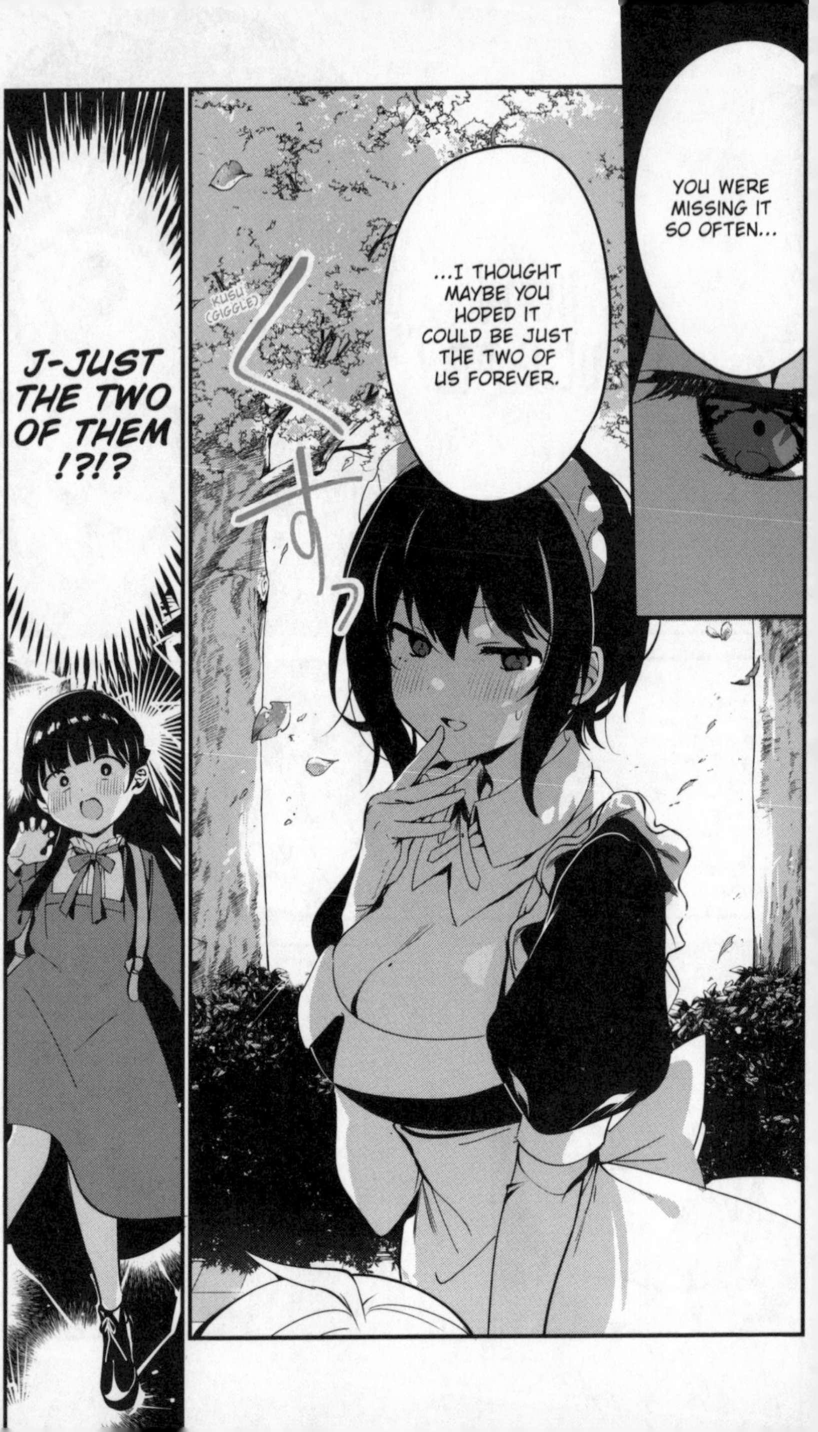
YOU WERE MISSING IT SO OFTEN...
...I THOUGHT MAYBE YOU HOPED IT COULD BE JUST THE TWO OF US FOREVER.
KUSU (GIGGLE)
J-JUST THE TWO OF THEM !?!?

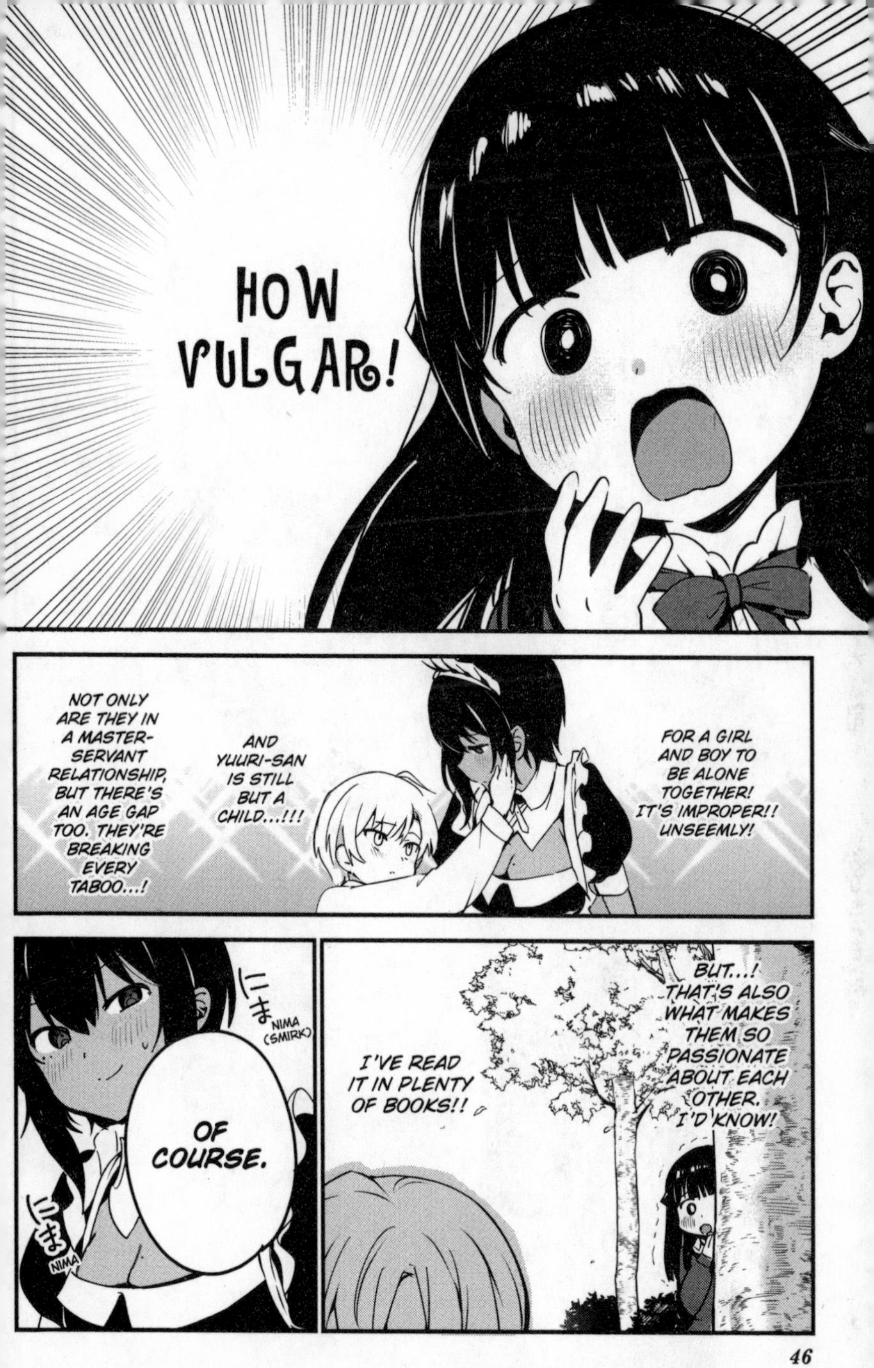
HOW VULGAR!
FOR A GIRL AND BOY TO BE ALONE TOGETHER! IT'S IMPROPER!! UNSEEMLY!
AND YUURI-SAN IS STILL BUT A CHILD...!!!
NOT ONLY ARE THEY IN A MASTER-SERVANT RELATIONSHIP, BUT THERE'S AN AGE GAP TOO. THEY'RE BREAKING EVERY TABOO...!
BUT...! THAT'S ALSO WHAT MAKES THEM SO PASSIONATE ABOUT EACH OTHER. I'D KNOW!
I'VE READ IT IN PLENTY OF BOOKS!!
にま
NIMA (SMIRK)
OF COURSE.
にま
NIMA

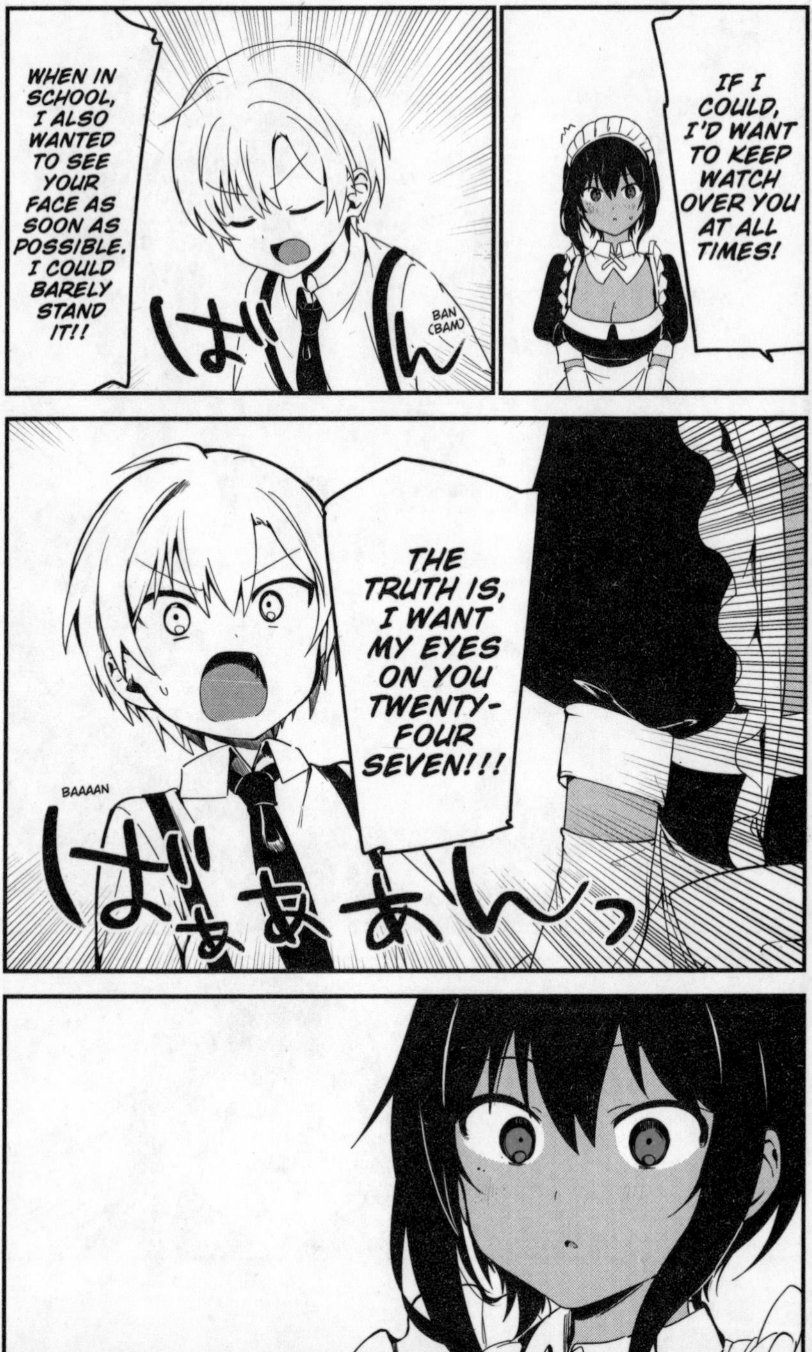
IF I COULD, I'D WANT TO KEEP WATCH OVER YOU AT ALL TIMES!
WHEN IN SCHOOL, I ALSO WANTED TO SEE YOUR FACE AS SOON AS POSSIBLE. I COULD BARELY STAND IT!!
BAN (BAM)
ばん
THE TRUTH IS, I WANT MY EYES ON YOU TWENTY-FOUR SEVEN!!!
BAAAAN
ばぁああんっ

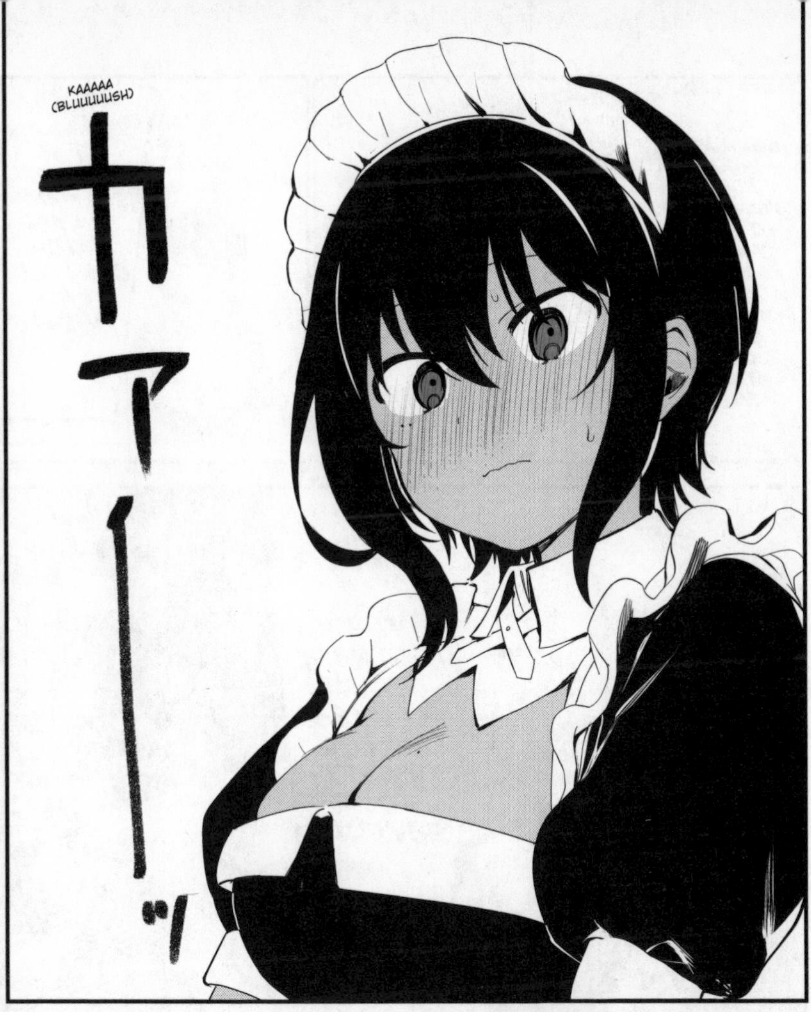
KAAAAA (BLUUUUUSH)
カアーッ
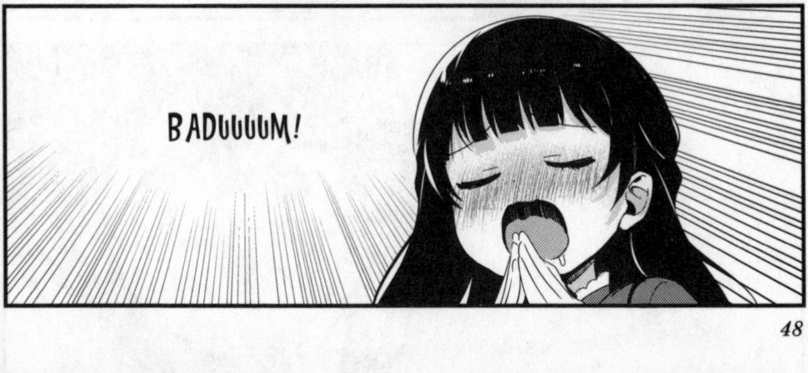
BADUUUUM!

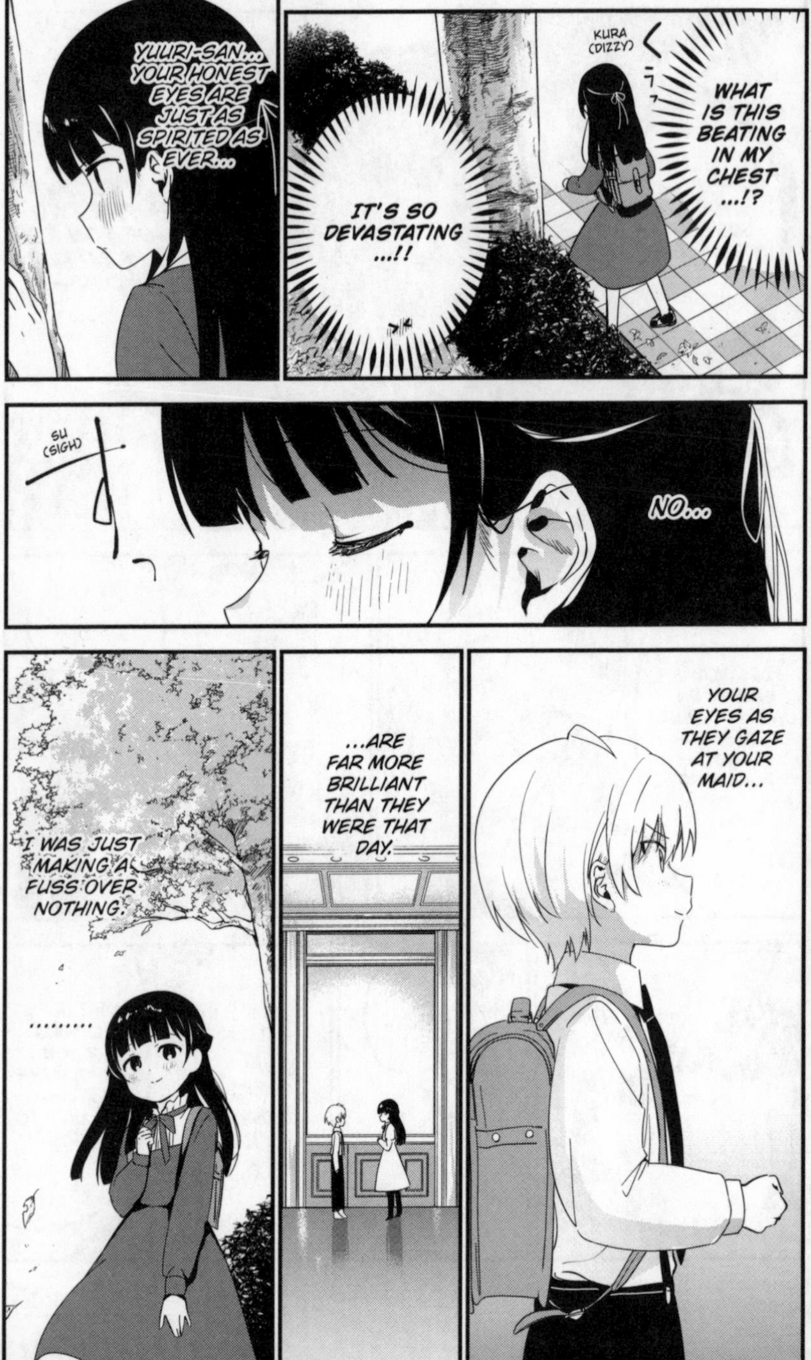
KURA (DIZZY)
WHAT IS THIS BEATING IN MY CHEST ...!?
IT'S SO DEVASTATING ...!!
YUURI-SAN... YOUR HONEST EYES ARE JUST AS SPIRITED AS EVER...
NO...
SU (SIGH)
YOUR EYES AS THEY GAZE AT YOUR MAID...
...ARE FAR MORE BRILLIANT THAN THEY WERE THAT DAY.
I WAS JUST MAKING A FUSS OVER NOTHING.
....

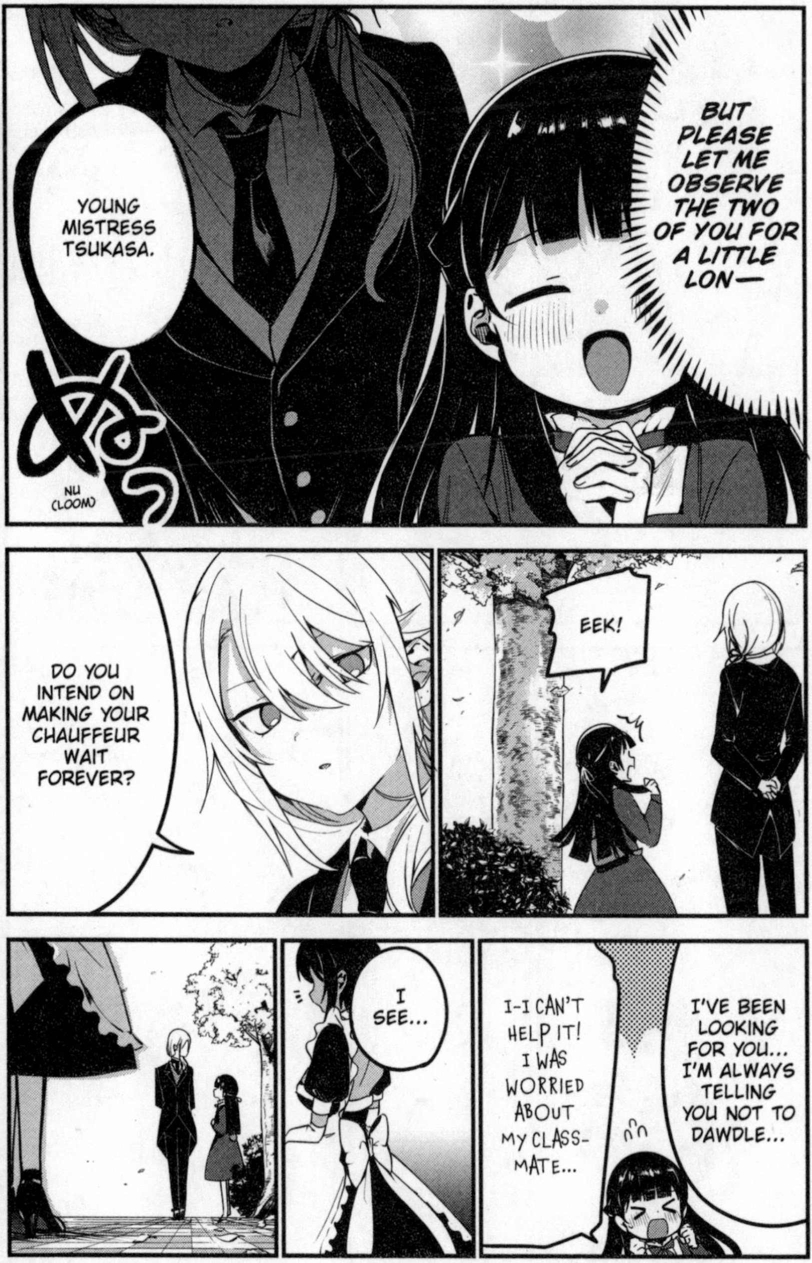
BUT PLEASE LET ME OBSERVE THE TWO OF YOU FOR A LITTLE LON—
YOUNG MISTRESS TSUKASA.
NU (LOOM)
EEK!
DO YOU INTEND ON MAKING YOUR CHAUFFEUR WAIT FOREVER?
I'VE BEEN LOOKING FOR YOU... I'M ALWAYS TELLING YOU NOT TO DAWDLE...
I-I CAN'T HELP IT! I WAS WORRIED ABOUT MY CLASS-MATE...
I SEE...

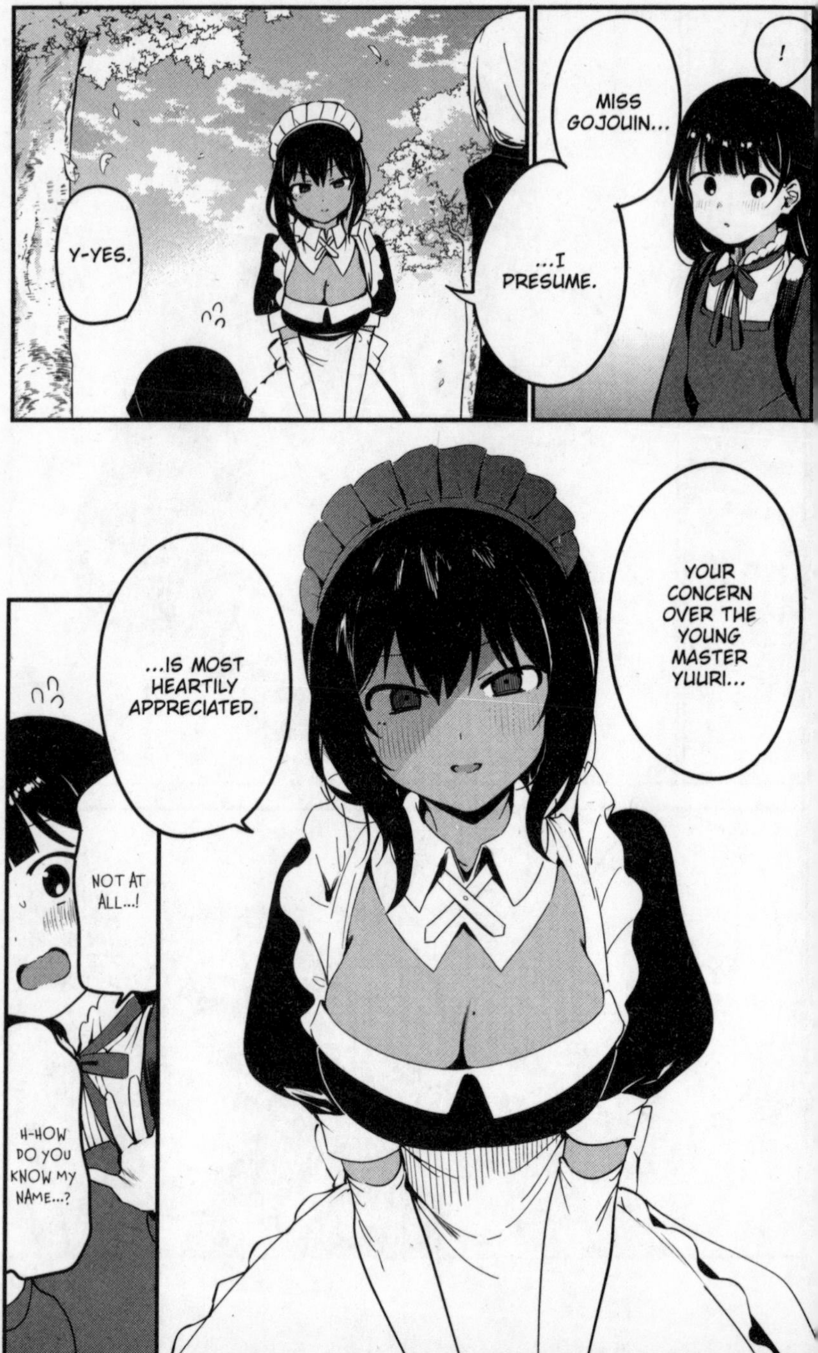
!
MISS GOJOUIN...
...I PRESUME.
Y-YES.
YOUR CONCERN OVER THE YOUNG MASTER YUURI...
...IS MOST HEARTILY APPRECIATED.
NOT AT ALL...!
H-HOW DO YOU KNOW MY NAME...?

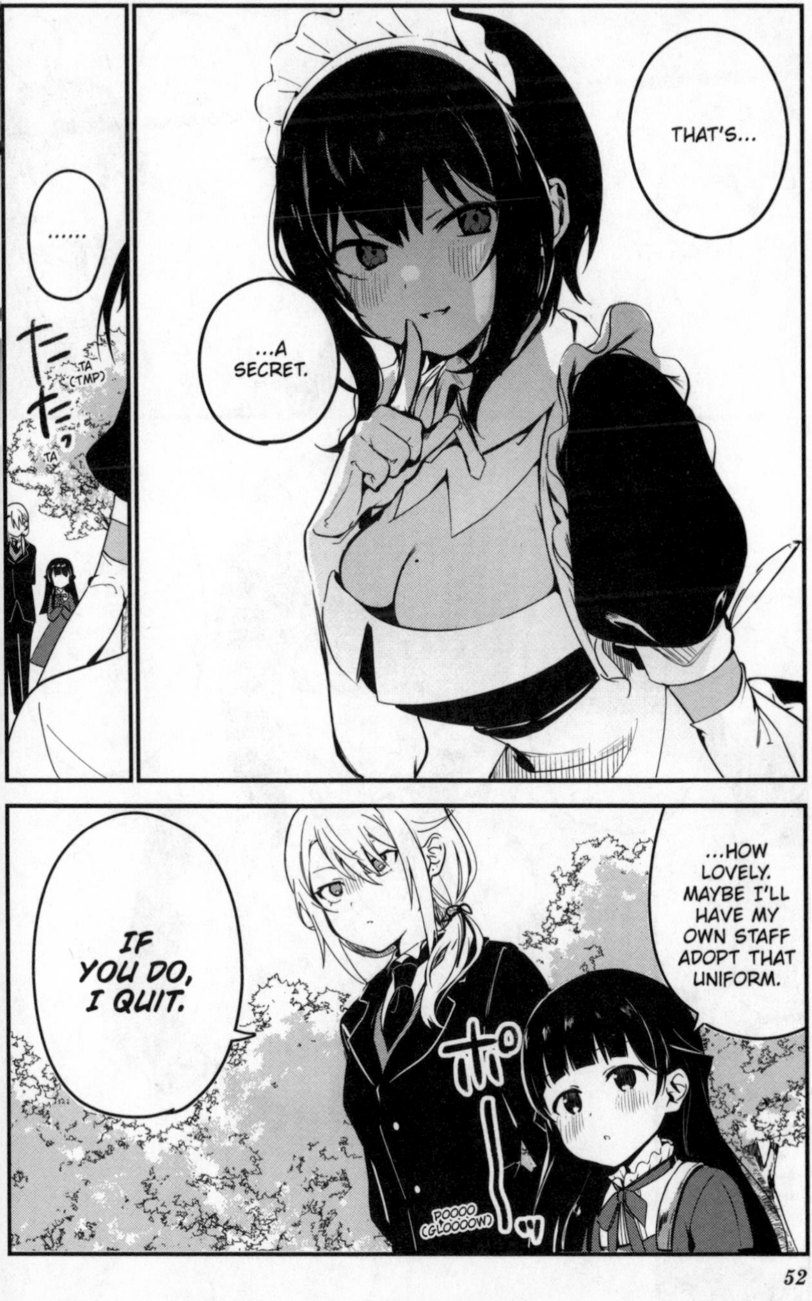
THAT'S...
...A SECRET.
......
TA (TMP)
TA
...HOW LOVELY. MAYBE I'LL HAVE MY OWN STAFF ADOPT THAT UNIFORM.
IF YOU DO, I QUIT.
POOOO (GLOOOOW)

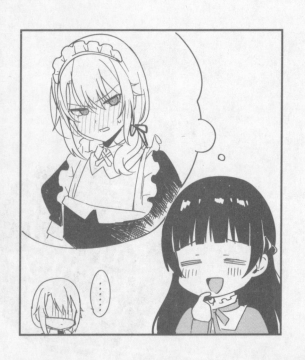

‥‥‥‥

The Maid I Hired Recently Is Mysterious

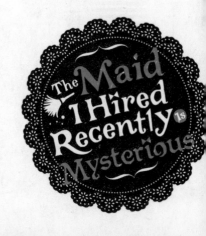

BONUS STORY ①

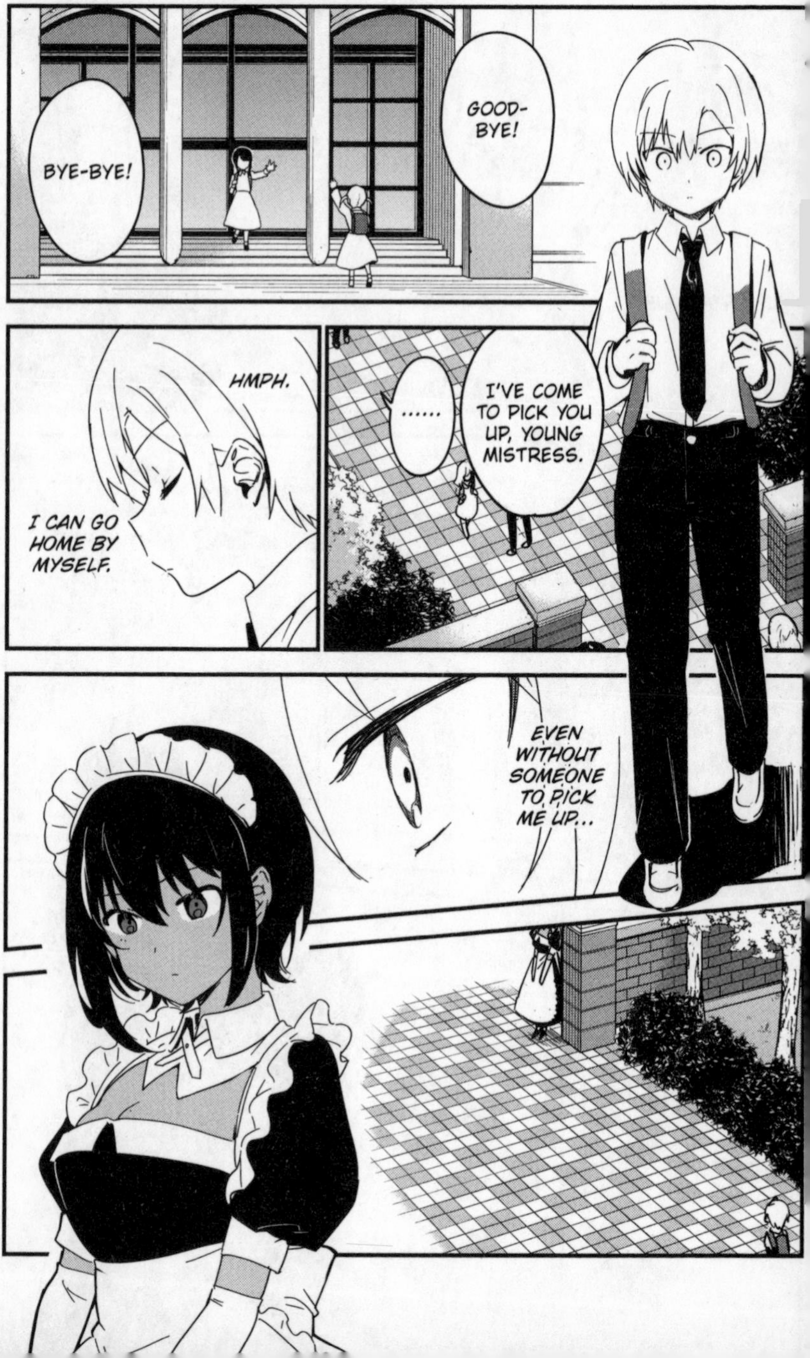
GOOD-BYE!
BYE-BYE!
I'VE COME TO PICK YOU UP, YOUNG MISTRESS.
......
HMPH.
I CAN GO HOME BY MYSELF.
EVEN WITHOUT SOMEONE TO PICK ME UP...

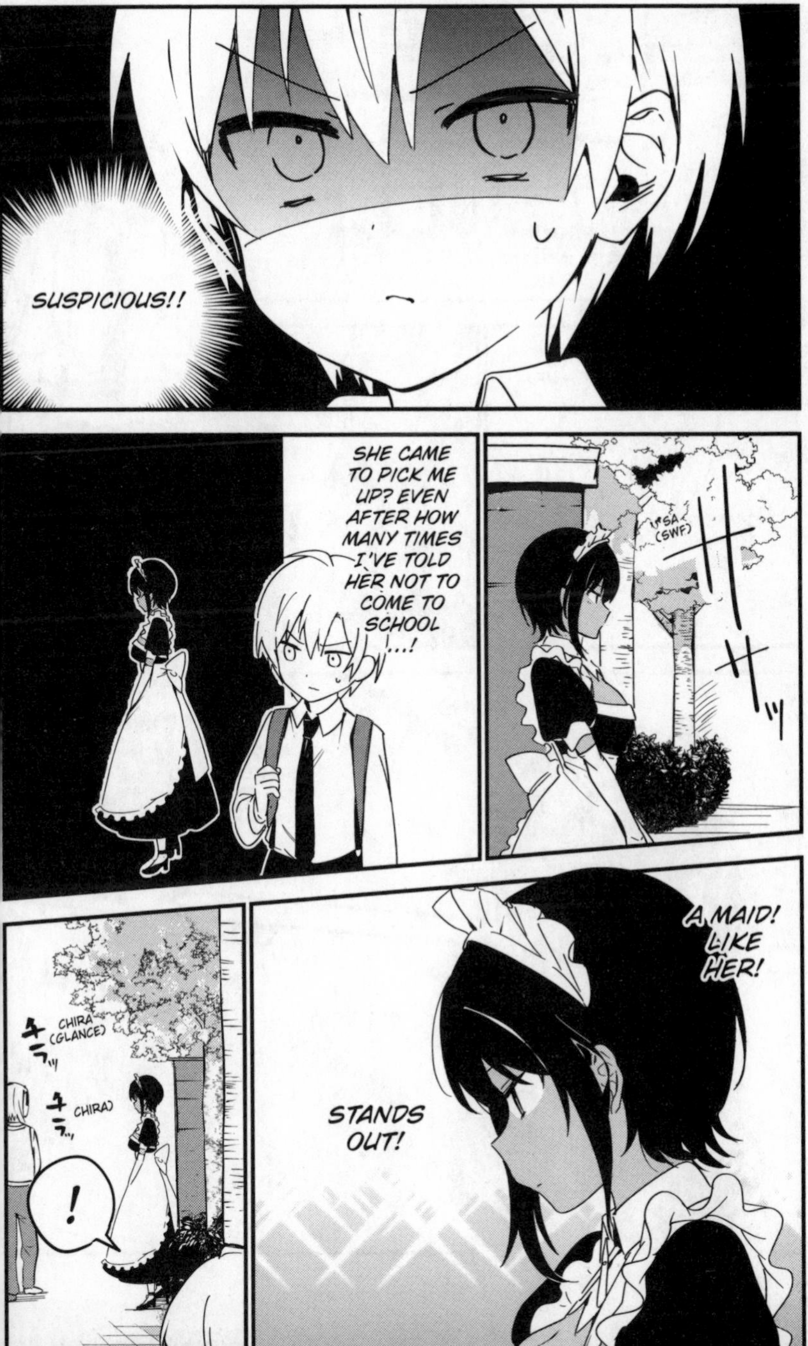
SUSPICIOUS!!
SA (SWF)
サッ
SHE CAME TO PICK ME UP? EVEN AFTER HOW MANY TIMES I'VE TOLD HER NOT TO COME TO SCHOOL...!
A MAID! LIKE HER!
STANDS OUT!
CHIRA (GLANCE)
チラッ
CHIRA)
チラッ
!

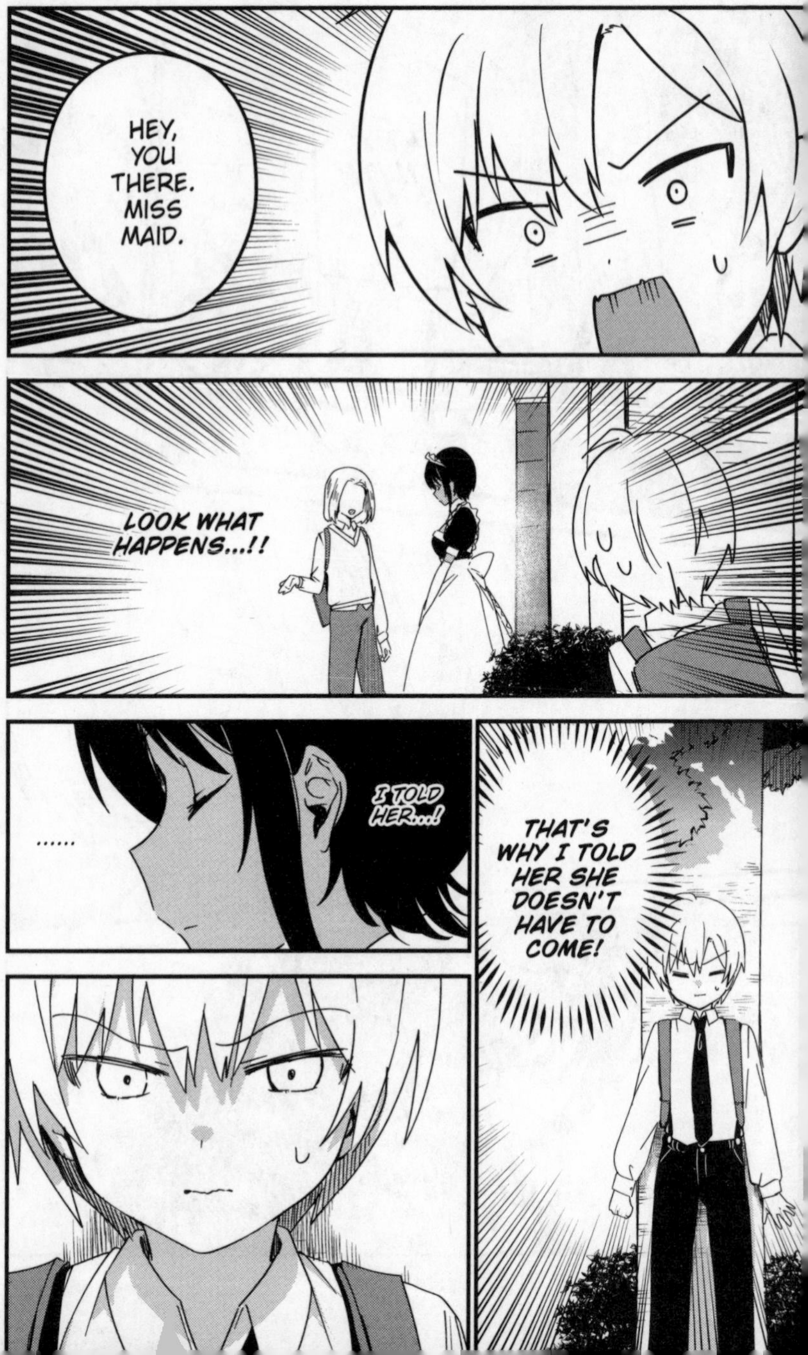
HEY, YOU THERE. MISS MAID.
LOOK WHAT HAPPENS...!!
THAT'S WHY I TOLD HER SHE DOESN'T HAVE TO COME!
I TOLD HER...!
......

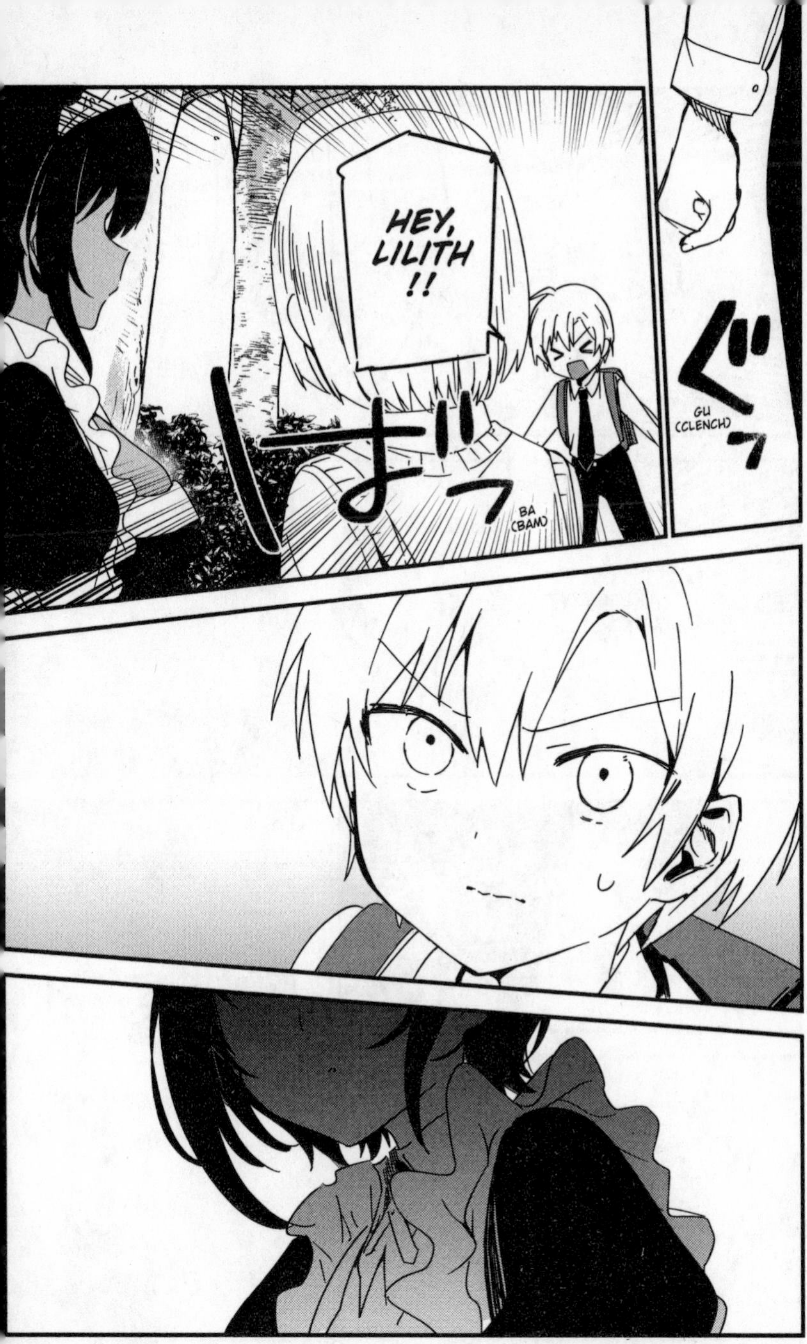
ぐっ
GU (CLENCH)
HEY, LILITH!!
ばっ
BA (BAM)

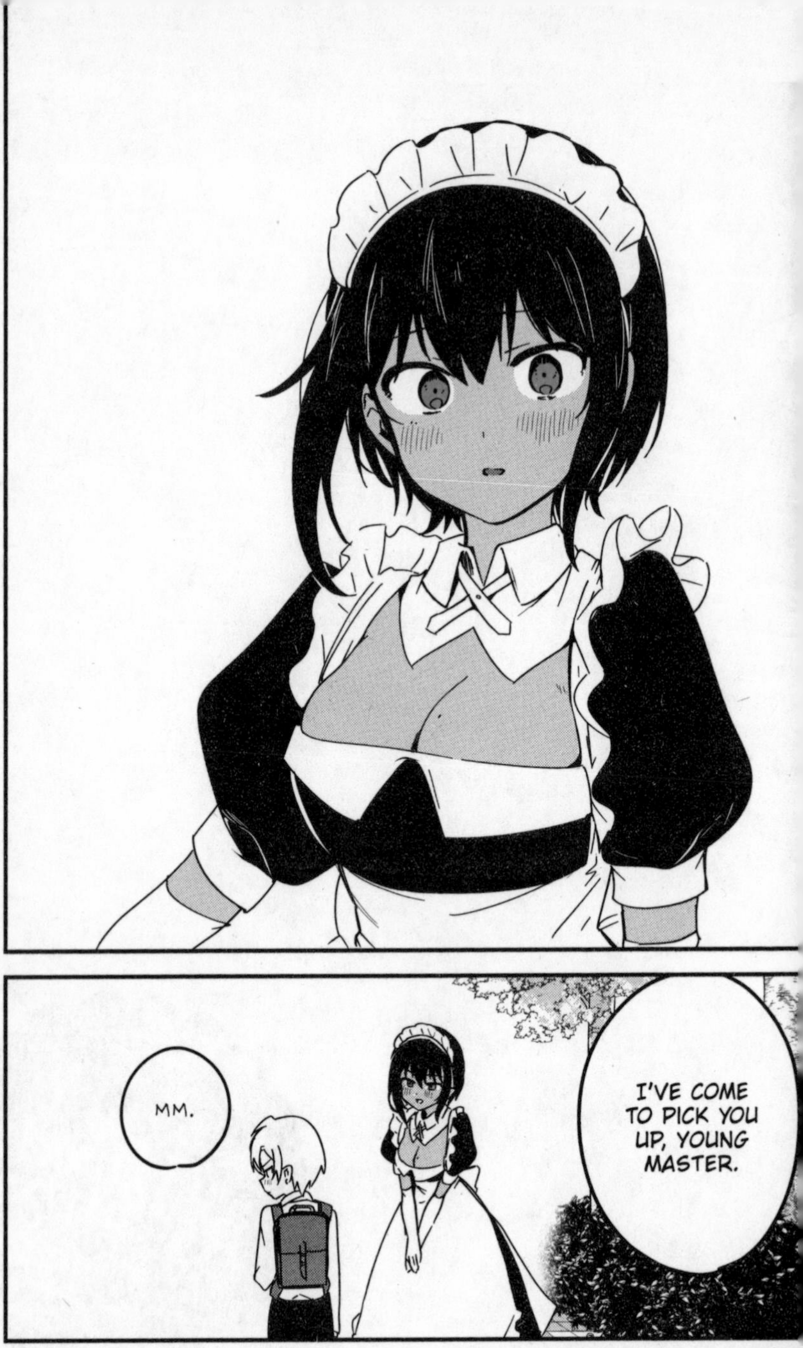
I'VE COME TO PICK YOU UP, YOUNG MASTER.
MM.

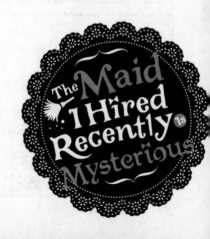

The Maid I Hired Recently is Mysterious

CHAPTER 20

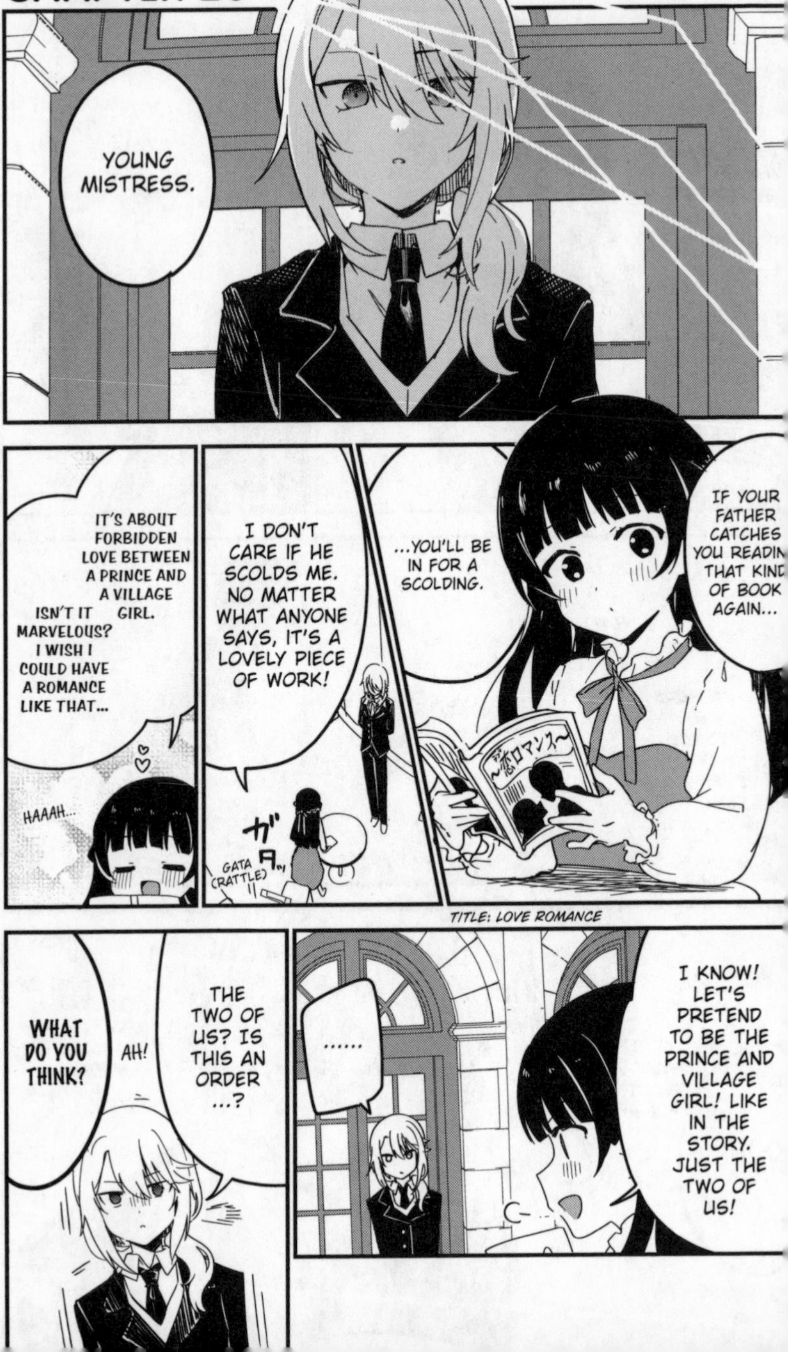

YOUNG MISTRESS.
IF YOUR FATHER CATCHES YOU READIN THAT KIND OF BOOK AGAIN...
...YOU'LL BE IN FOR A SCOLDING.
～恋ロマンス～
TITLE: LOVE ROMANCE
I DON'T CARE IF HE SCOLDS ME. NO MATTER WHAT ANYONE SAYS, IT'S A LOVELY PIECE OF WORK!
ガタッ
GATA (RATTLE)
IT'S ABOUT FORBIDDEN LOVE BETWEEN A PRINCE AND A VILLAGE GIRL.
ISN'T IT MARVELOUS? I WISH I COULD HAVE A ROMANCE LIKE THAT...
HAAAH...
I KNOW! LET'S PRETEND TO BE THE PRINCE AND VILLAGE GIRL! LIKE IN THE STORY. JUST THE TWO OF US!
......
THE TWO OF US? IS THIS AN ORDER ...?
AH!
WHAT DO YOU THINK?

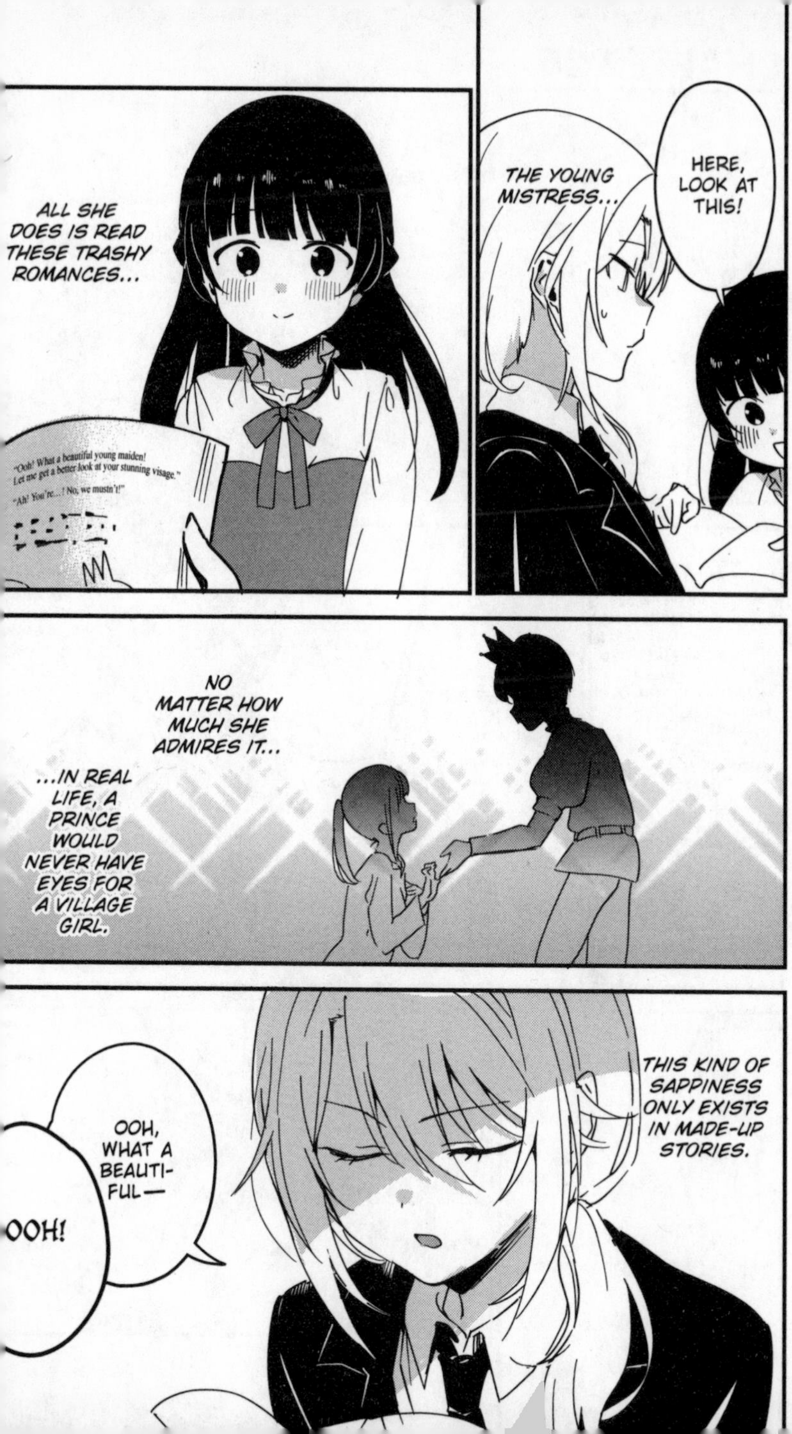
HERE, LOOK AT THIS!
THE YOUNG MISTRESS...
ALL SHE DOES IS READ THESE TRASHY ROMANCES...
"Ooh! What a beautiful young maiden! Let me get a better look at your stunning visage."
"Ah! You're...! No, we mustn't!"
NO MATTER HOW MUCH SHE ADMIRES IT...
...IN REAL LIFE, A PRINCE WOULD NEVER HAVE EYES FOR A VILLAGE GIRL.
THIS KIND OF SAPPINESS ONLY EXISTS IN MADE-UP STORIES.
OOH, WHAT A BEAUTI-FUL—
OOH!

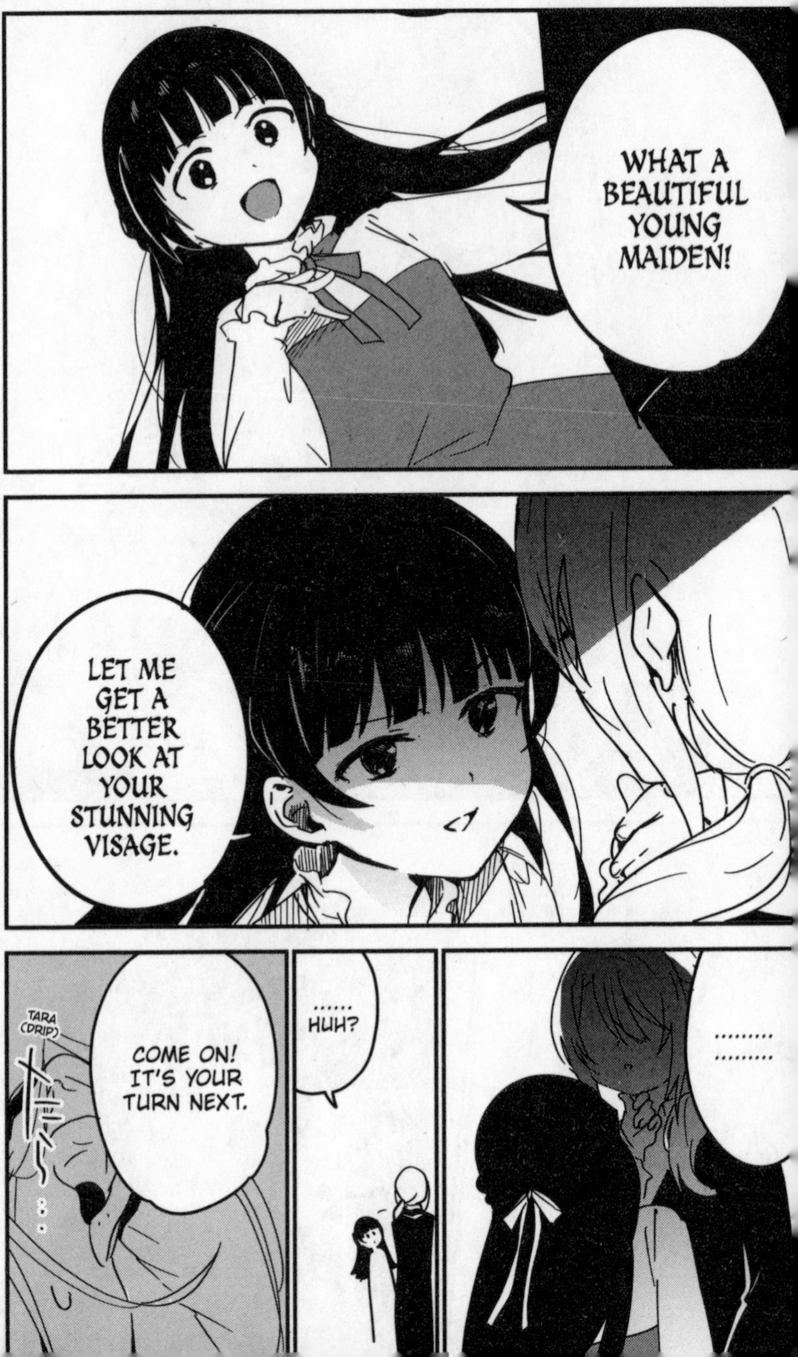
WHAT A BEAUTIFUL YOUNG MAIDEN!
LET ME GET A BETTER LOOK AT YOUR STUNNING VISAGE.
....
....
......
HUH?
TARA (DRIP)
COME ON! IT'S YOUR TURN NEXT.

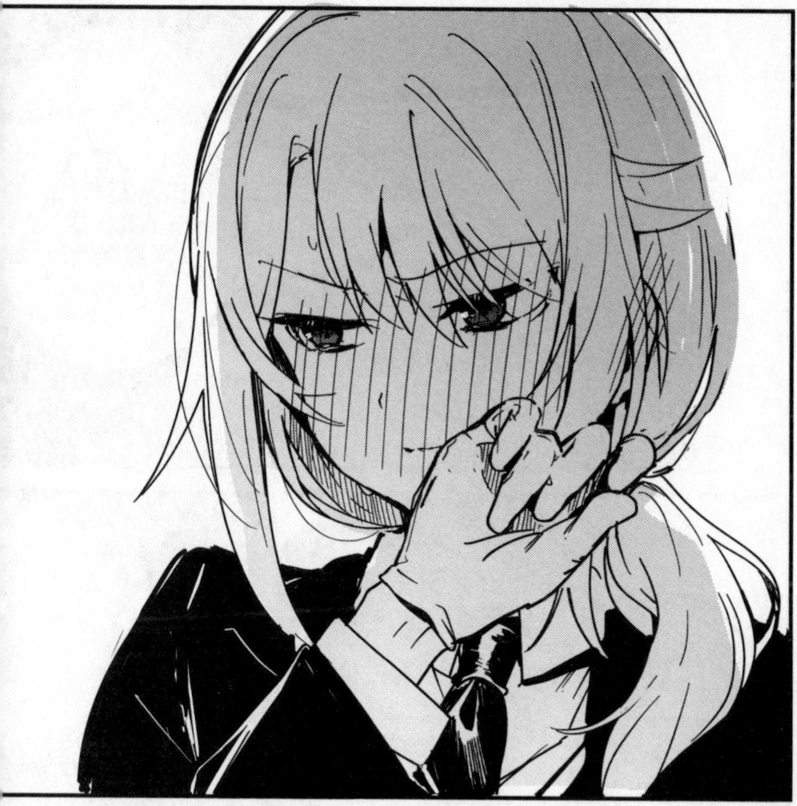

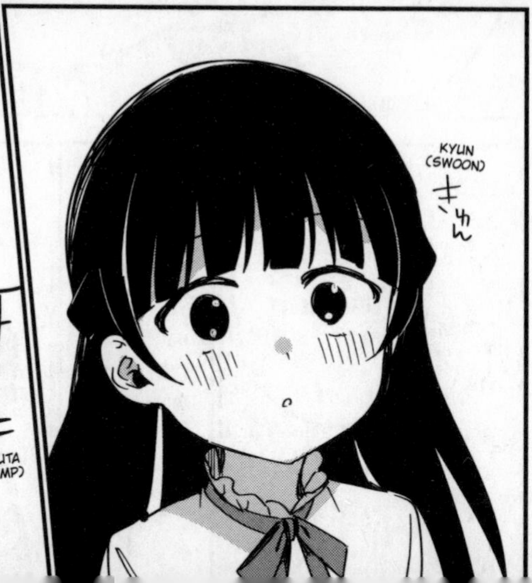

KYUN (SWOON)
きゅん

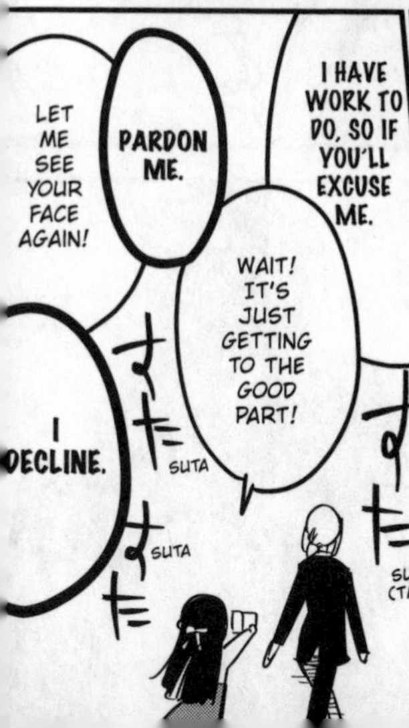

I HAVE WORK TO DO, SO IF YOU'LL EXCUSE ME.
PARDON ME.
LET ME SEE YOUR FACE AGAIN!
WAIT! IT'S JUST GETTING TO THE GOOD PART!
SUTA (TMP)
I DECLINE.
SUTA
SUTA

EEK!
HOW STUNNING!
OH MY!
......
NOBODY GETS IT AT ALL!
THEY SHOULD BE SAYING "HOW CUTE!"
?

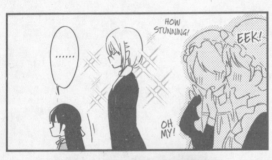

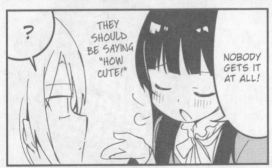

The Maid I Hired Recently Is Mysterious

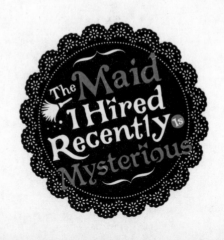

CHAPTER 21

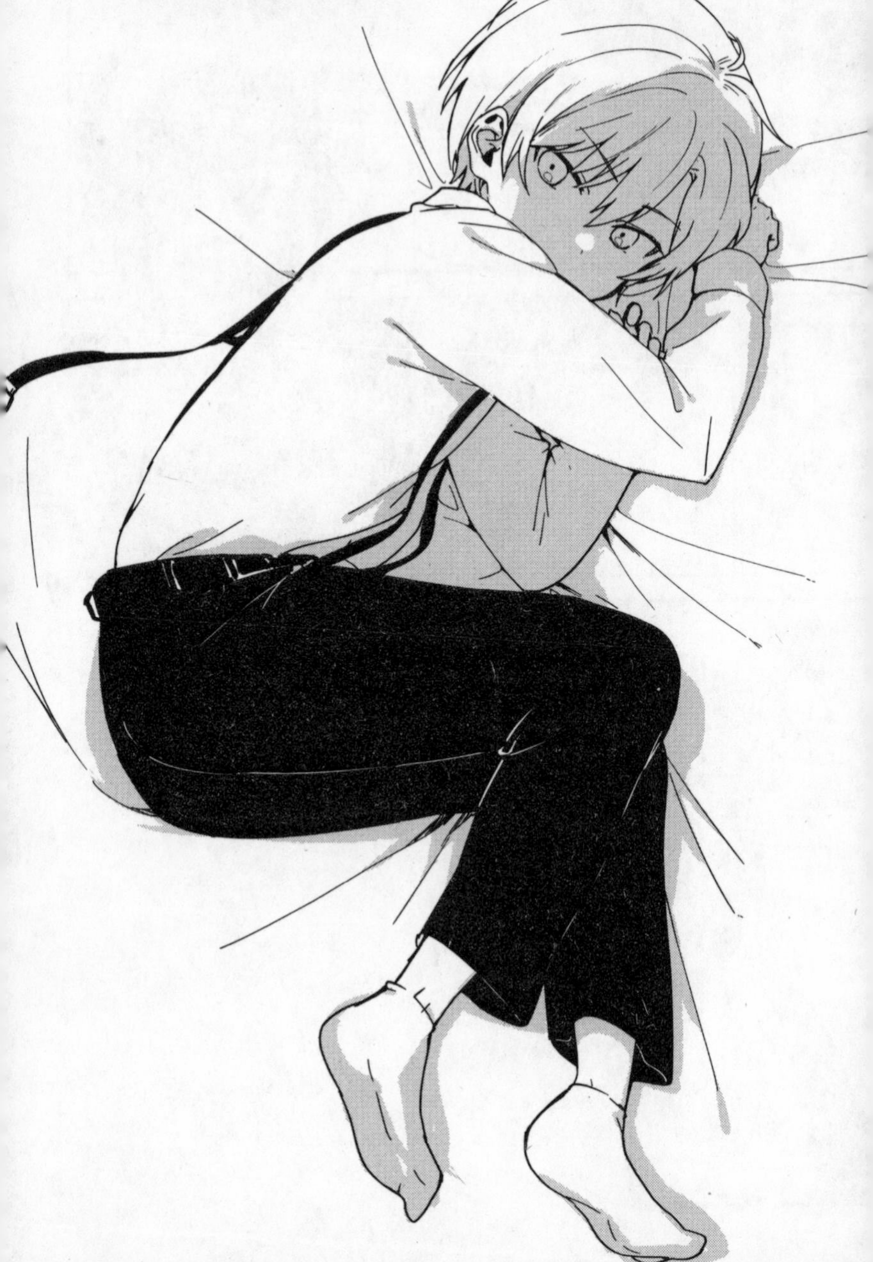

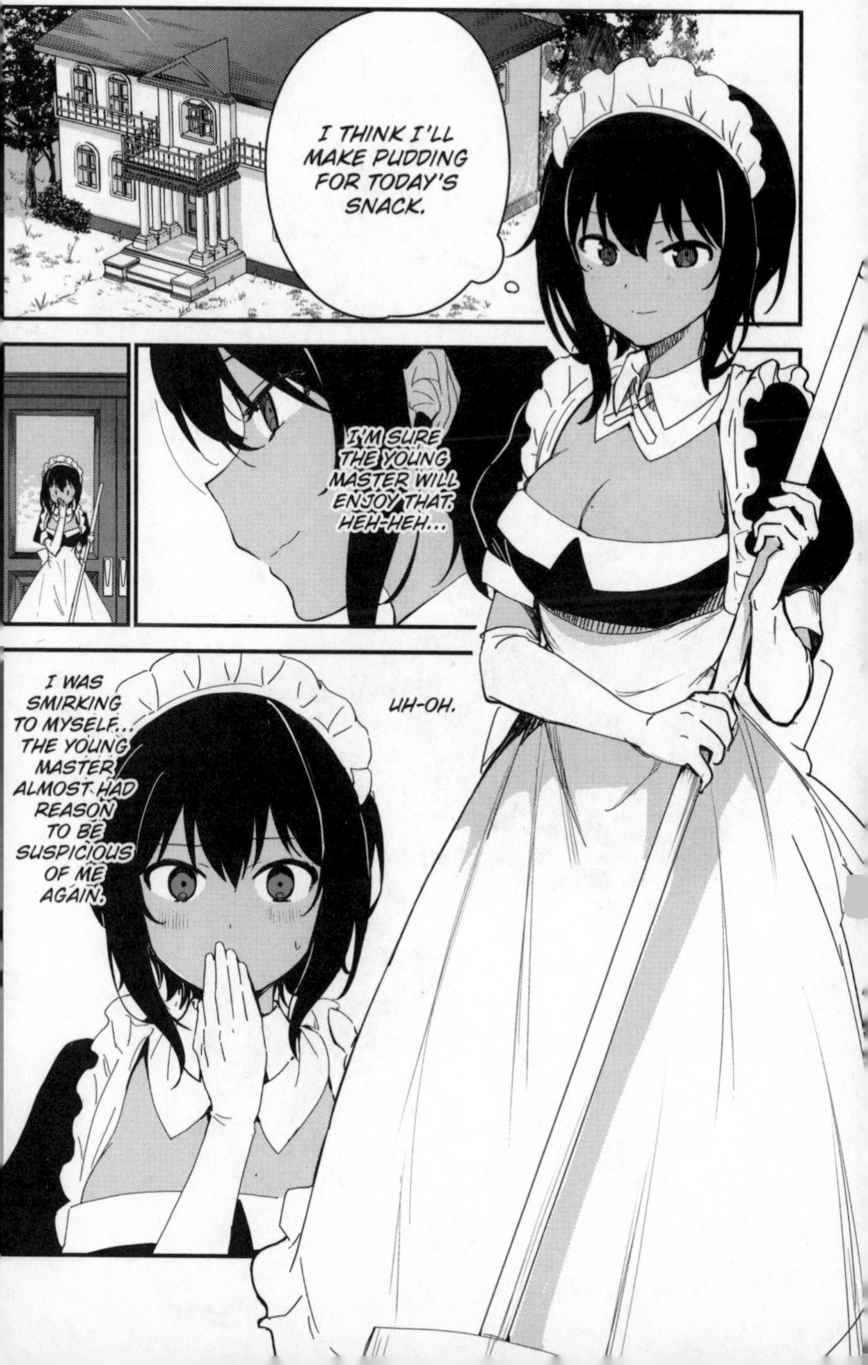
I THINK I'LL MAKE PUDDING FOR TODAY'S SNACK.
I'M SURE THE YOUNG MASTER WILL ENJOY THAT. HEH-HEH...
UH-OH.
I WAS SMIRKING TO MYSELF... THE YOUNG MASTER ALMOST HAD REASON TO BE SUSPICIOUS OF ME AGAIN.

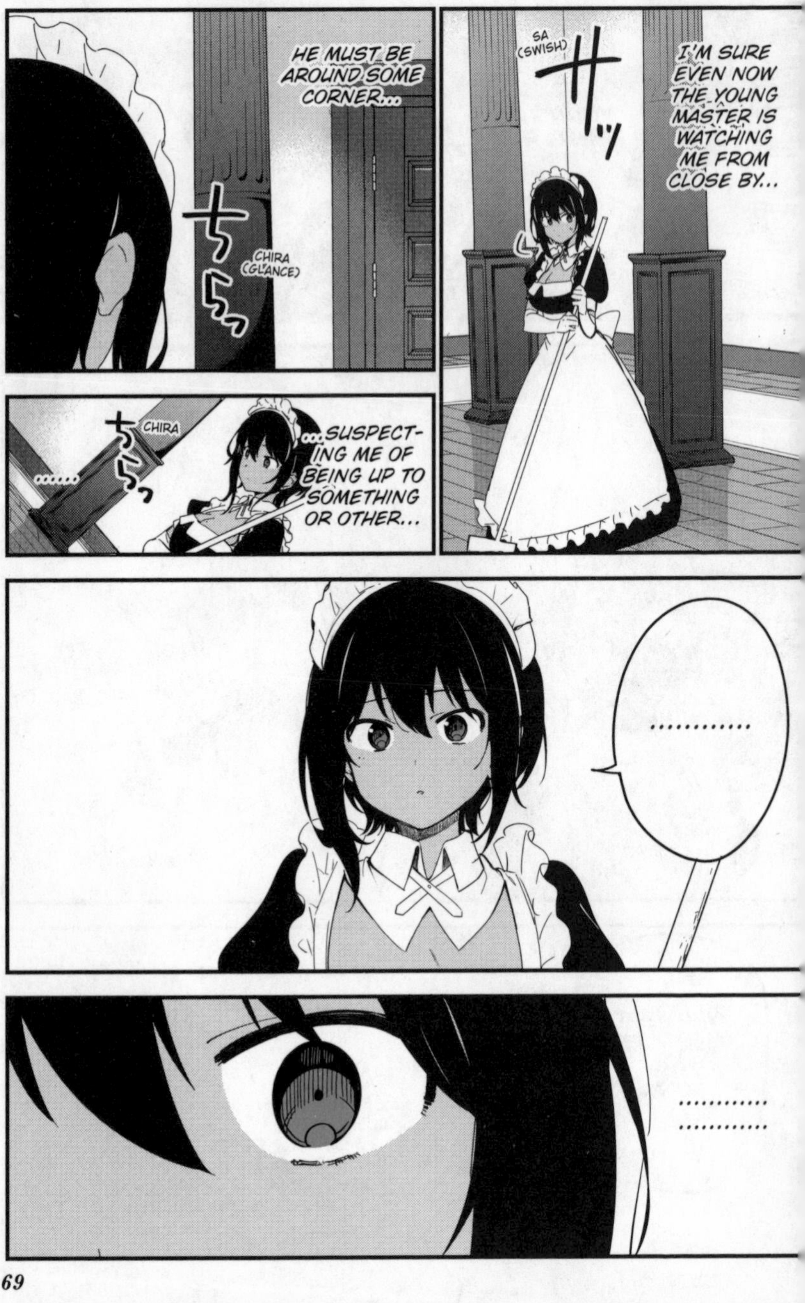
SA (SWISH)
サッ
I'M SURE EVEN NOW THE YOUNG MASTER IS WATCHING ME FROM CLOSE BY...
HE MUST BE AROUND SOME CORNER...
ちらっ
CHIRA (GLANCE)
...SUSPECTING ME OF BEING UP TO SOMETHING OR OTHER...
ちらっ
CHIRA
......
....
....
....

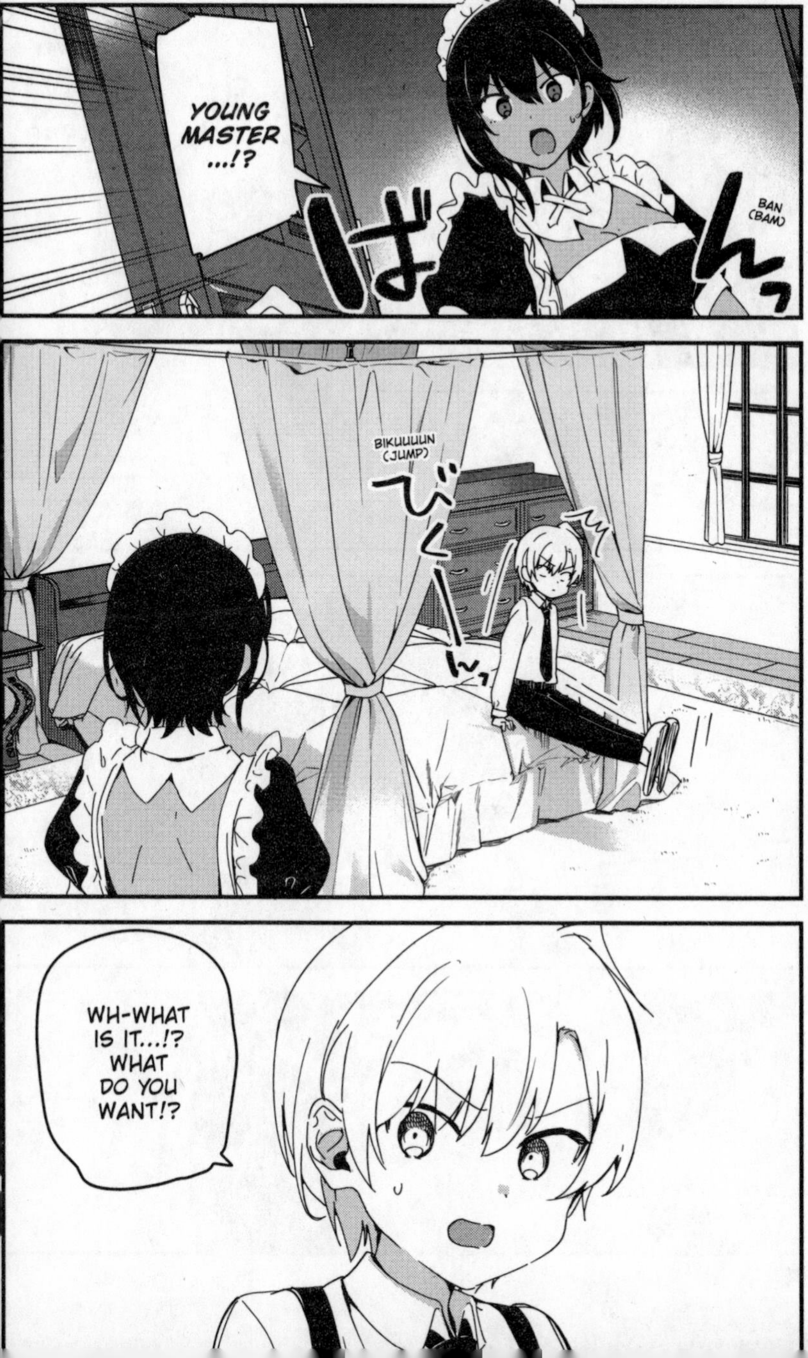
BAN (BAM)
YOUNG MASTER ...!?
BIKUUUUN (JUMP)
WH-WHAT IS IT...!? WHAT DO YOU WANT!?

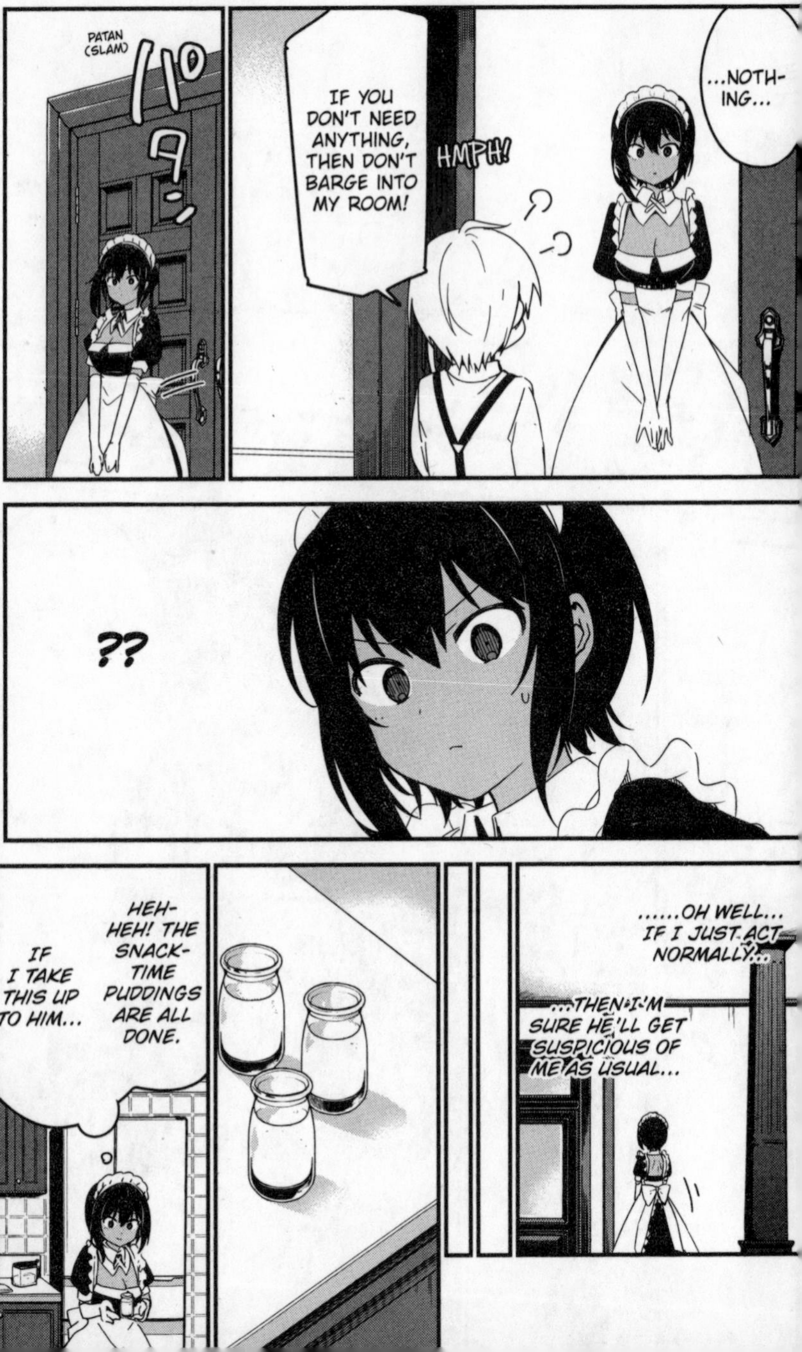
...NOTHING...
IF YOU DON'T NEED ANYTHING, THEN DON'T BARGE INTO MY ROOM!
HMPH!
PATAN (SLAM)
??
......OH WELL... IF I JUST ACT NORMALLY...
...THEN I'M SURE HE'LL GET SUSPICIOUS OF ME AS USUAL...
HEH-HEH! THE SNACK-TIME PUDDINGS ARE ALL DONE.
IF I TAKE THIS UP TO HIM...

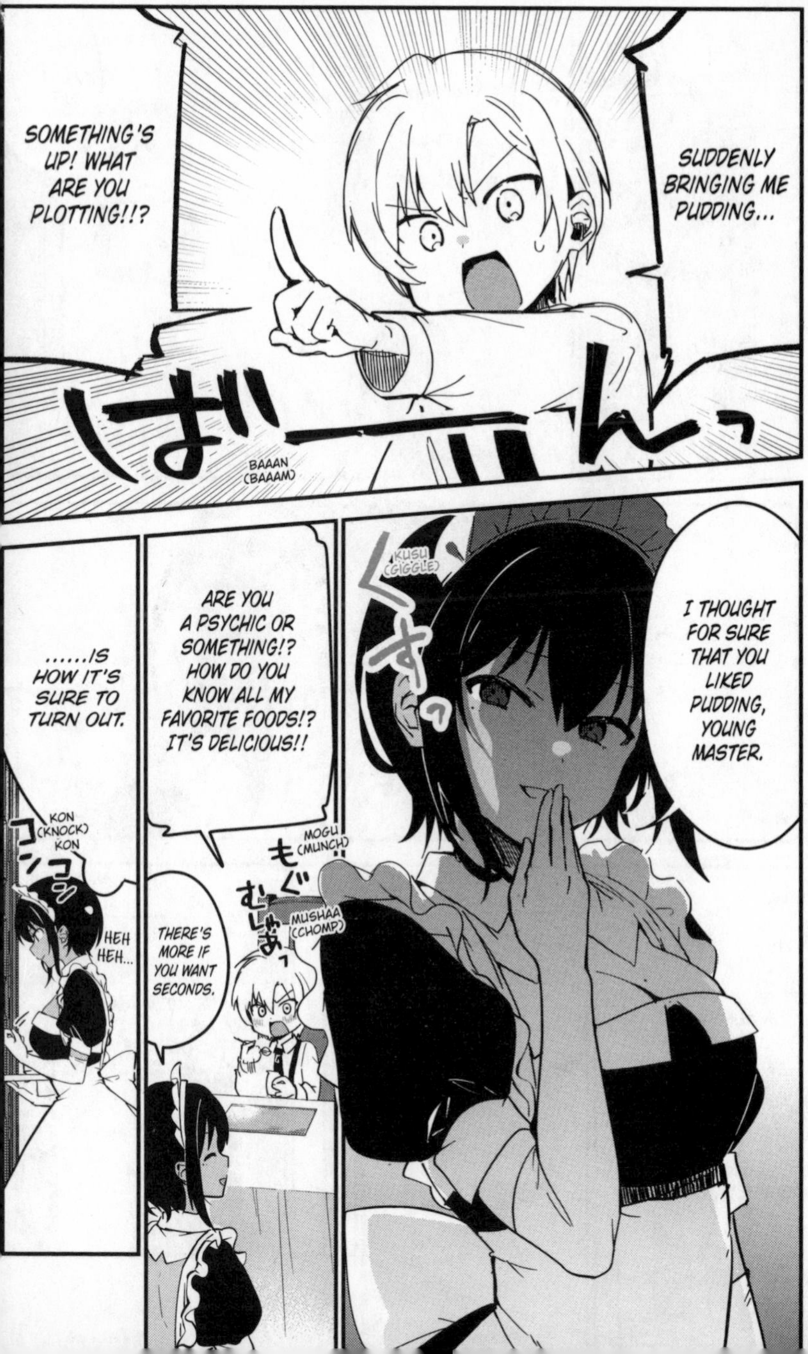
SUDDENLY BRINGING ME PUDDING...
SOMETHING'S UP! WHAT ARE YOU PLOTTING!!?
ばーーんっ
BAAAN (BAAAM)
くすっ
KUSU (GIGGLE)
I THOUGHT FOR SURE THAT YOU LIKED PUDDING, YOUNG MASTER.
ARE YOU A PSYCHIC OR SOMETHING!? HOW DO YOU KNOW ALL MY FAVORITE FOODS!? IT'S DELICIOUS!!
もぐ
MOGU (MUNCH)
むしゃあっ
MUSHAA (CHOMP)
THERE'S MORE IF YOU WANT SECONDS.
......IS HOW IT'S SURE TO TURN OUT.
コンコン
KON (KNOCK) KON
HEH HEH...

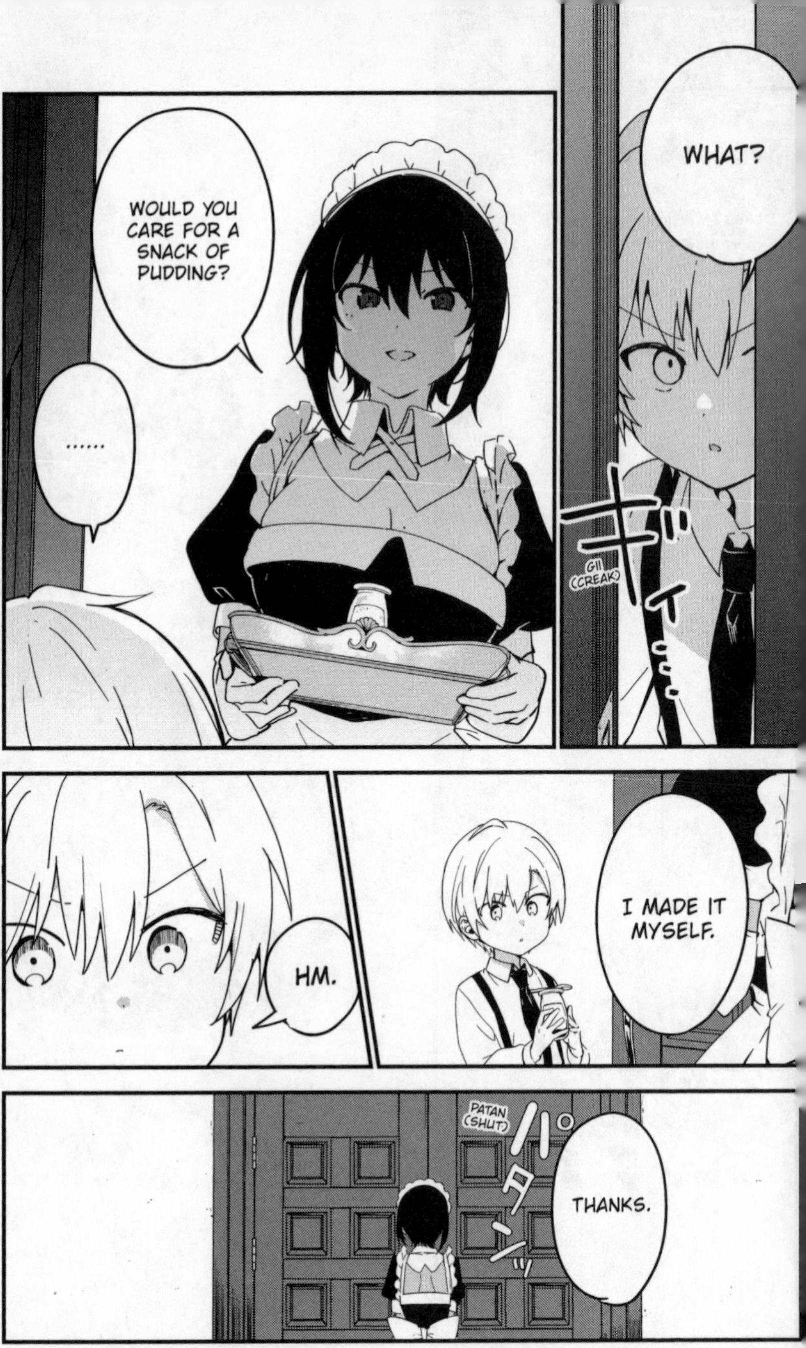
WHAT?
GII (CREAK)
WOULD YOU CARE FOR A SNACK OF PUDDING?
......
I MADE IT MYSELF.
HM.
PATAN (SHUT)
THANKS.

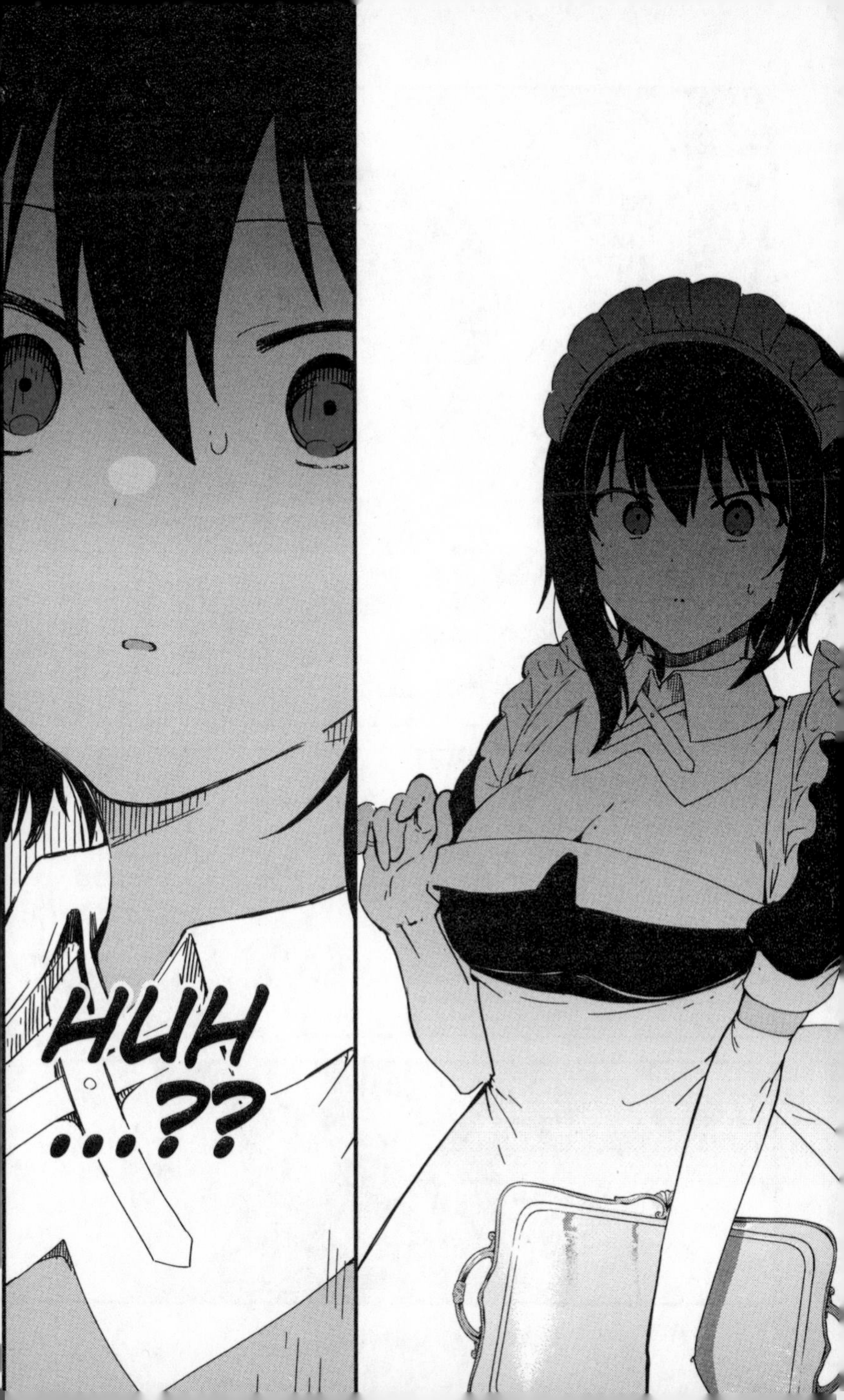
HUH ...??

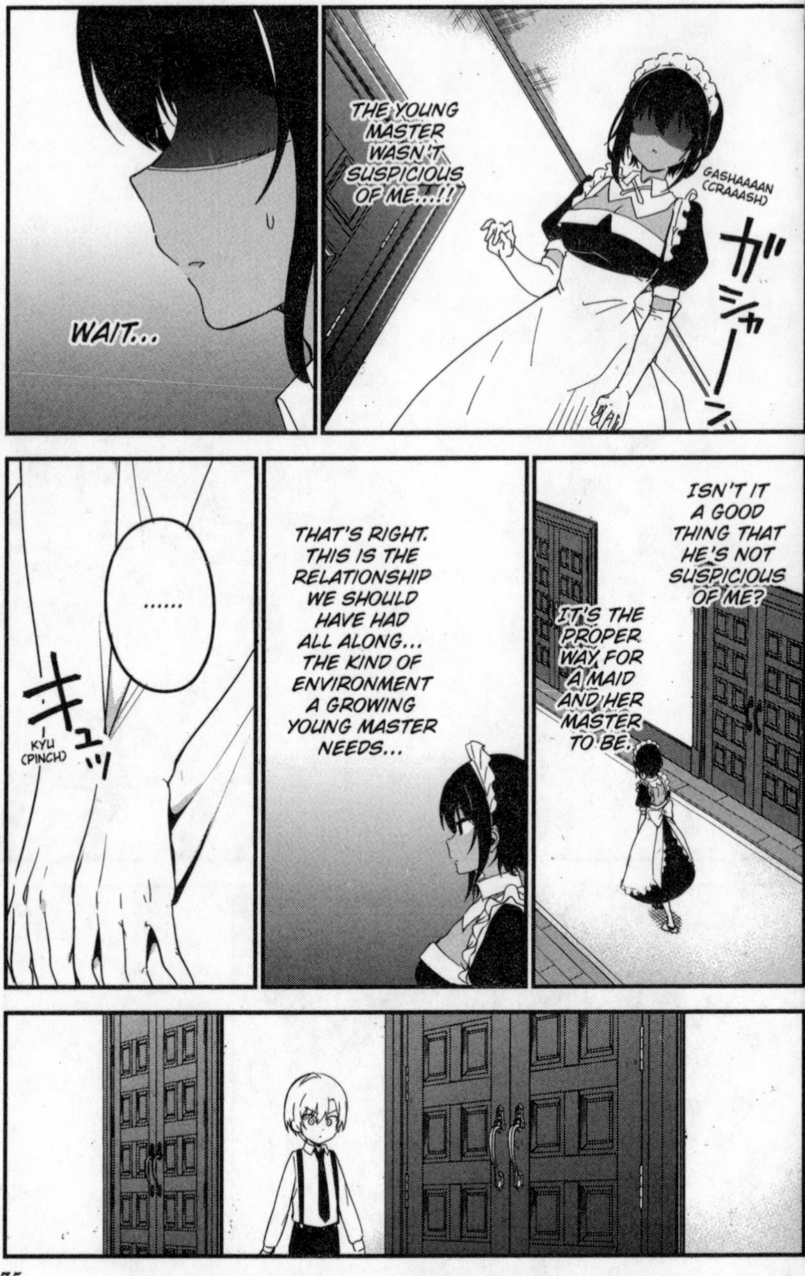
GASHAAAAN (CRAAASH)
ガシャーン
THE YOUNG MASTER WASN'T SUSPICIOUS OF ME...!!
WAIT...
ISN'T IT A GOOD THING THAT HE'S NOT SUSPICIOUS OF ME?
IT'S THE PROPER WAY FOR A MAID AND HER MASTER TO BE.
THAT'S RIGHT. THIS IS THE RELATIONSHIP WE SHOULD HAVE HAD ALL ALONG... THE KIND OF ENVIRONMENT A GROWING YOUNG MASTER NEEDS...
......
キュッ
KYU (PINCH)

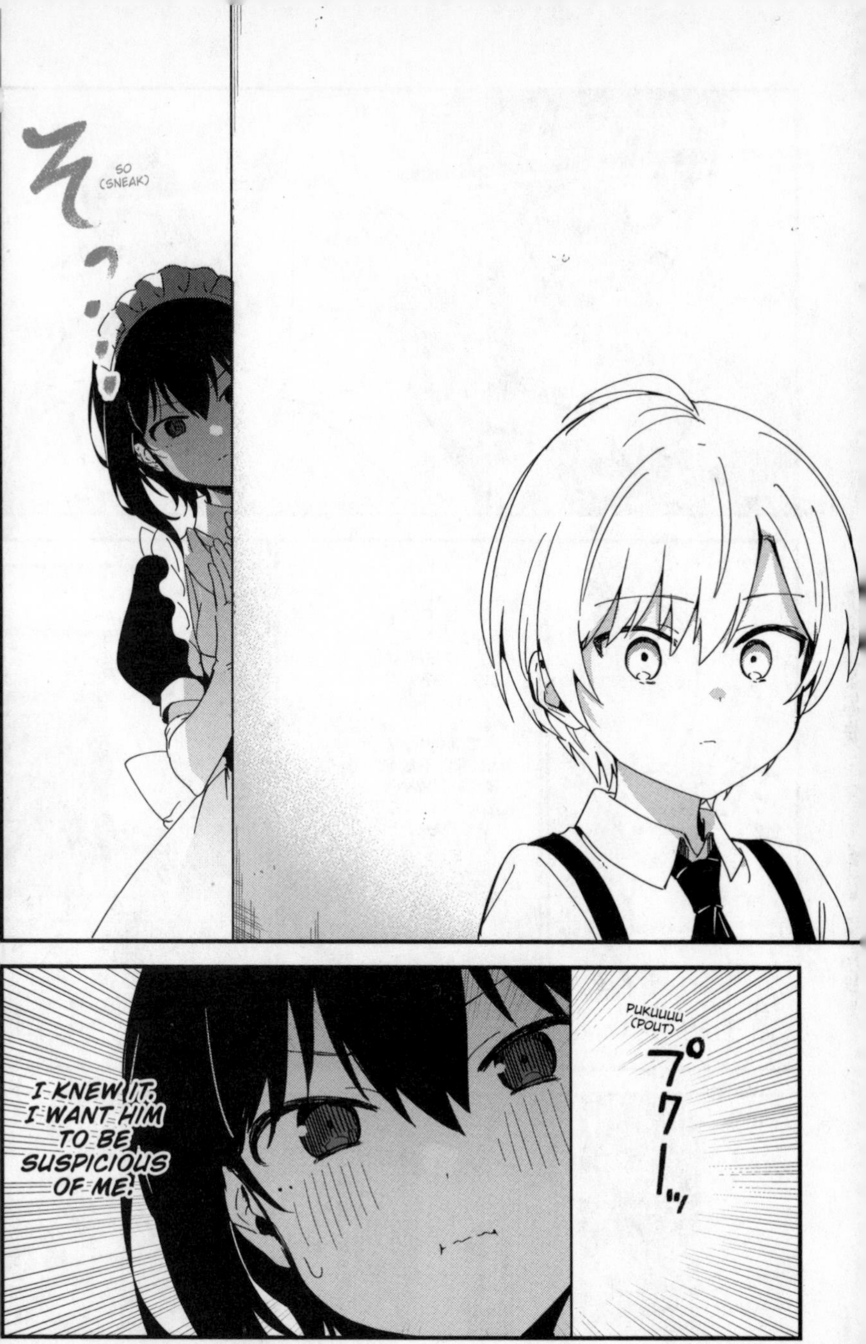
SO
(SNEAK)
PUKUUUU
(POUT)
I KNEW IT. I WANT HIM TO BE SUSPICIOUS OF ME!

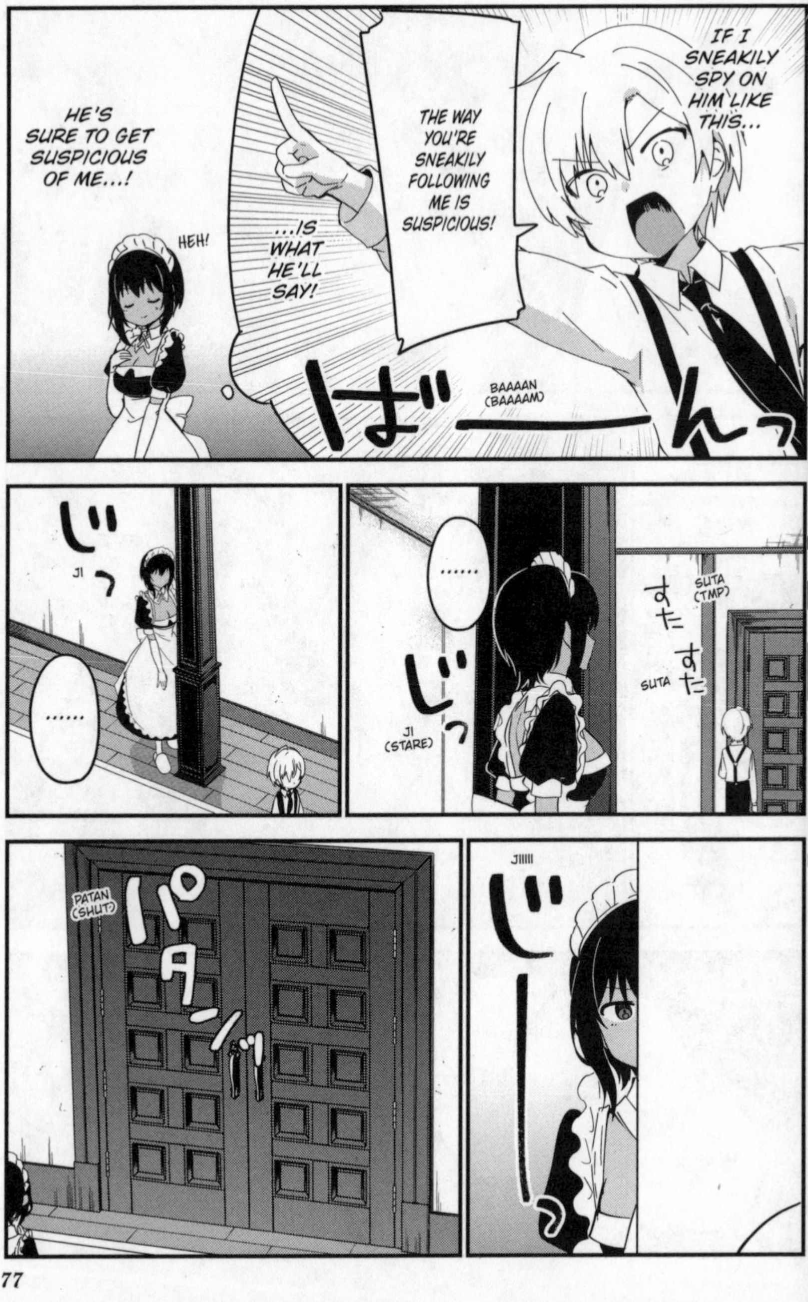
IF I SNEAKILY SPY ON HIM LIKE THIS...
THE WAY YOU'RE SNEAKILY FOLLOWING ME IS SUSPICIOUS!
...IS WHAT HE'LL SAY!
ばーーんっ
BAAAAN (BAAAAM)
HEH!
HE'S SURE TO GET SUSPICIOUS OF ME...!
すた
SUTA (TMP)
すた
SUTA
......
じっ
JI (STARE)
じっ
JI
......
じーっ
JIIII
パタンッ
PATAN (SHUT)

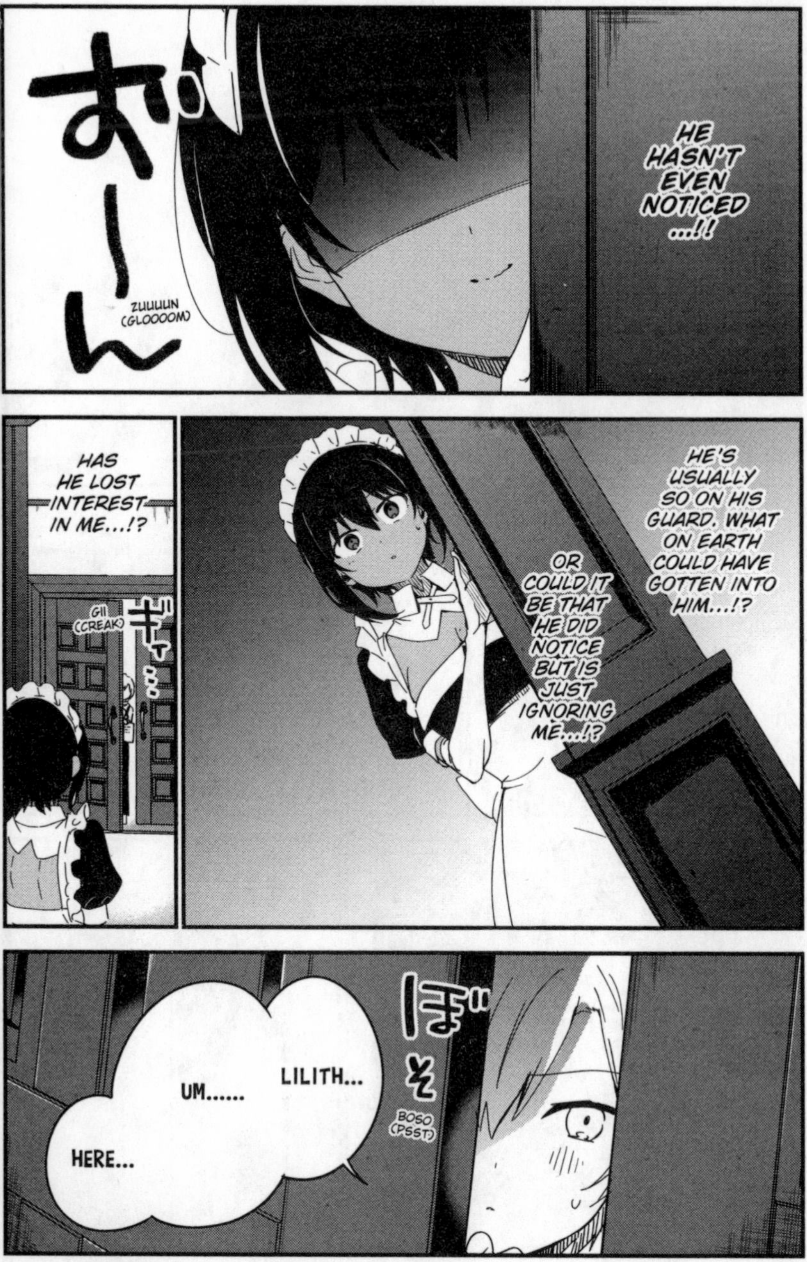
HE HASN'T EVEN NOTICED...!!
ZUUUUN (GLOOOOM)
HE'S USUALLY SO ON HIS GUARD. WHAT ON EARTH COULD HAVE GOTTEN INTO HIM...!?
OR COULD IT BE THAT HE DID NOTICE BUT IS JUST IGNORING ME...!?
HAS HE LOST INTEREST IN ME...!?
GII (CREAK)
BOSO (PSST)
LILITH...
UM......
HERE...

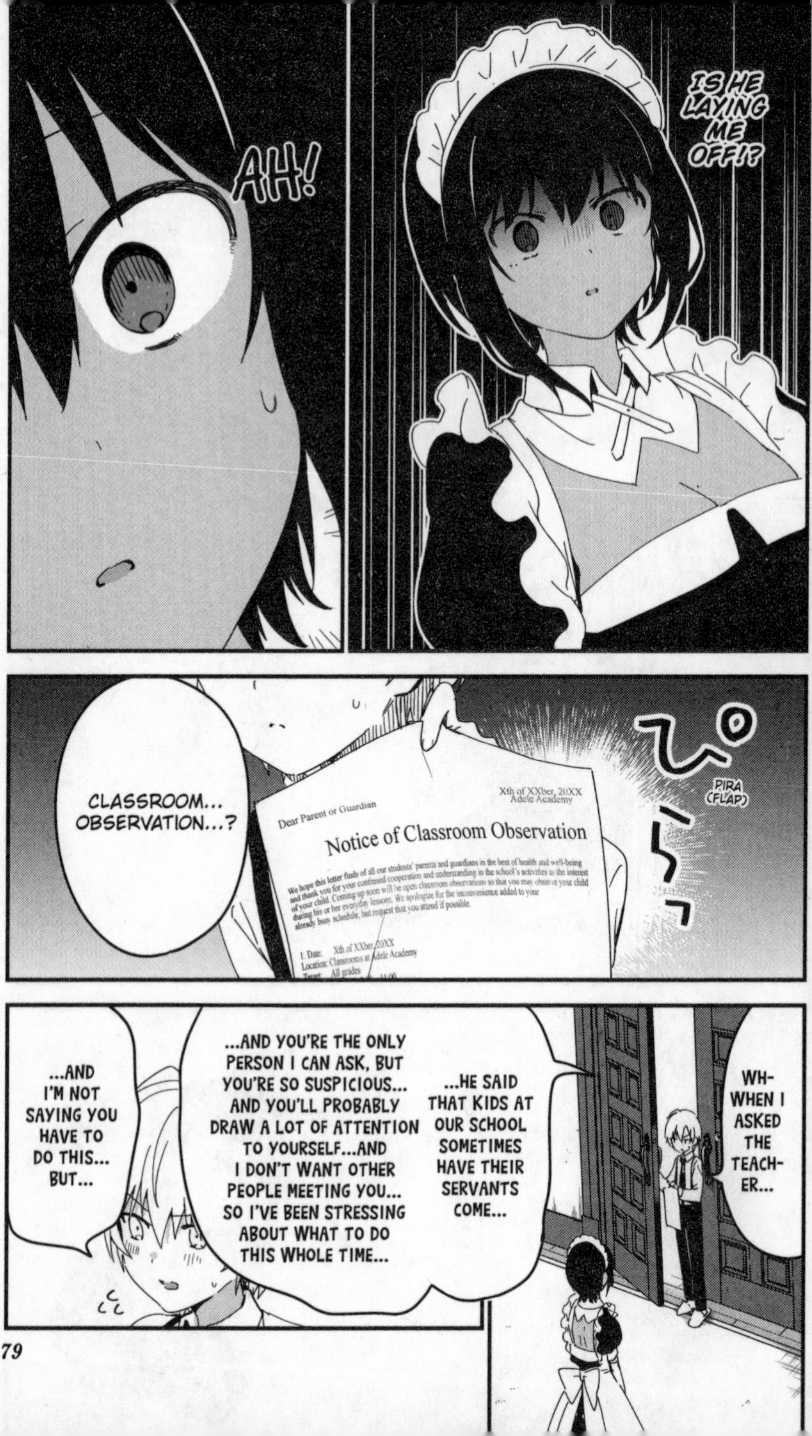
IS HE LAYING ME OFF!?
AH!
ぴら
PIRA (FLAP)
Xth of XXber, 20XX
Adele Academy
Dear Parent or Guardian
Notice of Classroom Observation
We hope this letter finds all of our students' parents and guardians in the best of health and well-being and thank you for your continued cooperation and understanding in the school's activities in the interest of your child. Coming up soon will be open classroom observations so that you may observe your child during his or her everyday lessons. We apologize for the inconvenience added to your already busy schedule, but request that you attend if possible.
1. Date: Xth of XXber, 20XX
Location: Classrooms at Adele Academy
Target: All grades
CLASSROOM... OBSERVATION...?
WH-WHEN I ASKED THE TEACHER...
...HE SAID THAT KIDS AT OUR SCHOOL SOMETIMES HAVE THEIR SERVANTS COME...
...AND YOU'RE THE ONLY PERSON I CAN ASK, BUT YOU'RE SO SUSPICIOUS... AND YOU'LL PROBABLY DRAW A LOT OF ATTENTION TO YOURSELF...AND I DON'T WANT OTHER PEOPLE MEETING YOU... SO I'VE BEEN STRESSING ABOUT WHAT TO DO THIS WHOLE TIME...
...AND I'M NOT SAYING YOU HAVE TO DO THIS... BUT...

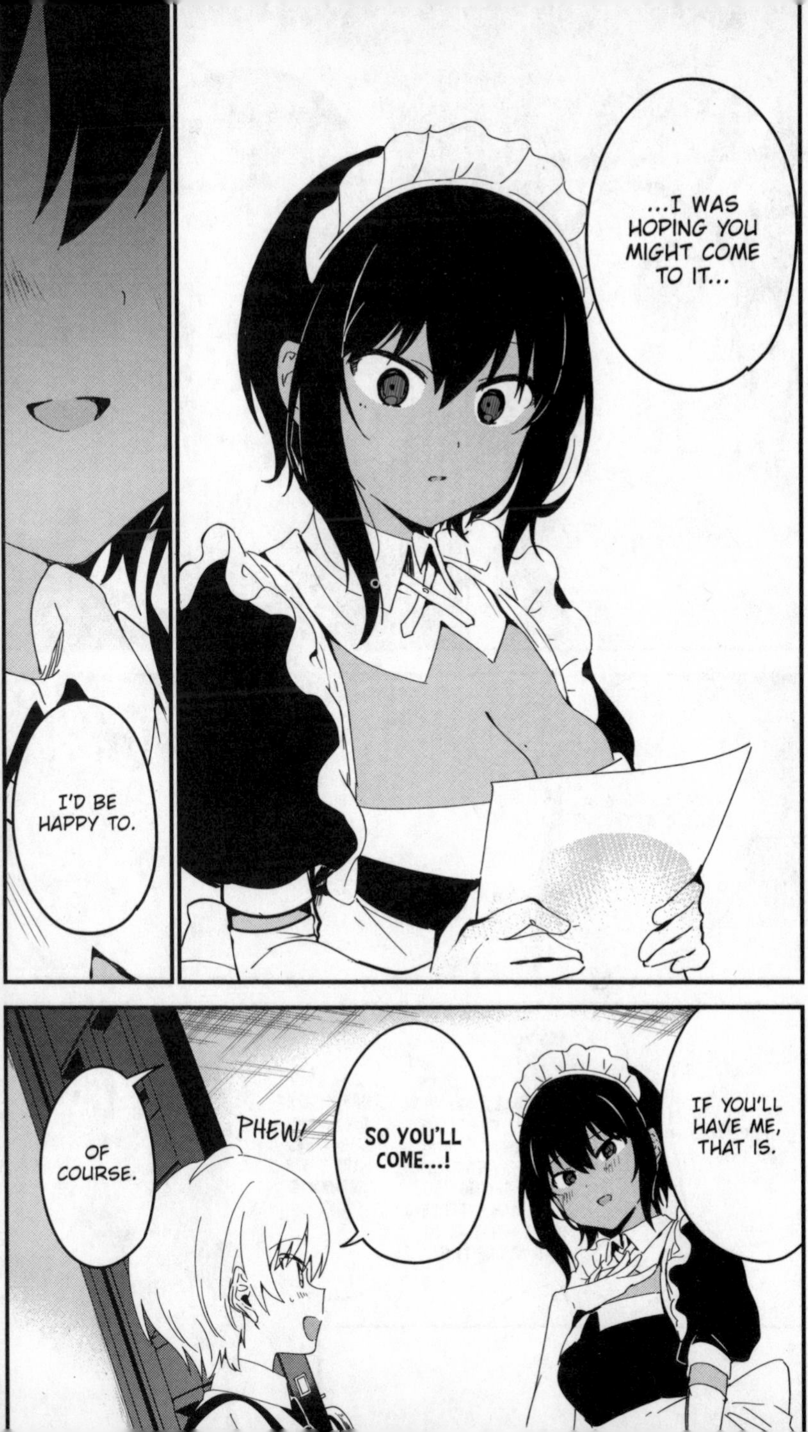
...I WAS HOPING YOU MIGHT COME TO IT...
I'D BE HAPPY TO.
IF YOU'LL HAVE ME, THAT IS.
SO YOU'LL COME...!
PHEW!
OF COURSE.

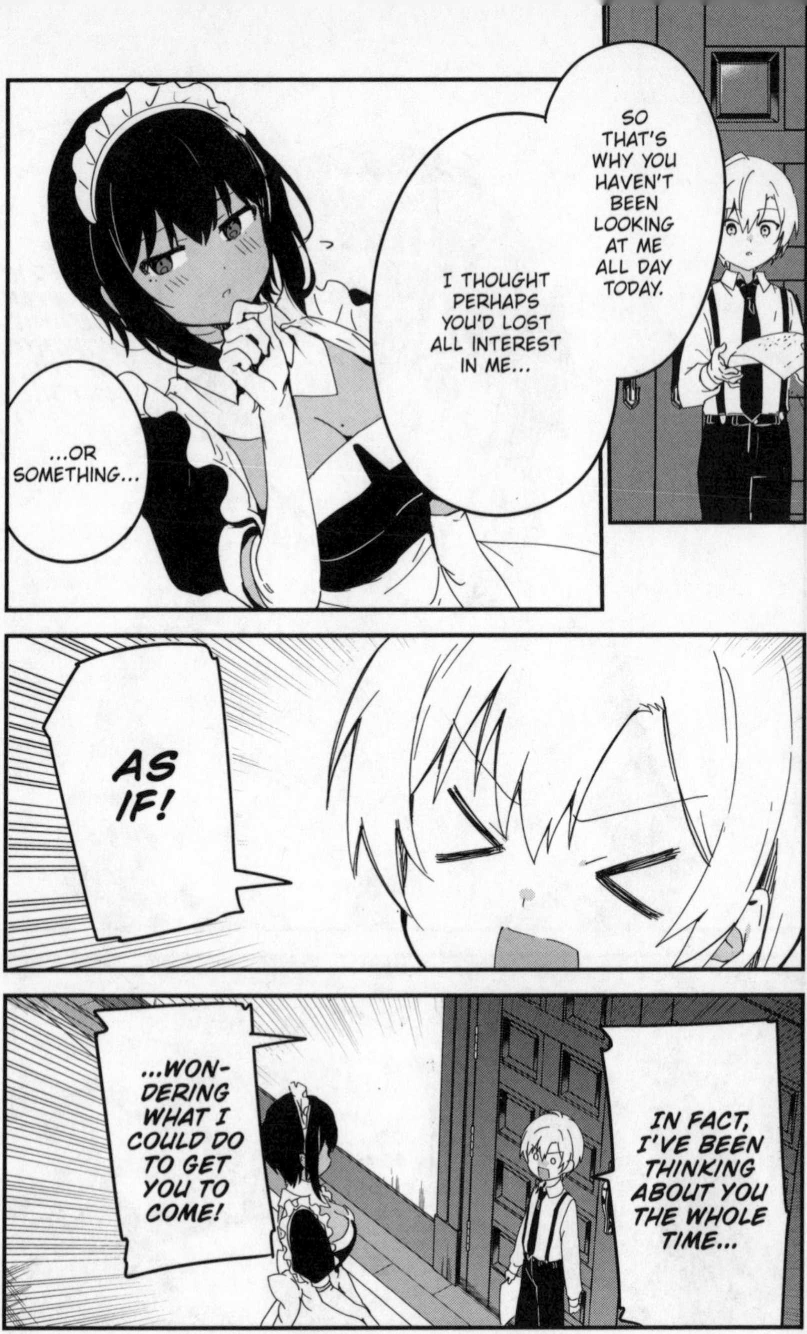
SO THAT'S WHY YOU HAVEN'T BEEN LOOKING AT ME ALL DAY TODAY.
I THOUGHT PERHAPS YOU'D LOST ALL INTEREST IN ME...
...OR SOMETHING...
AS IF!
IN FACT, I'VE BEEN THINKING ABOUT YOU THE WHOLE TIME...
...WON-DERING WHAT I COULD DO TO GET YOU TO COME!

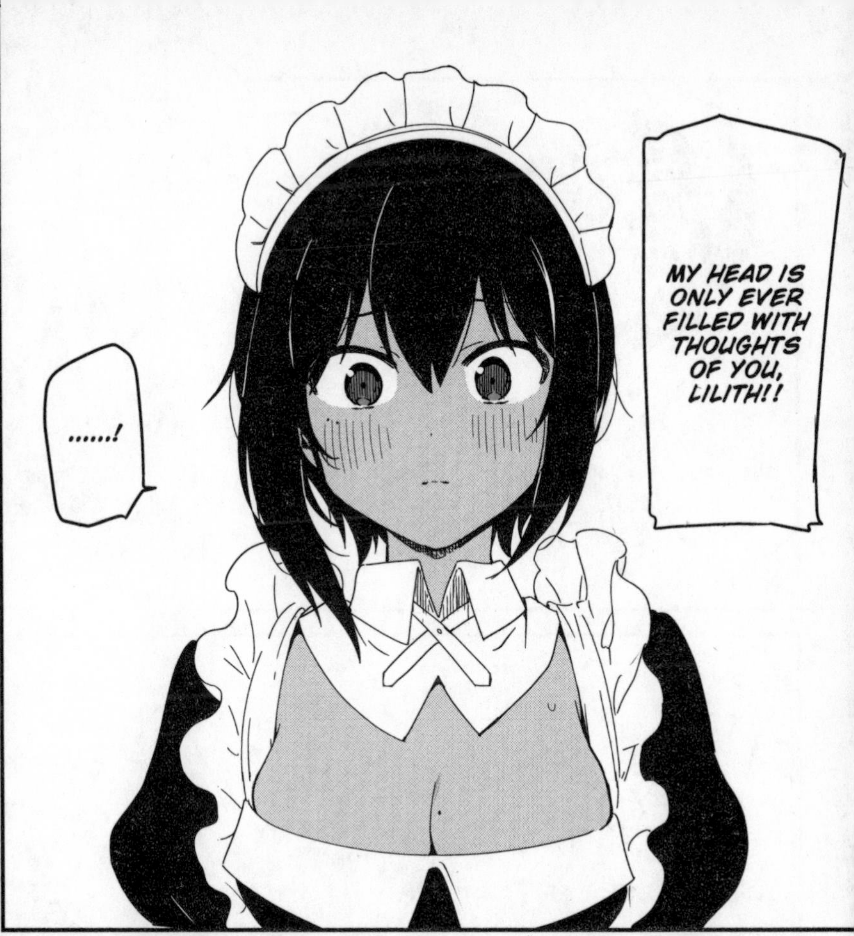
MY HEAD IS ONLY EVER FILLED WITH THOUGHTS OF YOU, LILITH!!
......!

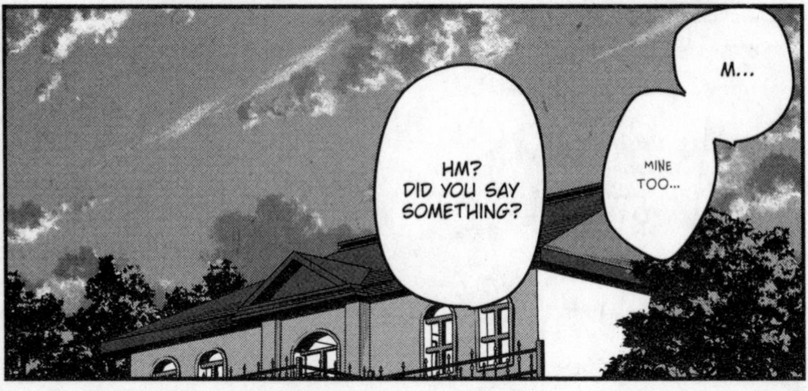
M...
MINE TOO...
HM? DID YOU SAY SOMETHING?

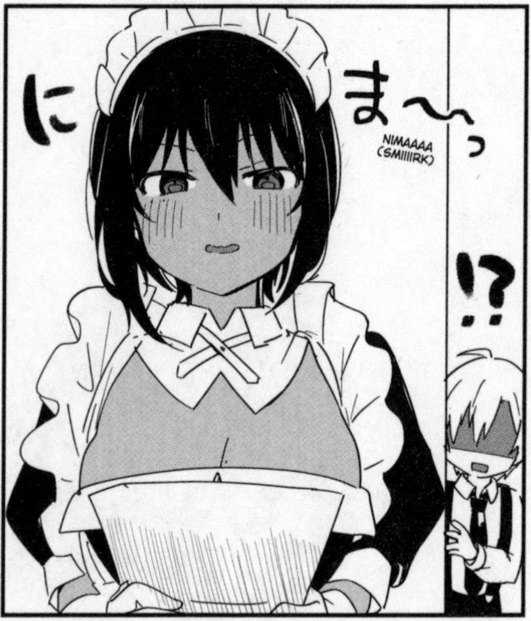
にま〜っ
NIMAAAA
(SMIIIIRK)
!?

The Maid I Hired Recently Is Mysterious

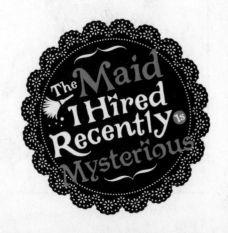

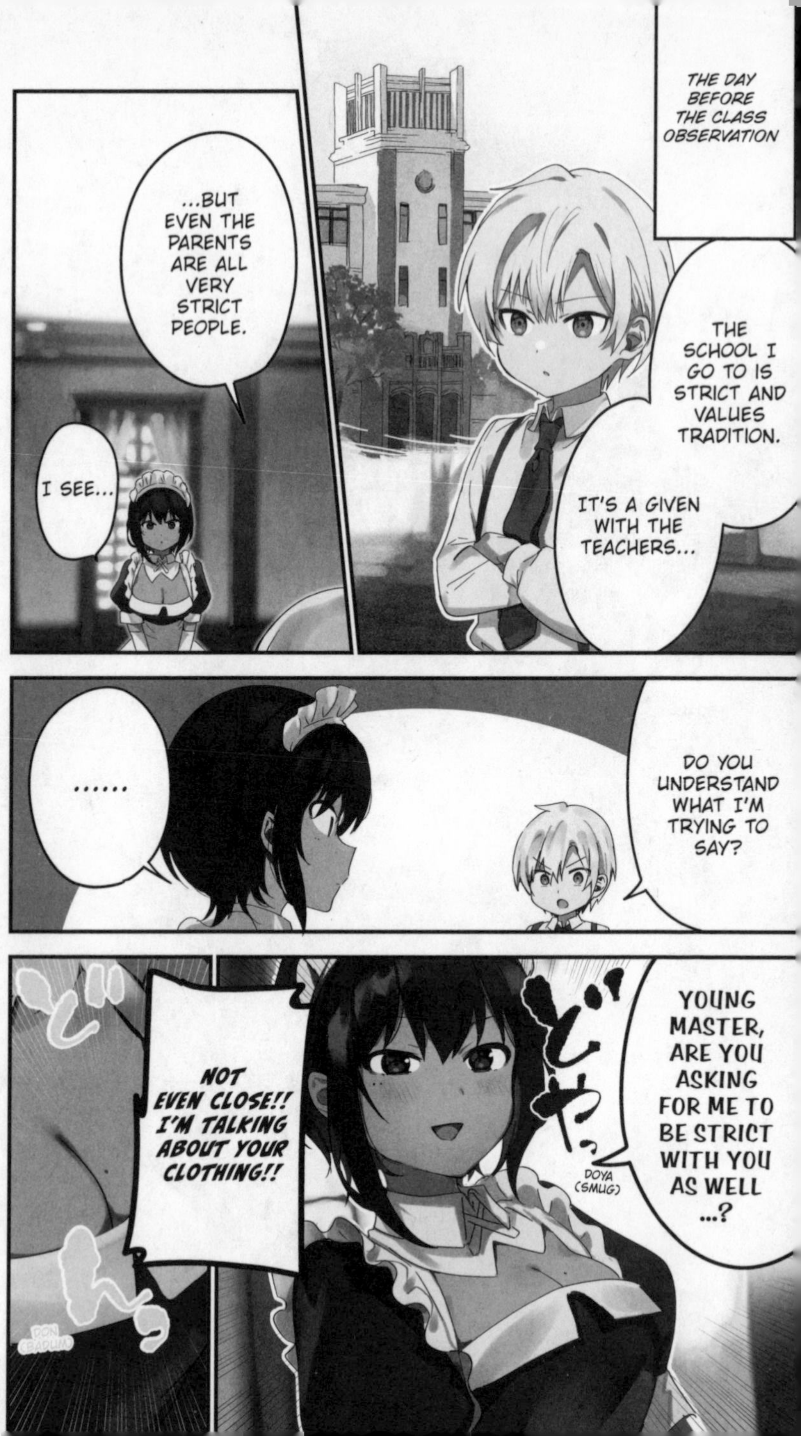
THE DAY BEFORE THE CLASS OBSERVATION
THE SCHOOL I GO TO IS STRICT AND VALUES TRADITION.
IT'S A GIVEN WITH THE TEACHERS...
...BUT EVEN THE PARENTS ARE ALL VERY STRICT PEOPLE.
I SEE...
DO YOU UNDERSTAND WHAT I'M TRYING TO SAY?
......
YOUNG MASTER, ARE YOU ASKING FOR ME TO BE STRICT WITH YOU AS WELL...?
DOYA (SMUG)
NOT EVEN CLOSE!! I'M TALKING ABOUT YOUR CLOTHING!!
DON (BADUM)

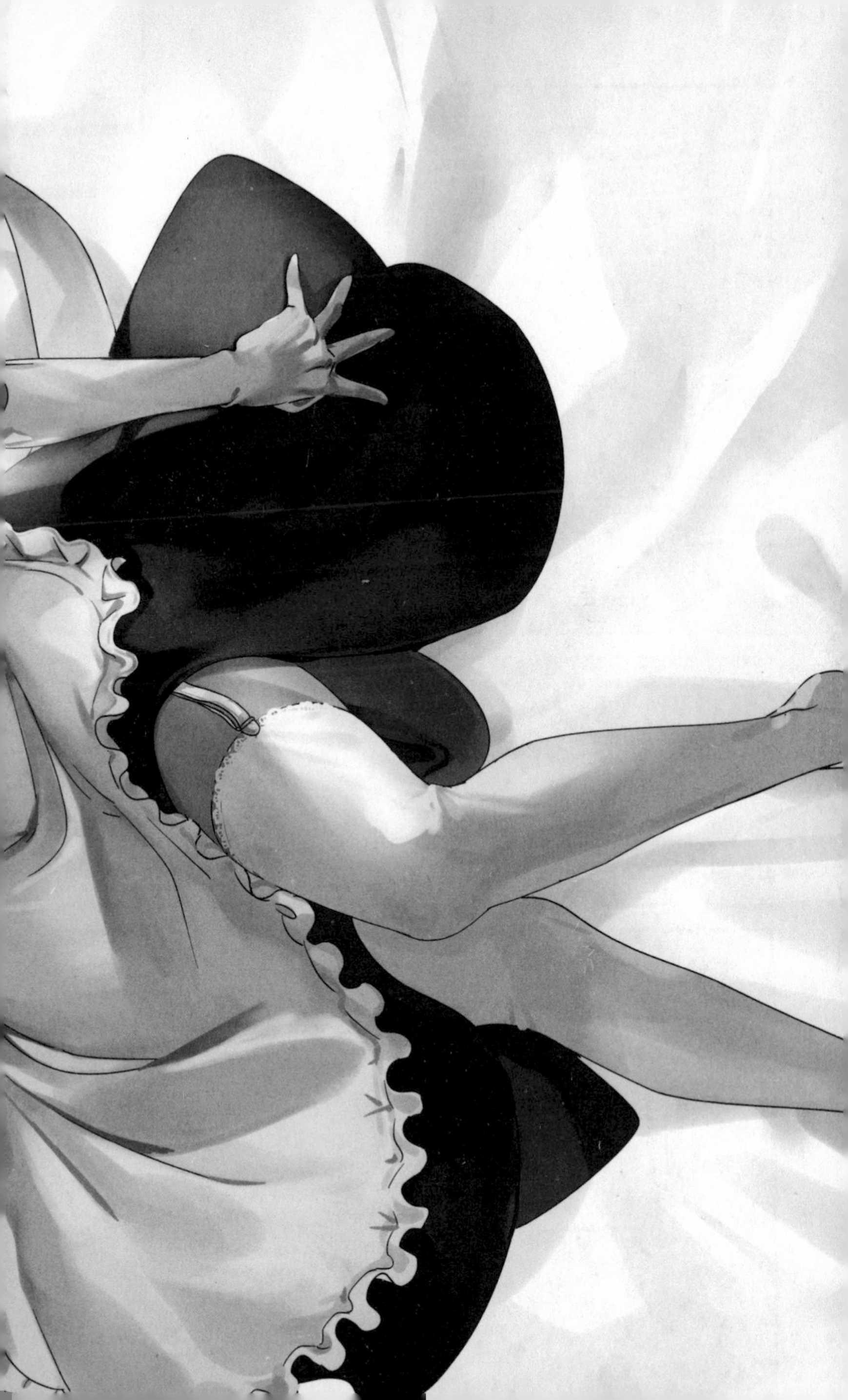

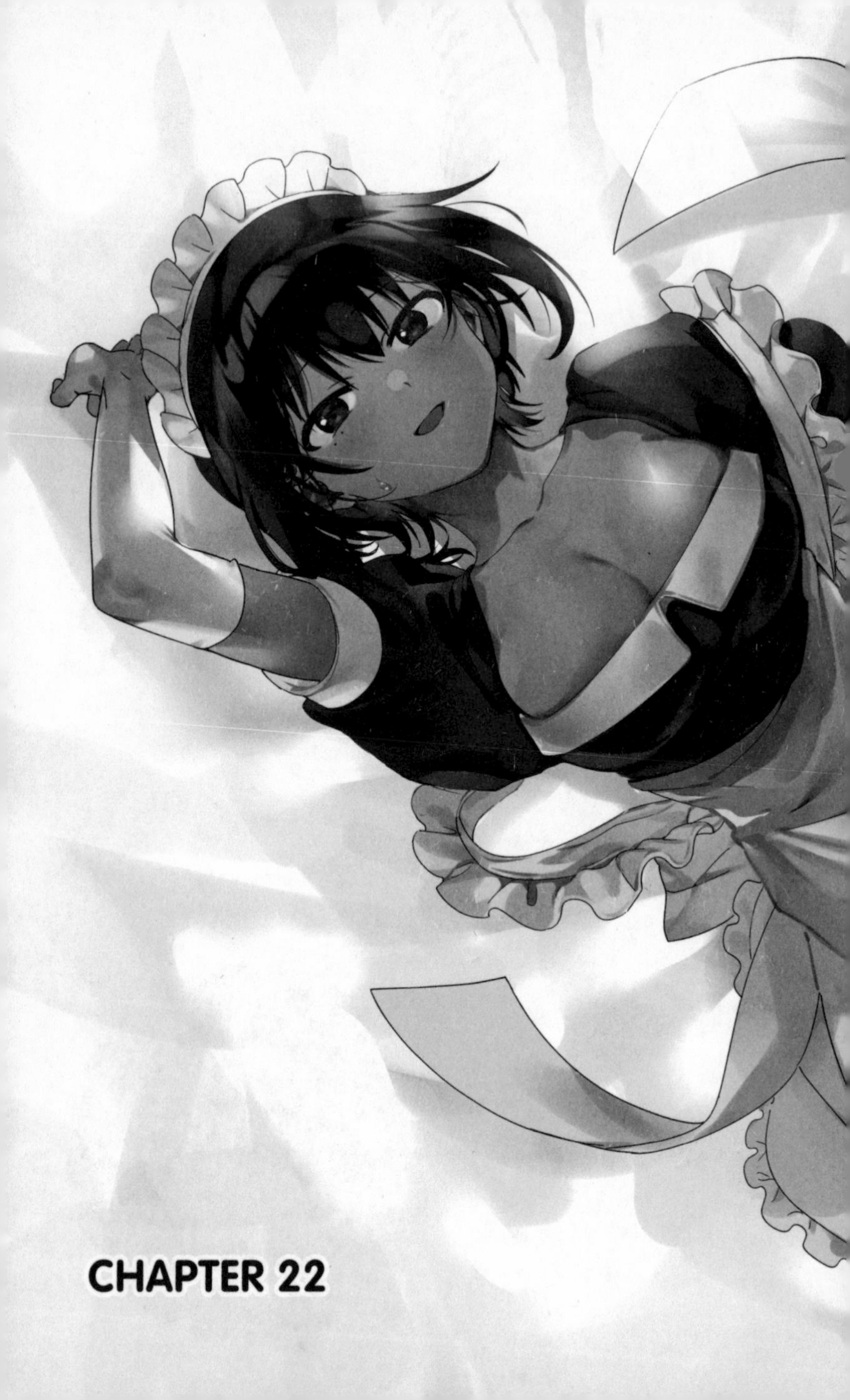

CHAPTER 22

The Maid I Hired Recently Is Mysterious

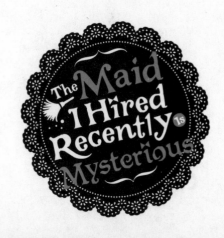

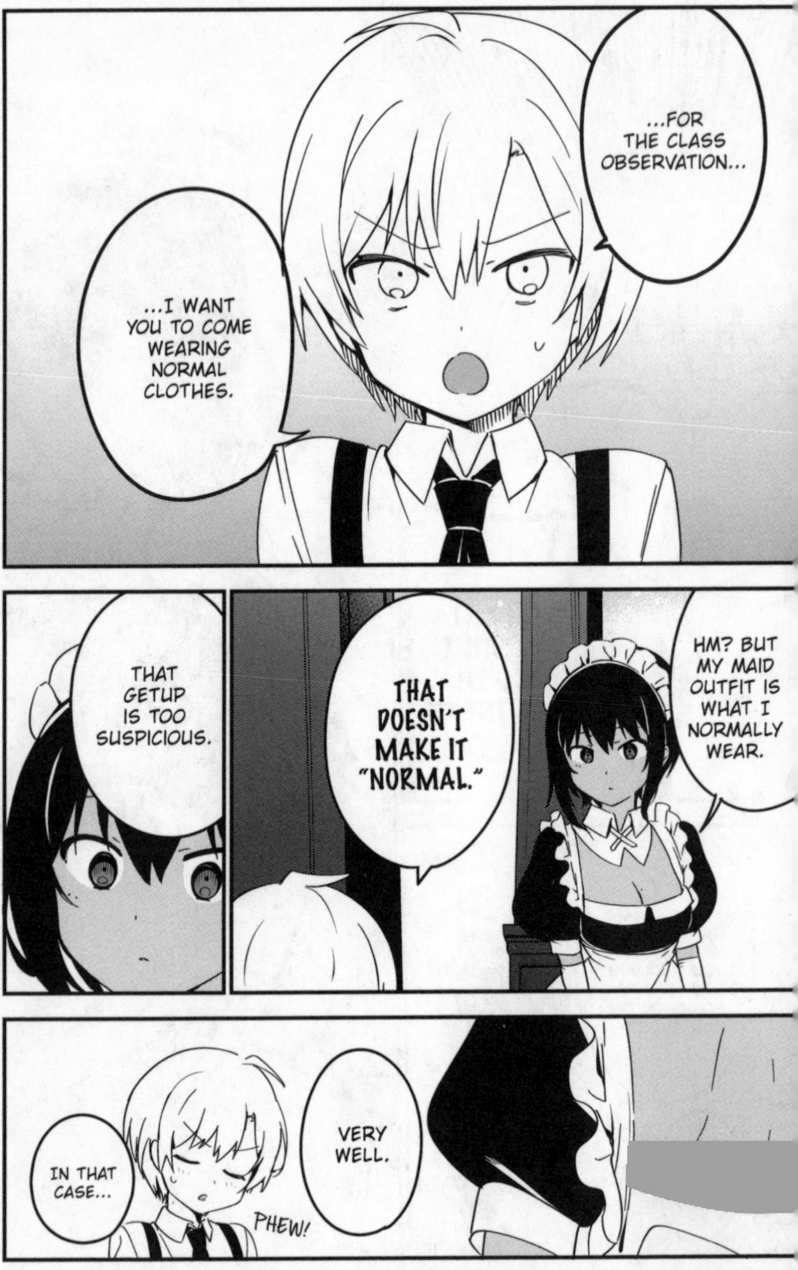
...FOR THE CLASS OBSERVATION...
...I WANT YOU TO COME WEARING NORMAL CLOTHES.
HM? BUT MY MAID OUTFIT IS WHAT I NORMALLY WEAR.
THAT DOESN'T MAKE IT "NORMAL."
THAT GETUP IS TOO SUSPICIOUS.
VERY WELL.
IN THAT CASE...
PHEW!

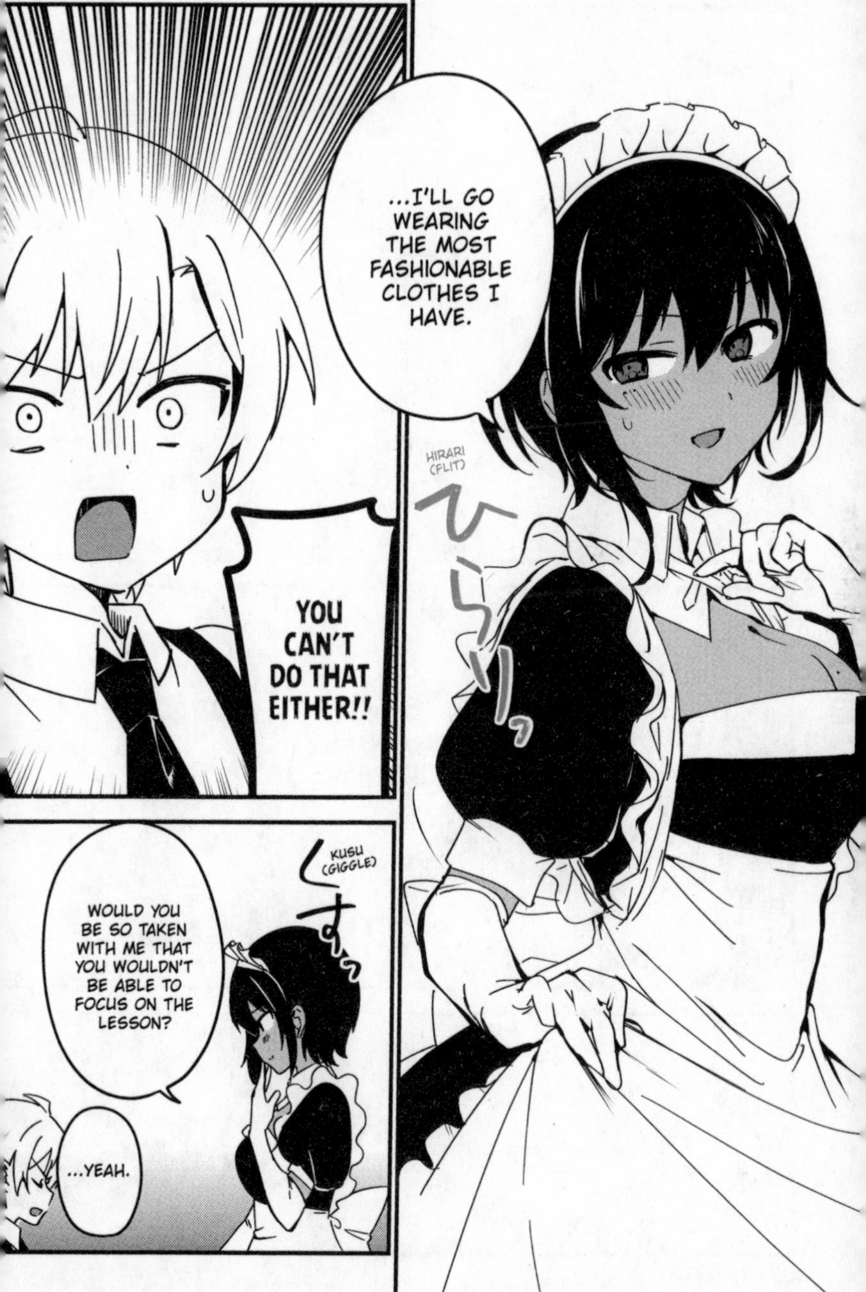
...I'LL GO WEARING THE MOST FASHIONABLE CLOTHES I HAVE.
HIRARI (FLIT)
YOU CAN'T DO THAT EITHER!!
KUSU (GIGGLE)
WOULD YOU BE SO TAKEN WITH ME THAT YOU WOULDN'T BE ABLE TO FOCUS ON THE LESSON?
...YEAH.

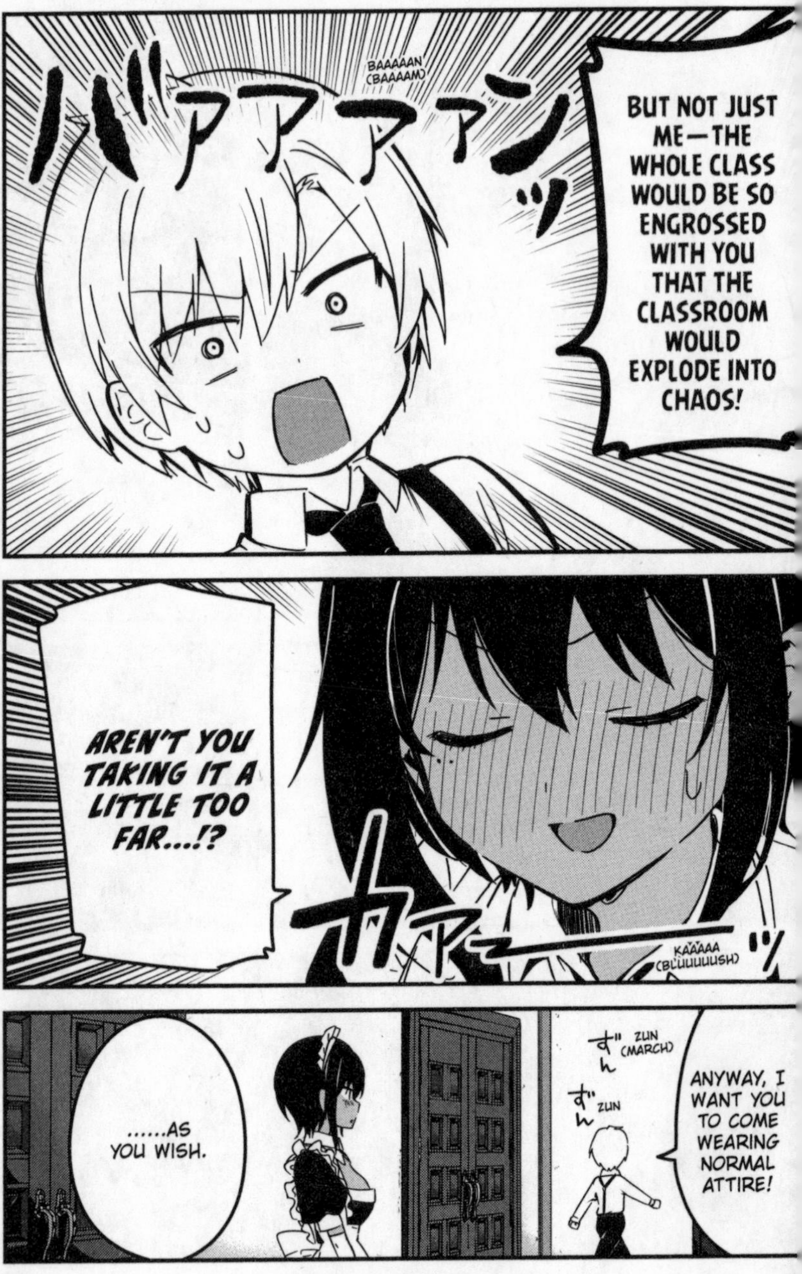
BUT NOT JUST ME—THE WHOLE CLASS WOULD BE SO ENGROSSED WITH YOU THAT THE CLASSROOM WOULD EXPLODE INTO CHAOS!
バアアアンッ
BAAAAAN (BAAAAAM)
AREN'T YOU TAKING IT A LITTLE TOO FAR...!?
カアーッ
KAAAAA (BLUUUUUSH)
ANYWAY, I WANT YOU TO COME WEARING NORMAL ATTIRE!
ずん
ZUN (MARCH)
ずん
ZUN
......AS YOU WISH.

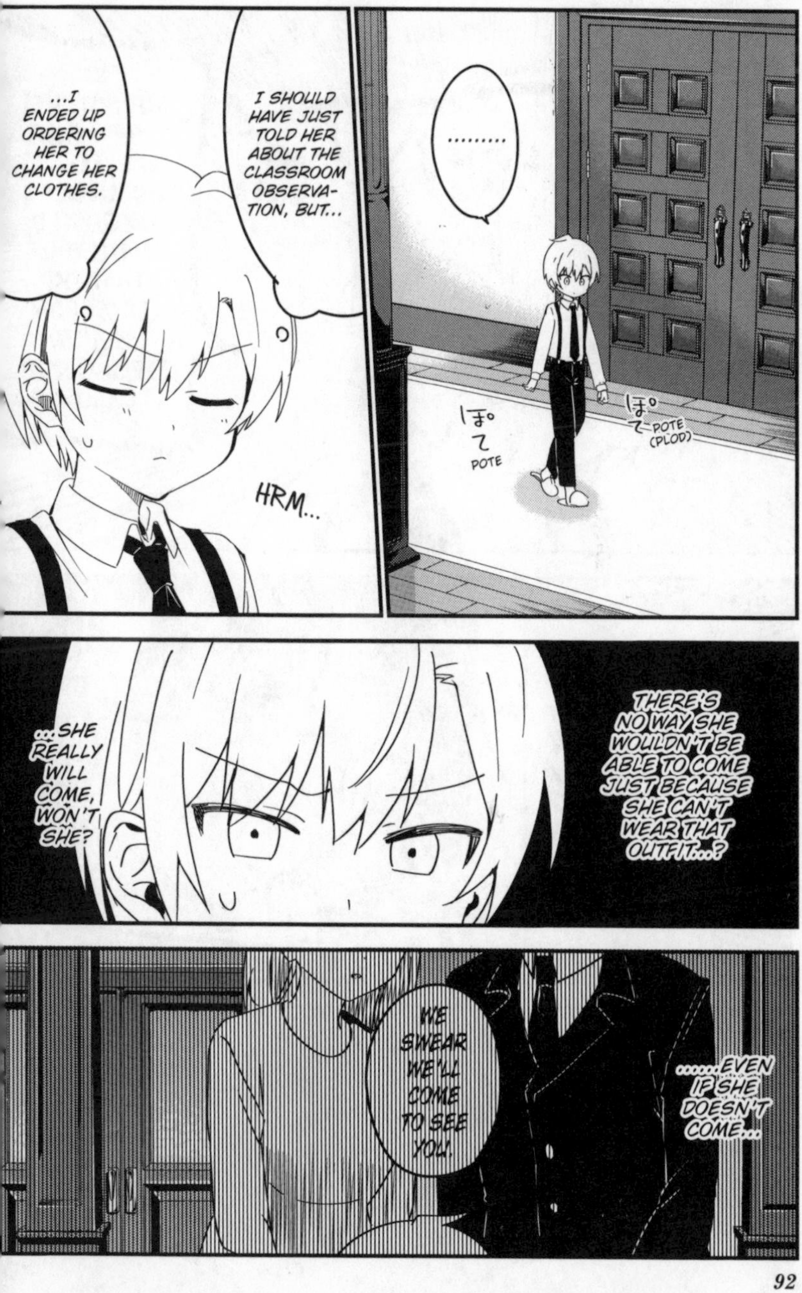
....
ぽて POTE (PLOD)
ぽて POTE
I SHOULD HAVE JUST TOLD HER ABOUT THE CLASSROOM OBSERVATION, BUT...
...I ENDED UP ORDERING HER TO CHANGE HER CLOTHES.
HRM...
THERE'S NO WAY SHE WOULDN'T BE ABLE TO COME JUST BECAUSE SHE CAN'T WEAR THAT OUTFIT...?
...SHE REALLY WILL COME, WON'T SHE?
......EVEN IF SHE DOESN'T COME...
WE SWEAR WE'LL COME TO SEE YOU!

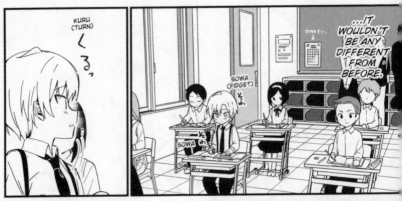

KURU
(TURN)

SOWA
(FIDGET)

SOWA

...IT WOULDN'T BE ANY DIFFERENT FROM BEFORE.

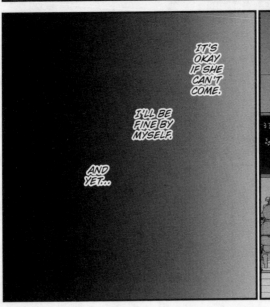

IT'S OKAY IF SHE CAN'T COME.

I'LL BE FINE BY MYSELF.

AND YET...

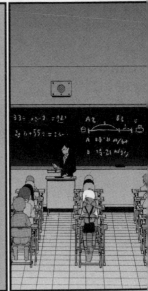

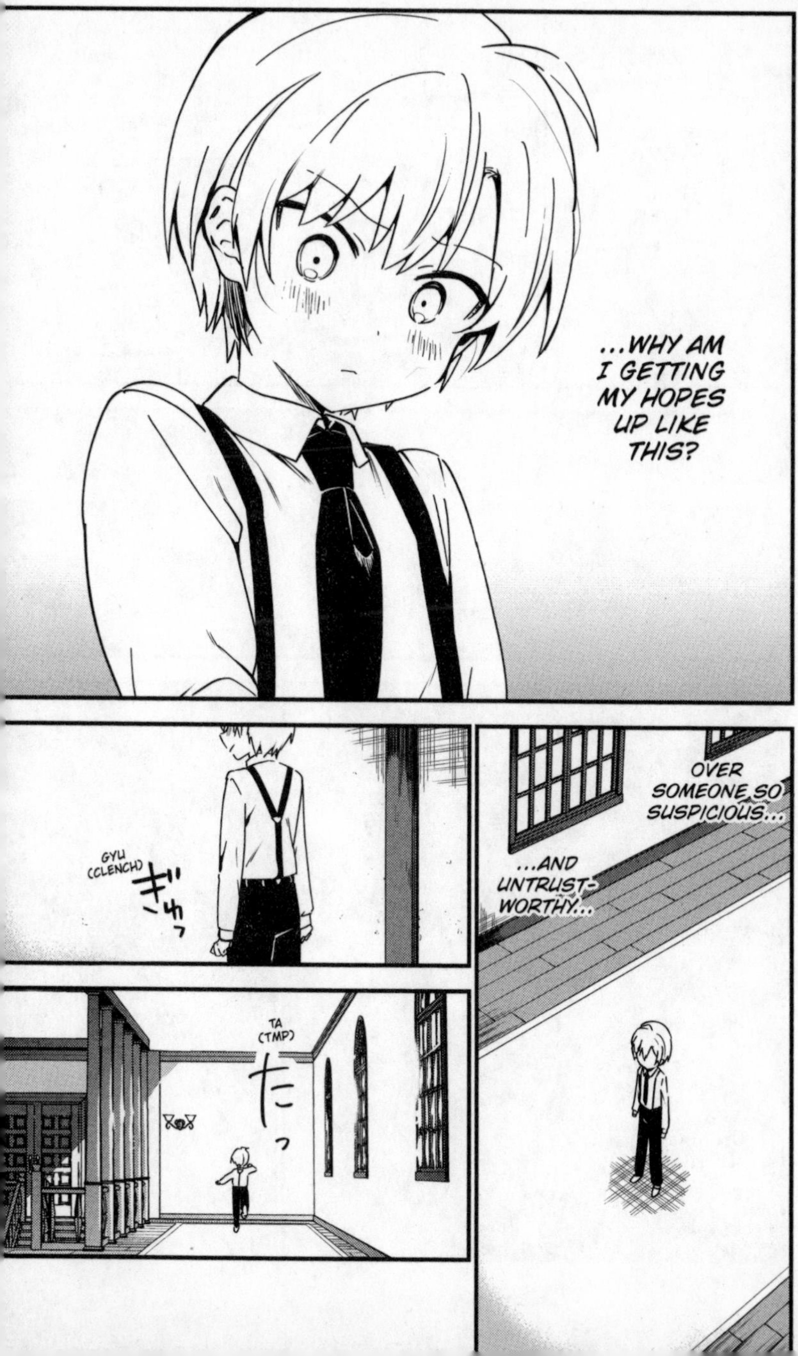
...WHY AM I GETTING MY HOPES UP LIKE THIS?
OVER SOMEONE SO SUSPICIOUS...
...AND UNTRUST-WORTHY...
GYU (CLENCH)
ぎゅっ
TA (TMP)
たっ

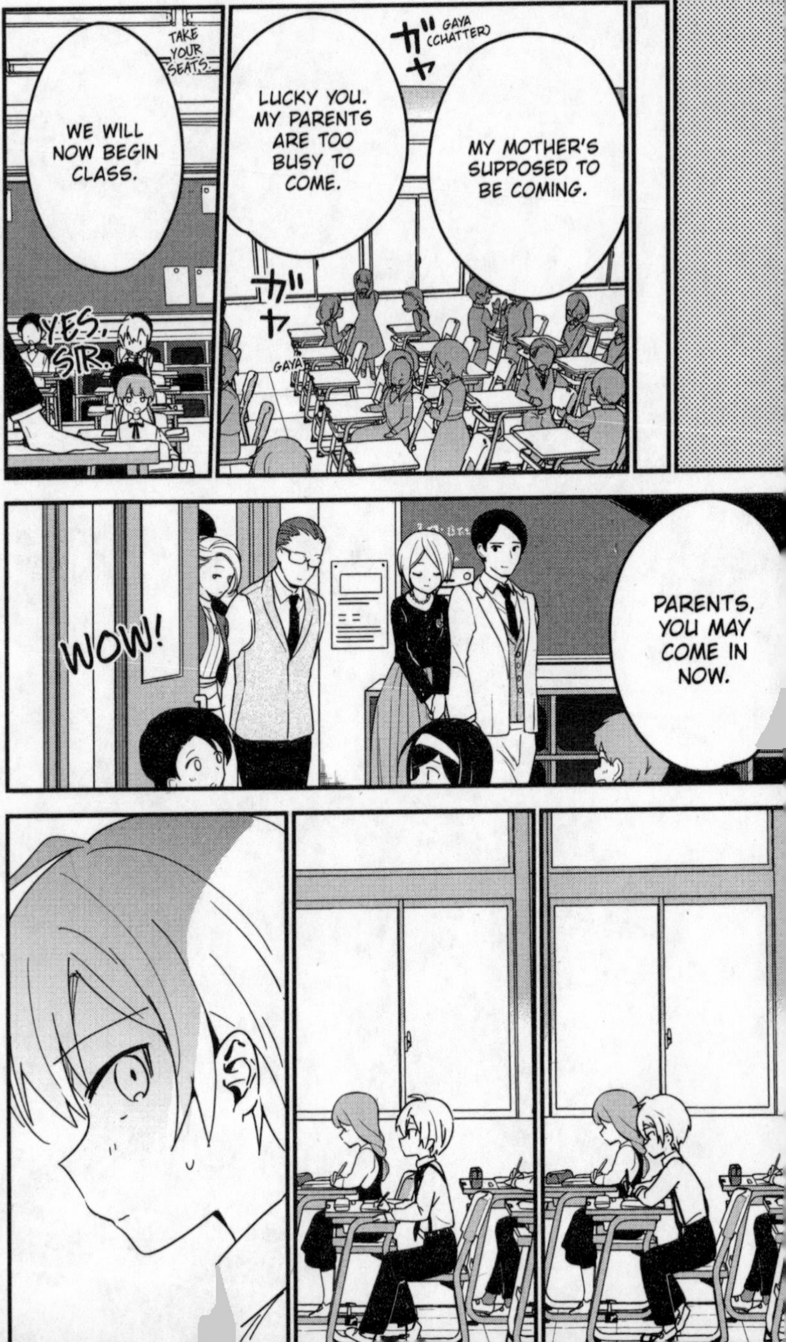
ガヤ
GAYA (CHATTER)
MY MOTHER'S SUPPOSED TO BE COMING.
LUCKY YOU. MY PARENTS ARE TOO BUSY TO COME.
ガヤ
GAYA
WE WILL NOW BEGIN CLASS.
TAKE YOUR SEATS.
YES, SIR.
PARENTS, YOU MAY COME IN NOW.
WOW!

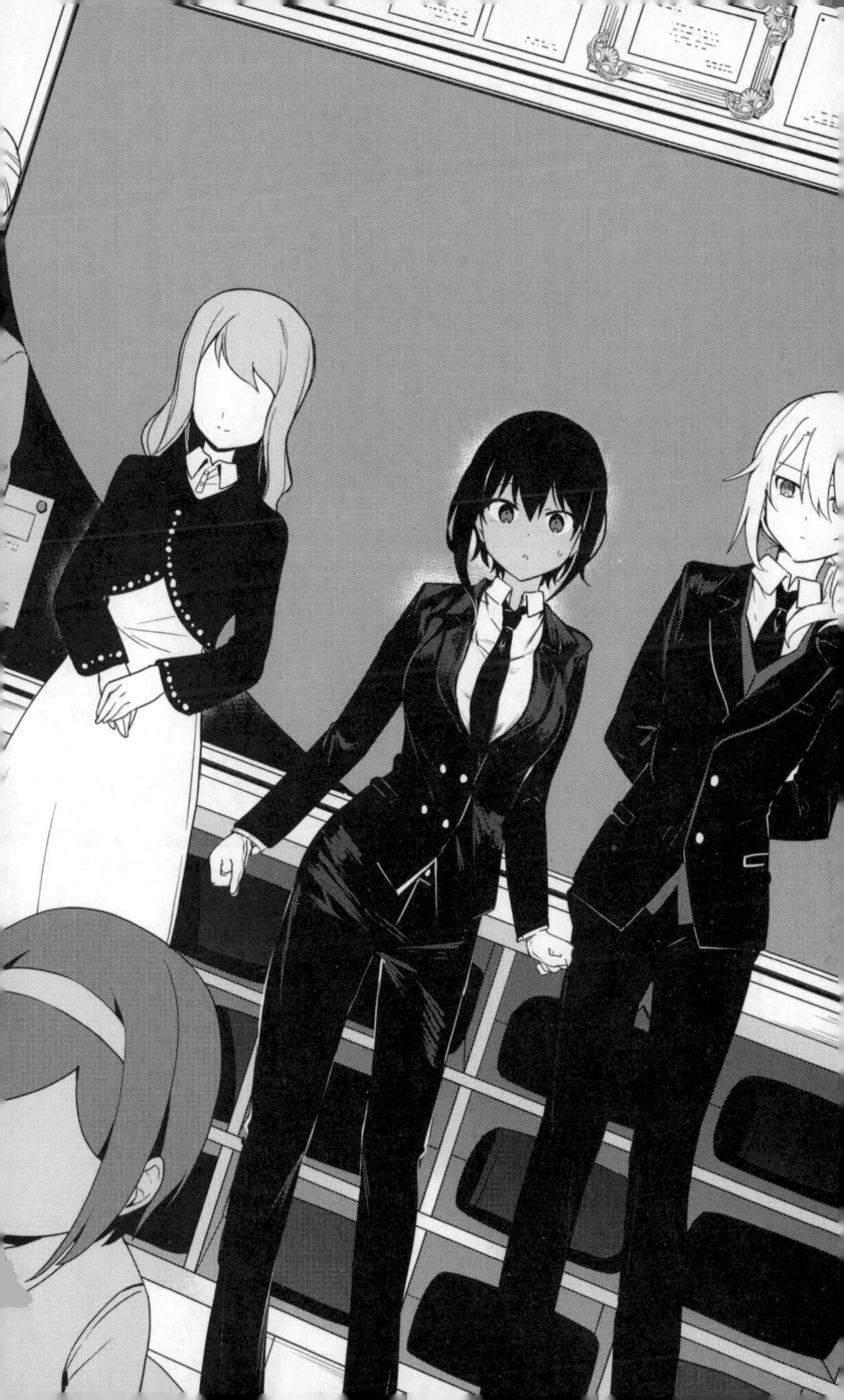

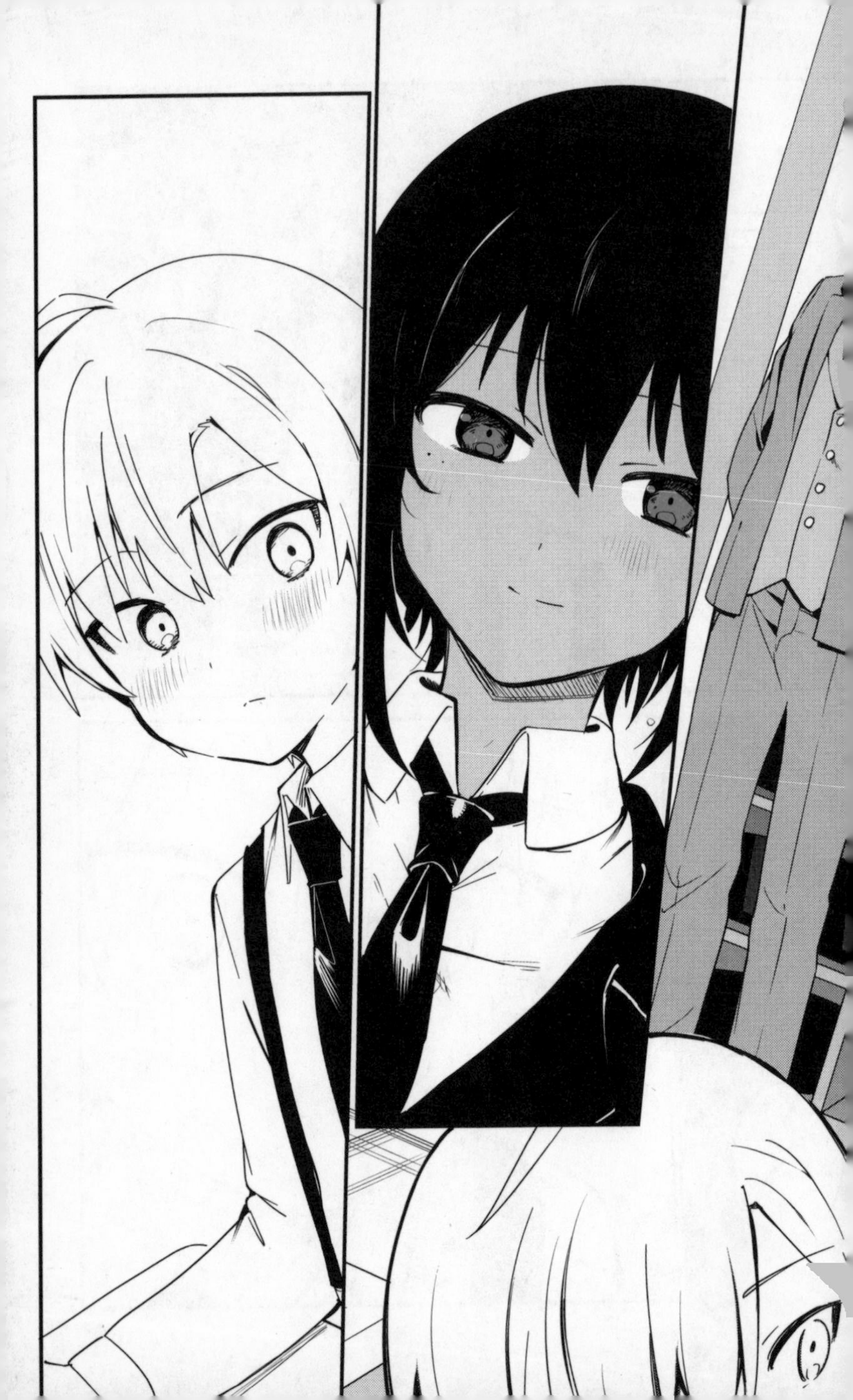

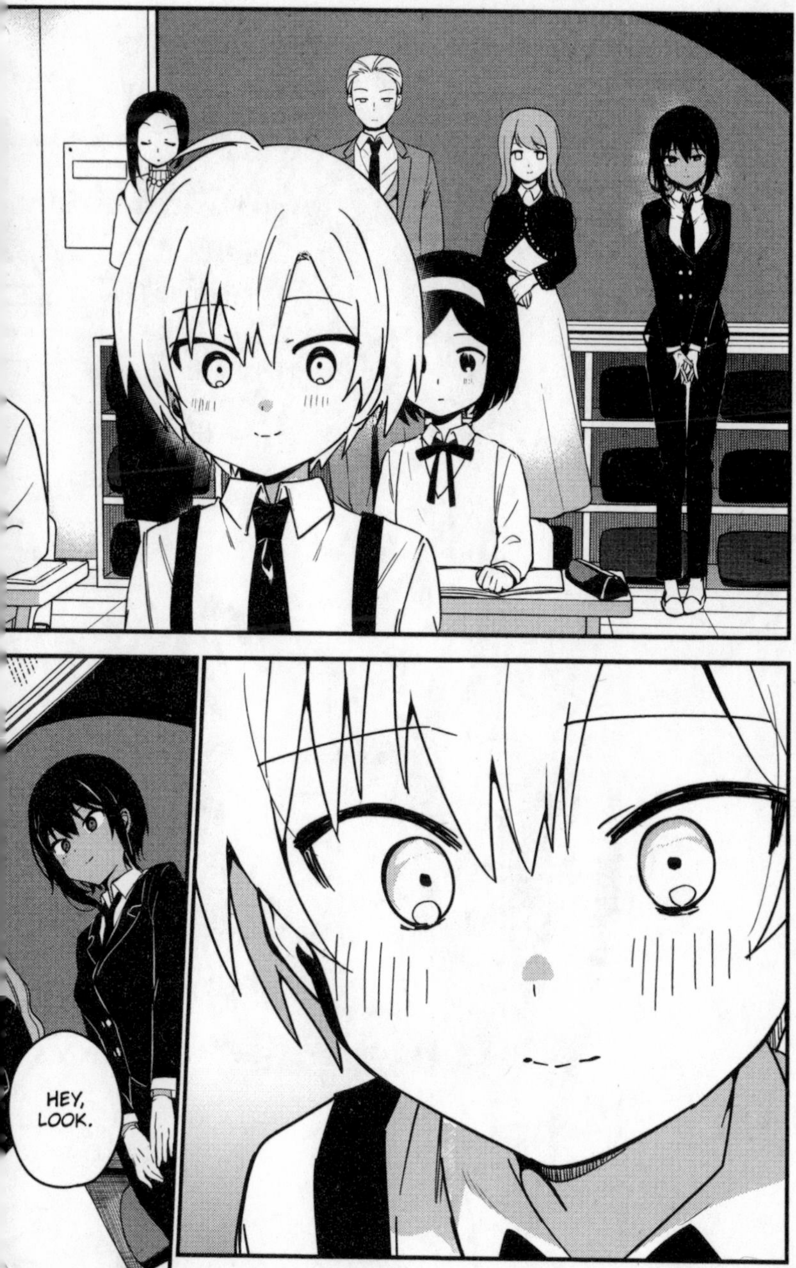
HEY, LOOK.

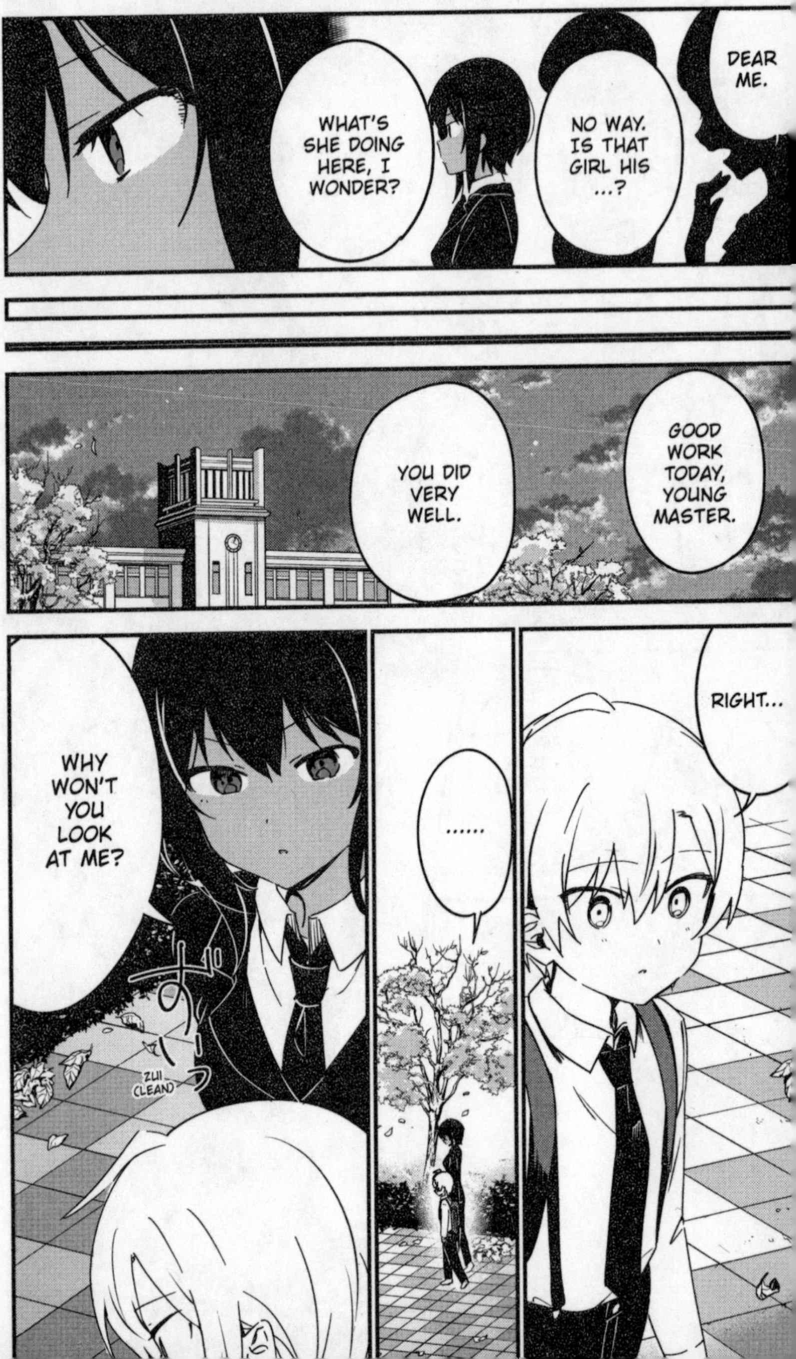
DEAR ME.
NO WAY. IS THAT GIRL HIS ...?
WHAT'S SHE DOING HERE, I WONDER?
GOOD WORK TODAY, YOUNG MASTER.
YOU DID VERY WELL.
RIGHT...
......
WHY WON'T YOU LOOK AT ME?
ZUI (LEAN)

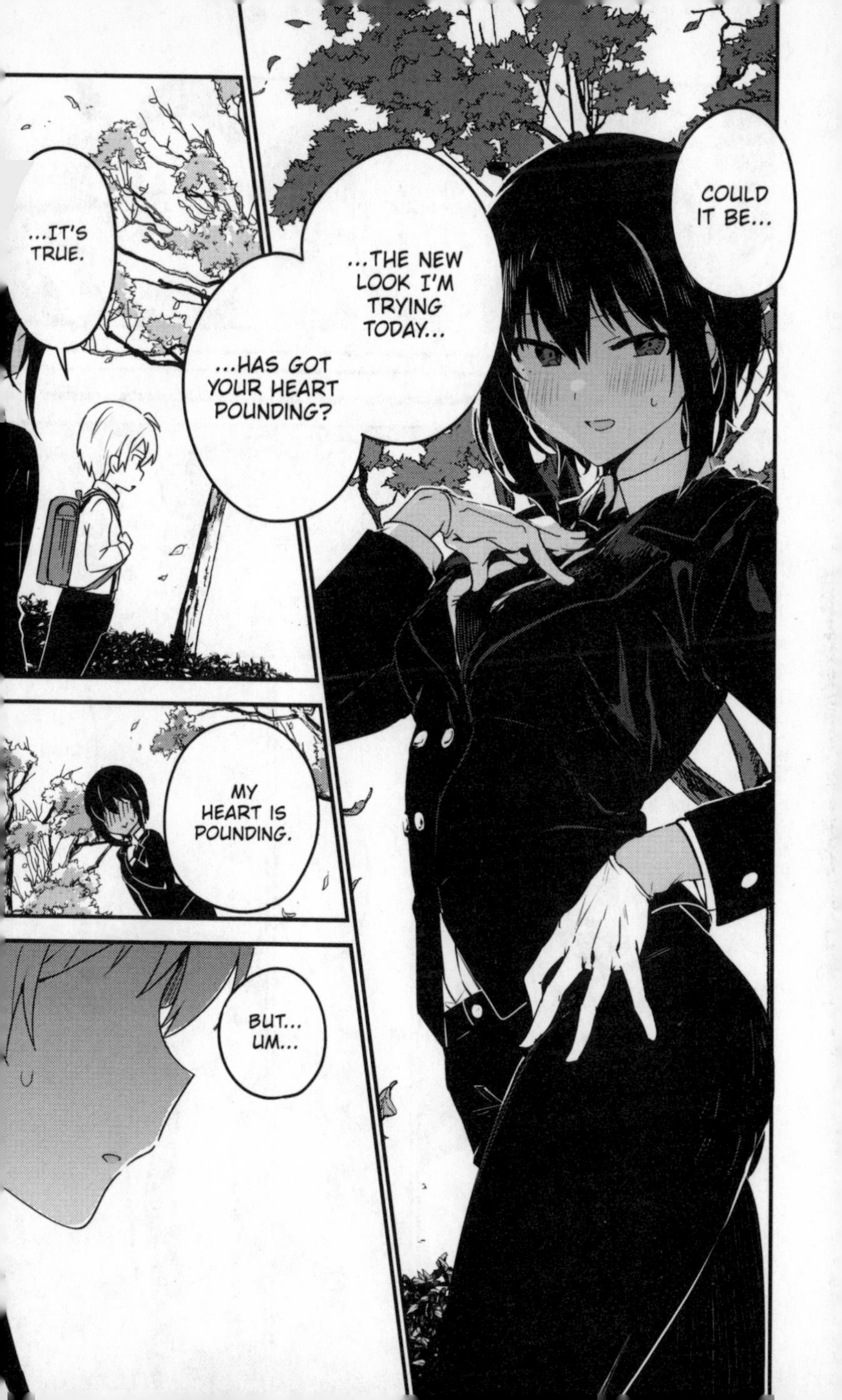
COULD IT BE...
...THE NEW LOOK I'M TRYING TODAY...
...HAS GOT YOUR HEART POUNDING?
...IT'S TRUE.
MY HEART IS POUNDING.
BUT... UM...

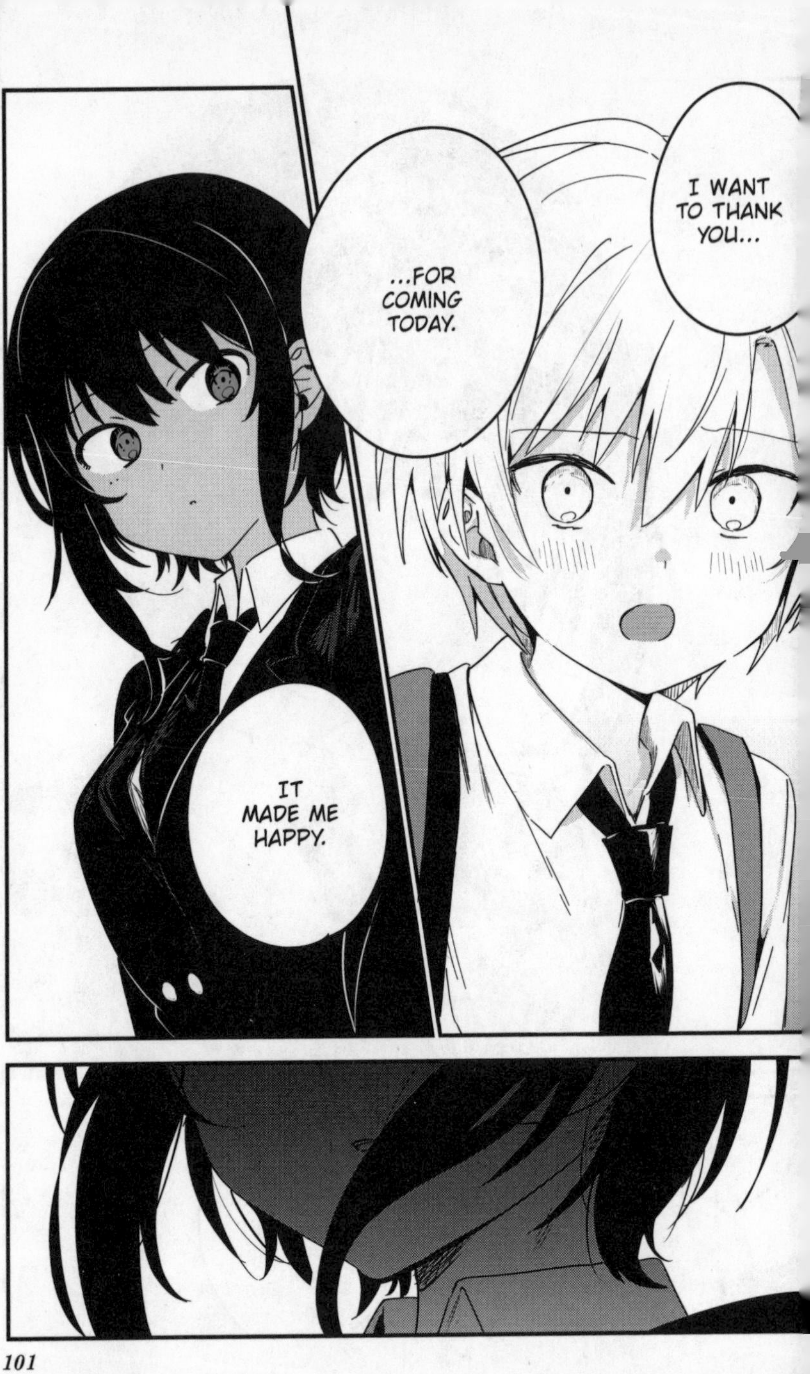
I WANT TO THANK YOU...
...FOR COMING TODAY.
IT MADE ME HAPPY.

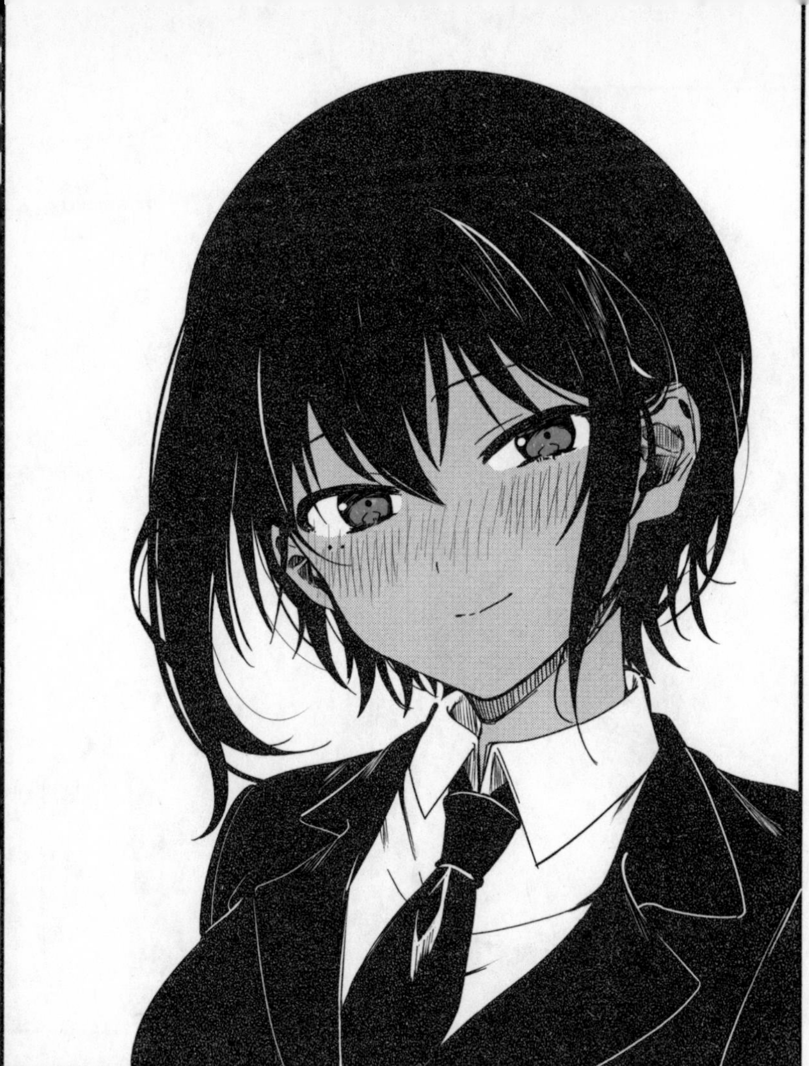

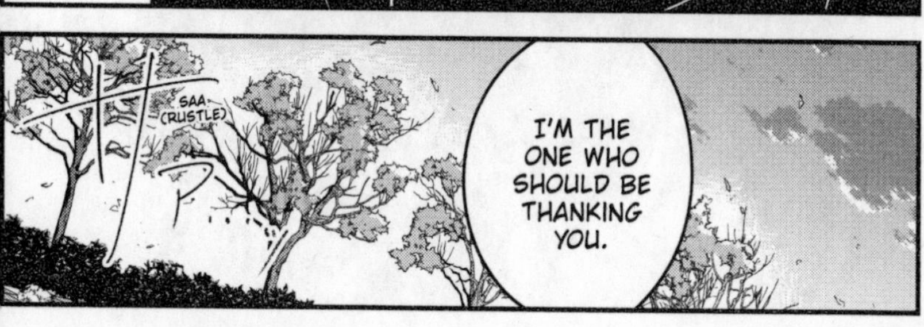
I'M THE ONE WHO SHOULD BE THANKING YOU.
SAA (RUSTLE)

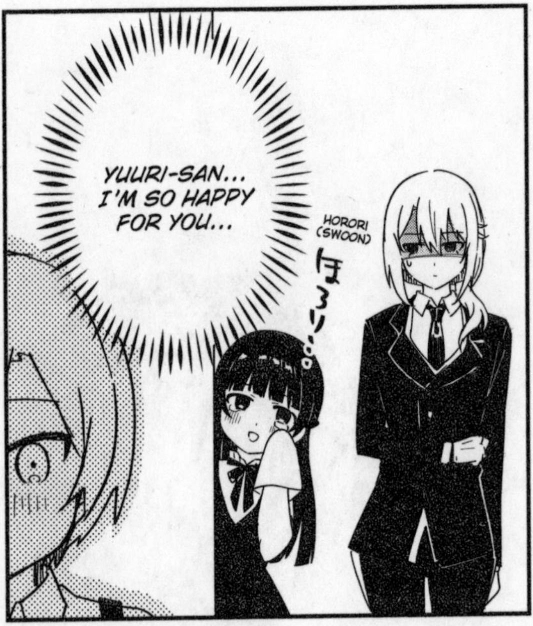
YUURI-SAN... I'M SO HAPPY FOR YOU...
HORORI (SWOON)
ほろリ

The Maid I Hired Recently Is Mysterious

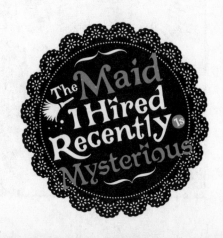

CHAPTER 23

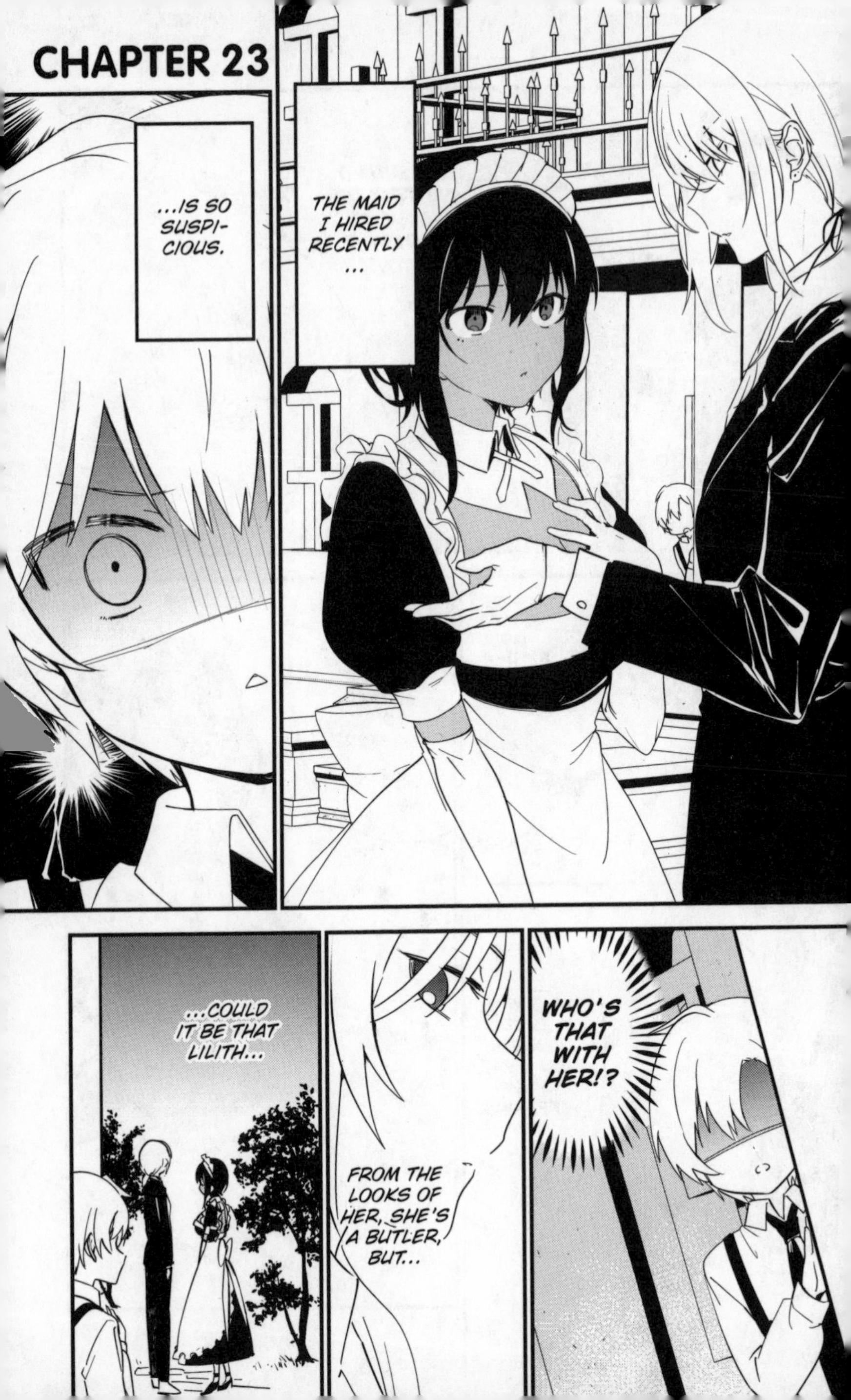
THE MAID I HIRED RECENTLY...
...IS SO SUSPICIOUS.
WHO'S THAT WITH HER!?
FROM THE LOOKS OF HER, SHE'S A BUTLER, BUT...
...COULD IT BE THAT LILITH...

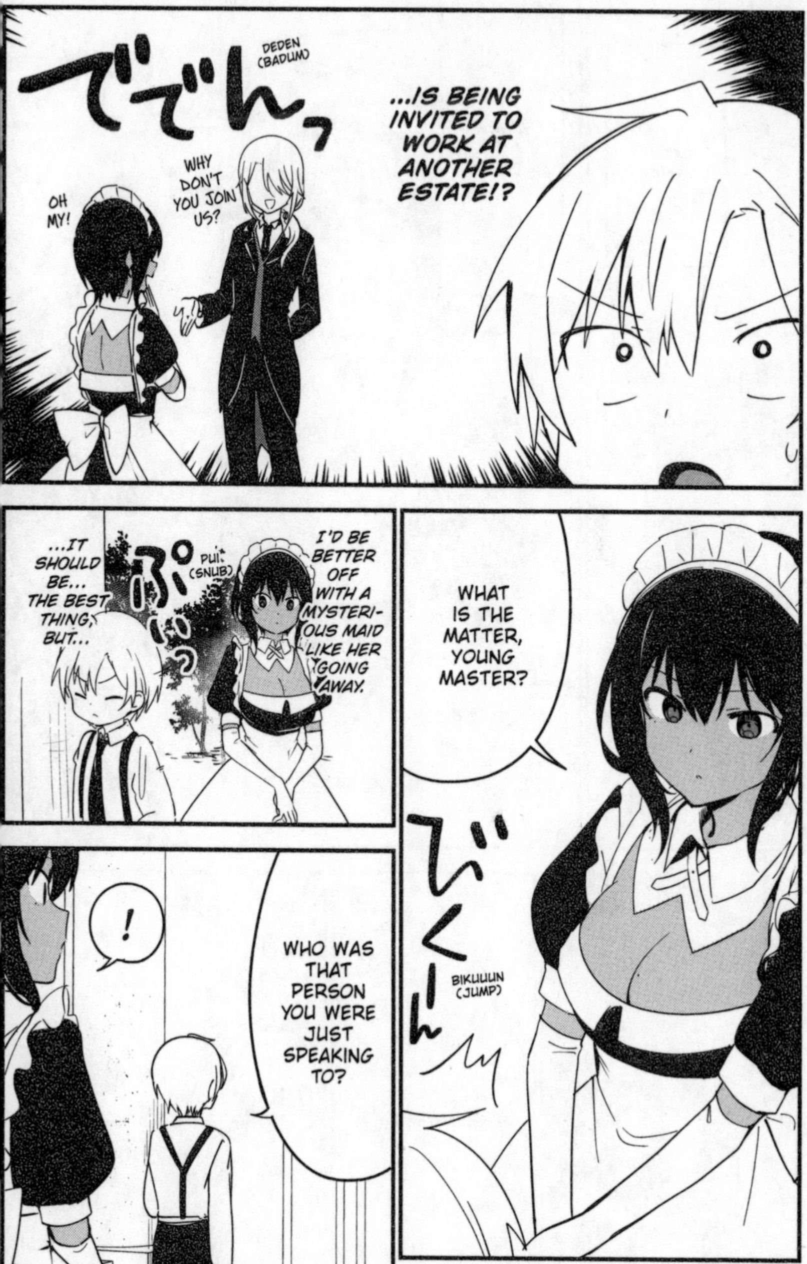
...IS BEING INVITED TO WORK AT ANOTHER ESTATE!?
ででんっ
DEDEN (BADUM)
WHY DON'T YOU JOIN US?
OH MY!
WHAT IS THE MATTER, YOUNG MASTER?
びくーん
BIKUUUN (JUMP)
I'D BE BETTER OFF WITH A MYSTERIOUS MAID LIKE HER GOING AWAY.
ぷいっ
PUI (SNUB)
...IT SHOULD BE... THE BEST THING, BUT...
WHO WAS THAT PERSON YOU WERE JUST SPEAKING TO?
!

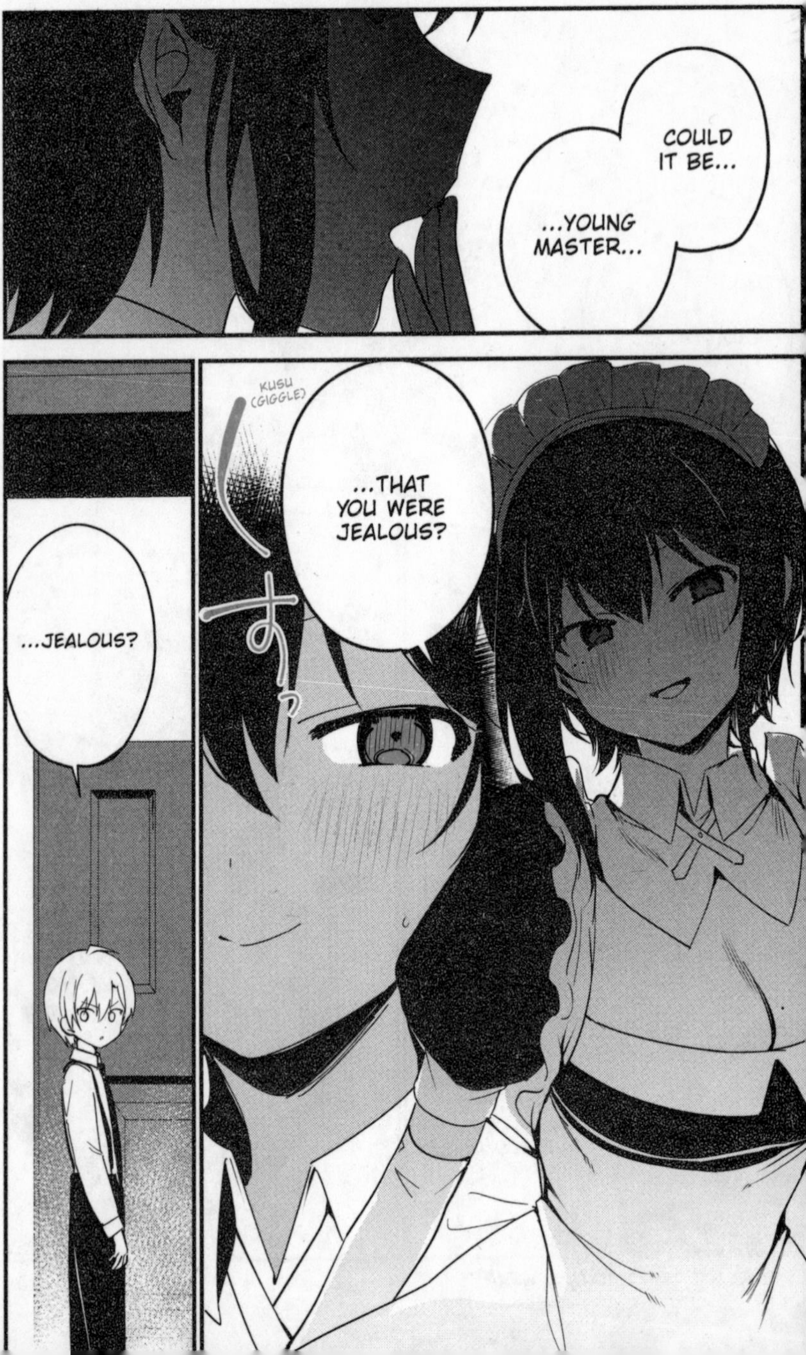
COULD IT BE...
...YOUNG MASTER...
くすっ
KUSU (GIGGLE)
...THAT YOU WERE JEALOUS?
...JEALOUS?

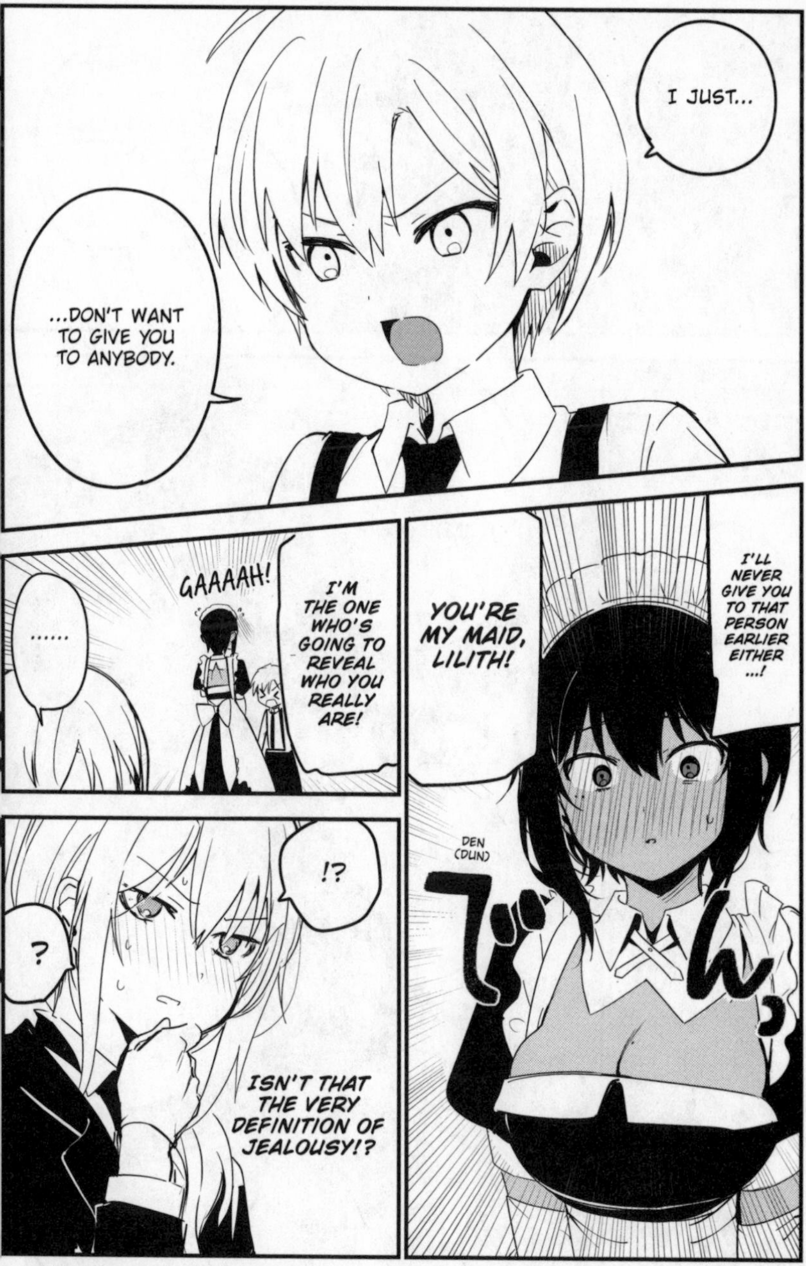
I JUST...
...DON'T WANT TO GIVE YOU TO ANYBODY.
I'LL NEVER GIVE YOU TO THAT PERSON EARLIER EITHER ...!
YOU'RE MY MAID, LILITH!
DEN (DUN)
I'M THE ONE WHO'S GOING TO REVEAL WHO YOU REALLY ARE!
GAAAAH!
......
!?
?
ISN'T THAT THE VERY DEFINITION OF JEALOUSY!?

SHE HAPPENED TO OVERHEAR.

BONUS STORY ②

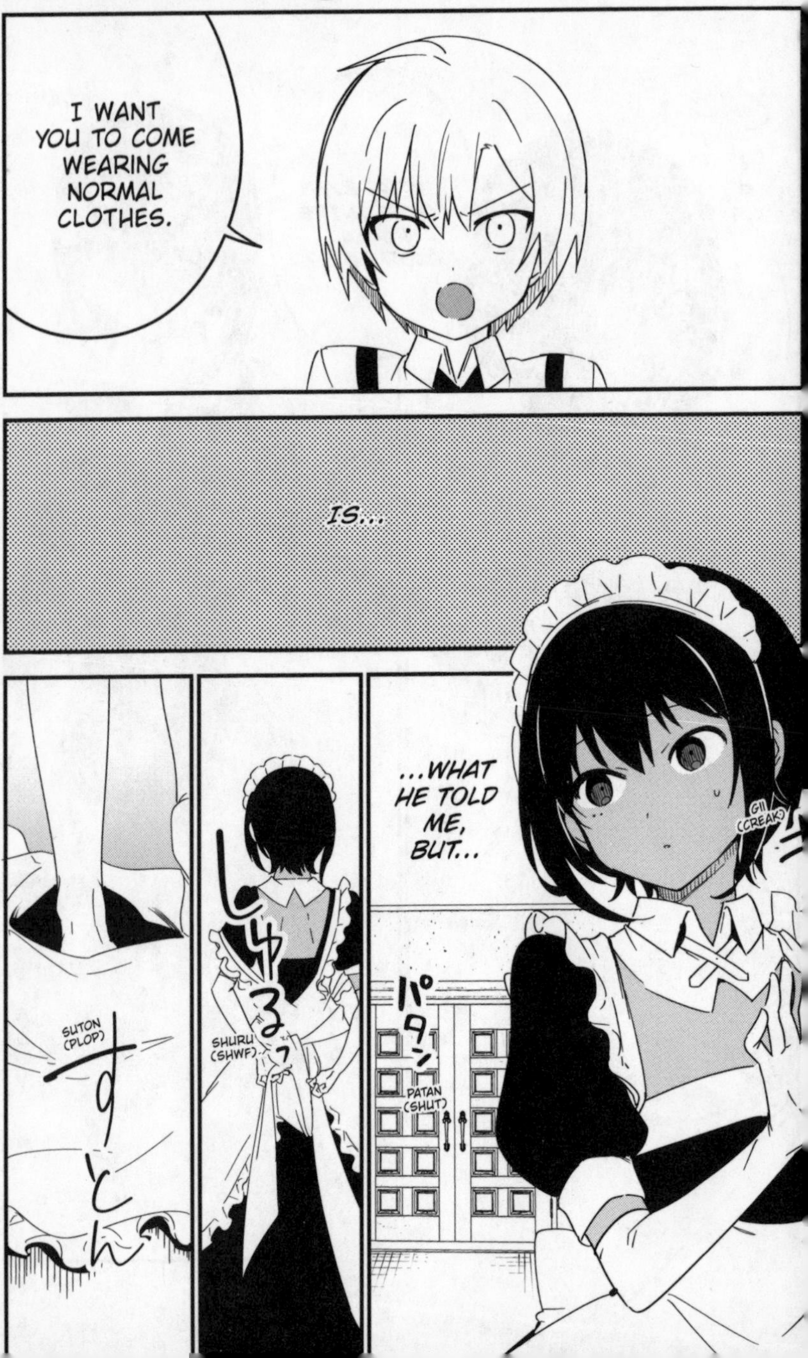
I WANT YOU TO COME WEARING NORMAL CLOTHES.
IS...
...WHAT HE TOLD ME, BUT...
GII (CREAK)
パタン
PATAN (SHUT)
SHURU (SHWF)
SUTON (PLOP)

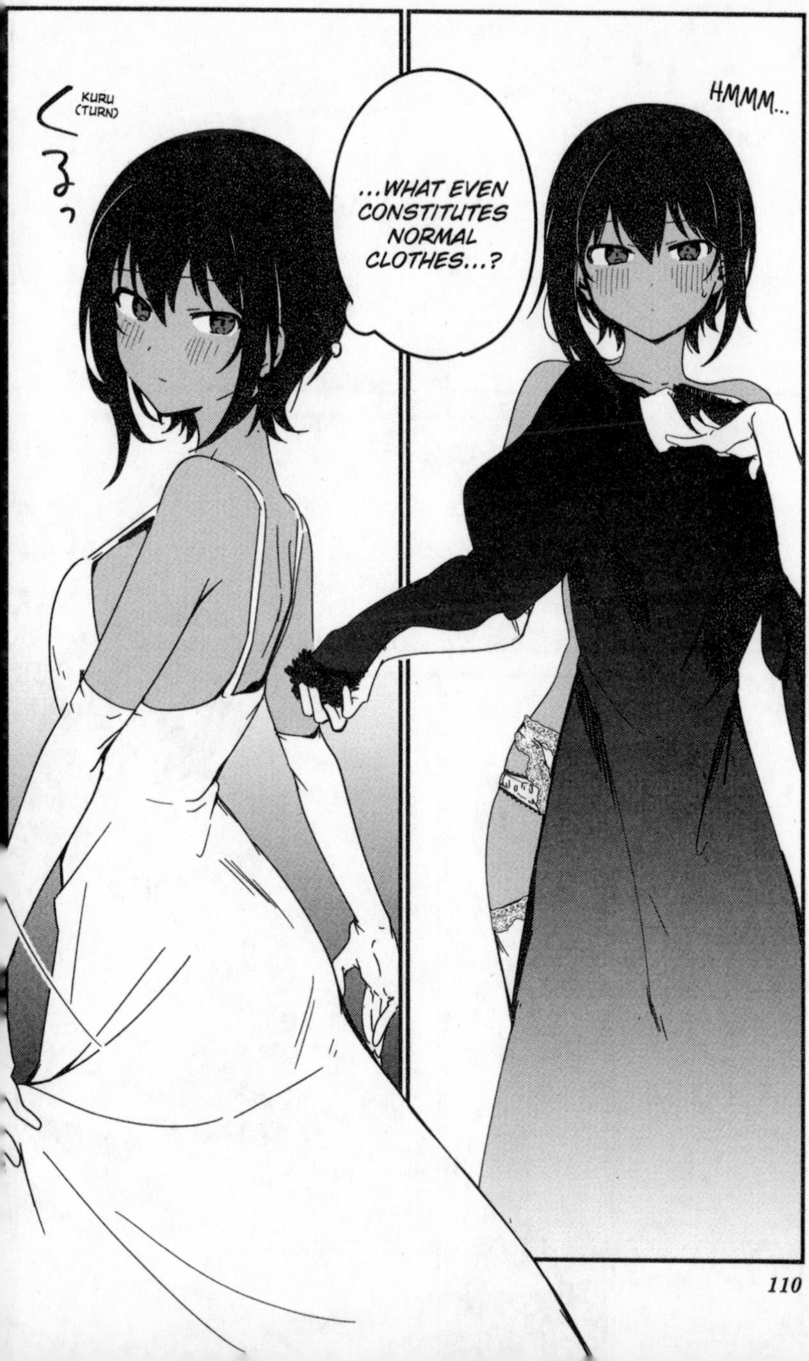
HMMM...
...WHAT EVEN CONSTITUTES NORMAL CLOTHES...?
くるっ
KURU (TURN)

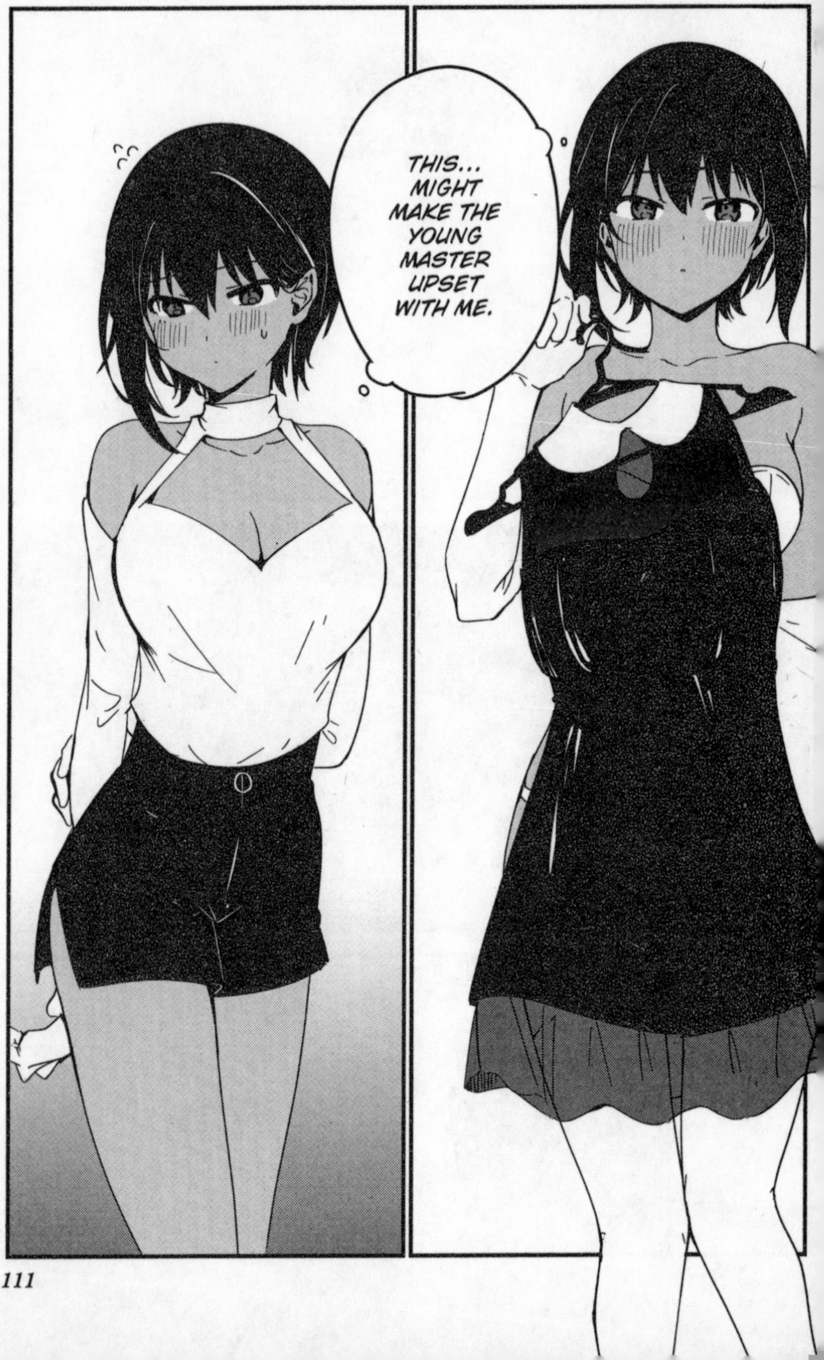
THIS... MIGHT MAKE THE YOUNG MASTER UPSET WITH ME.

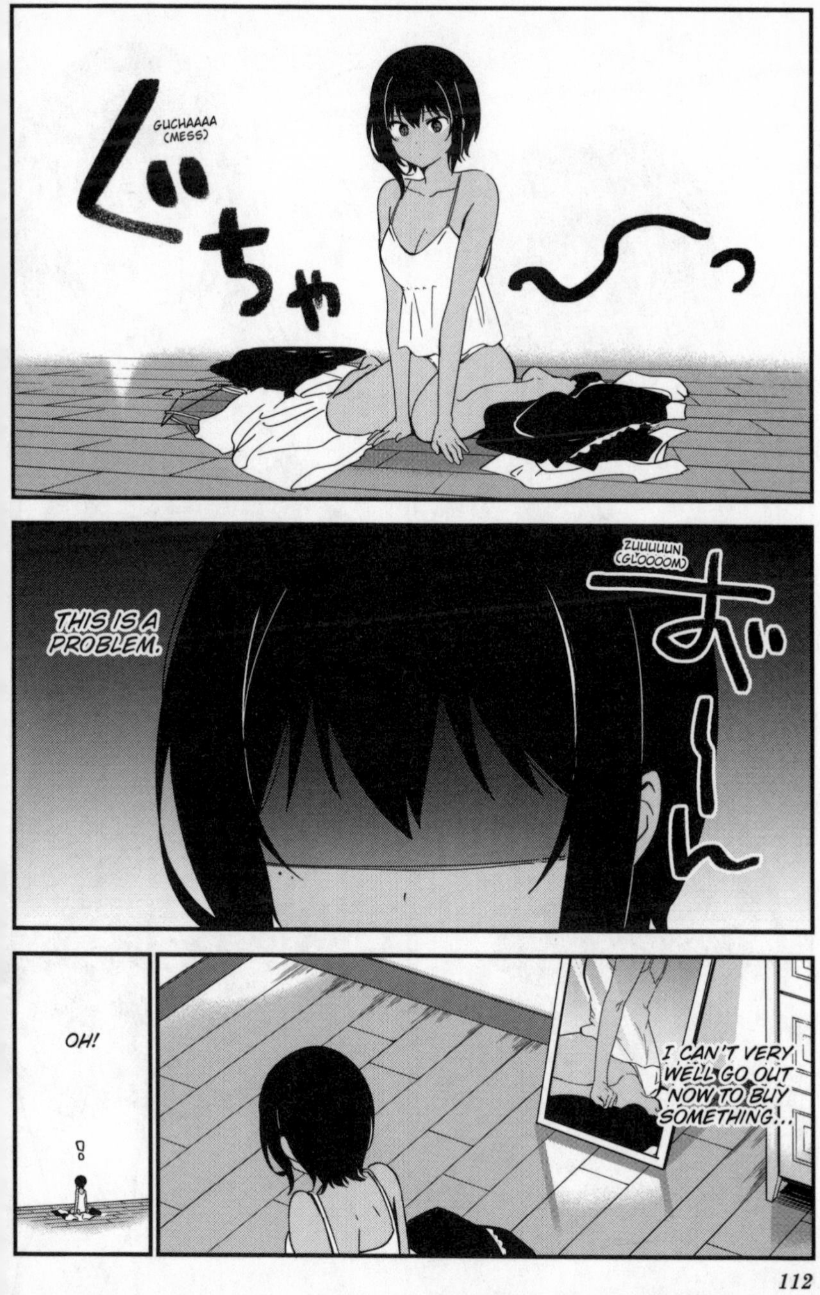
ぐちゃ〜っ
GUCHAAAA (MESS)
ず〜ん
ZUUUUUN (GLOOOOM)
THIS IS A PROBLEM.
I CAN'T VERY WELL GO OUT NOW TO BUY SOMETHING...
OH!
!?

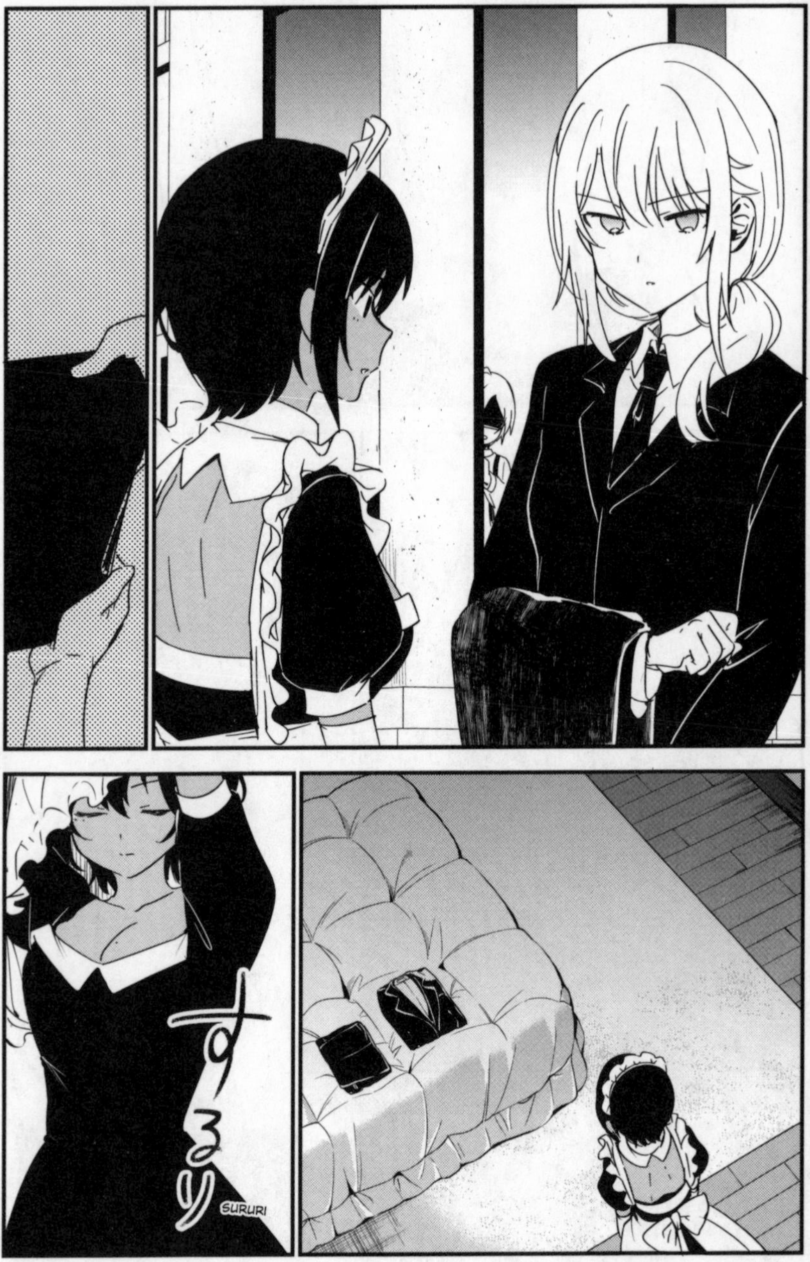
するり
SURURI

PICHI (TIGHT)
ぴちっ

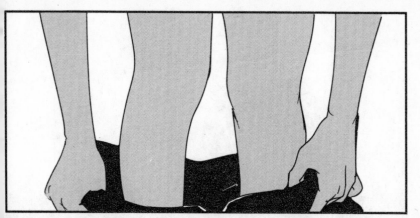

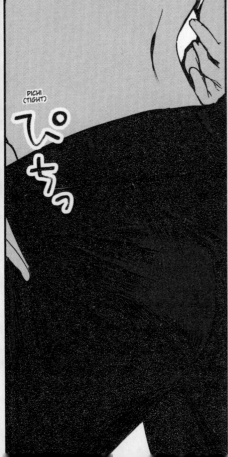

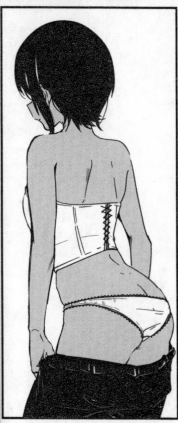

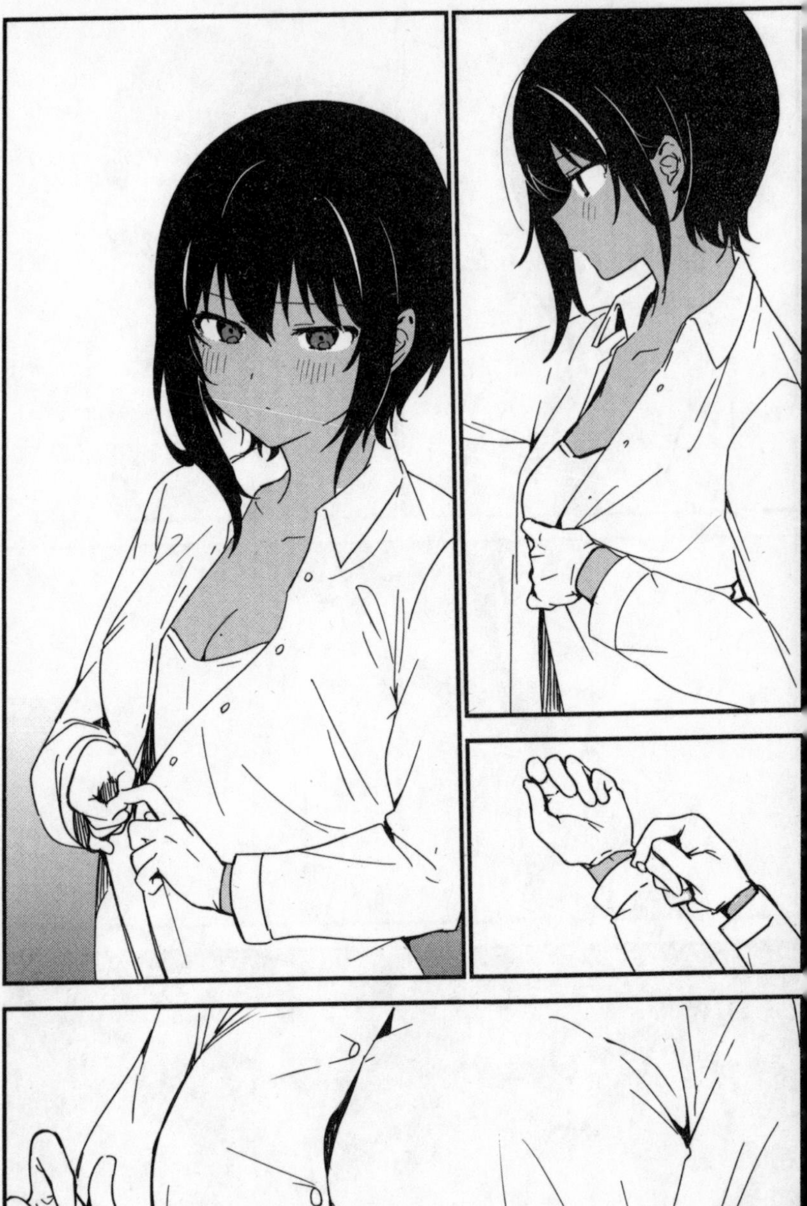

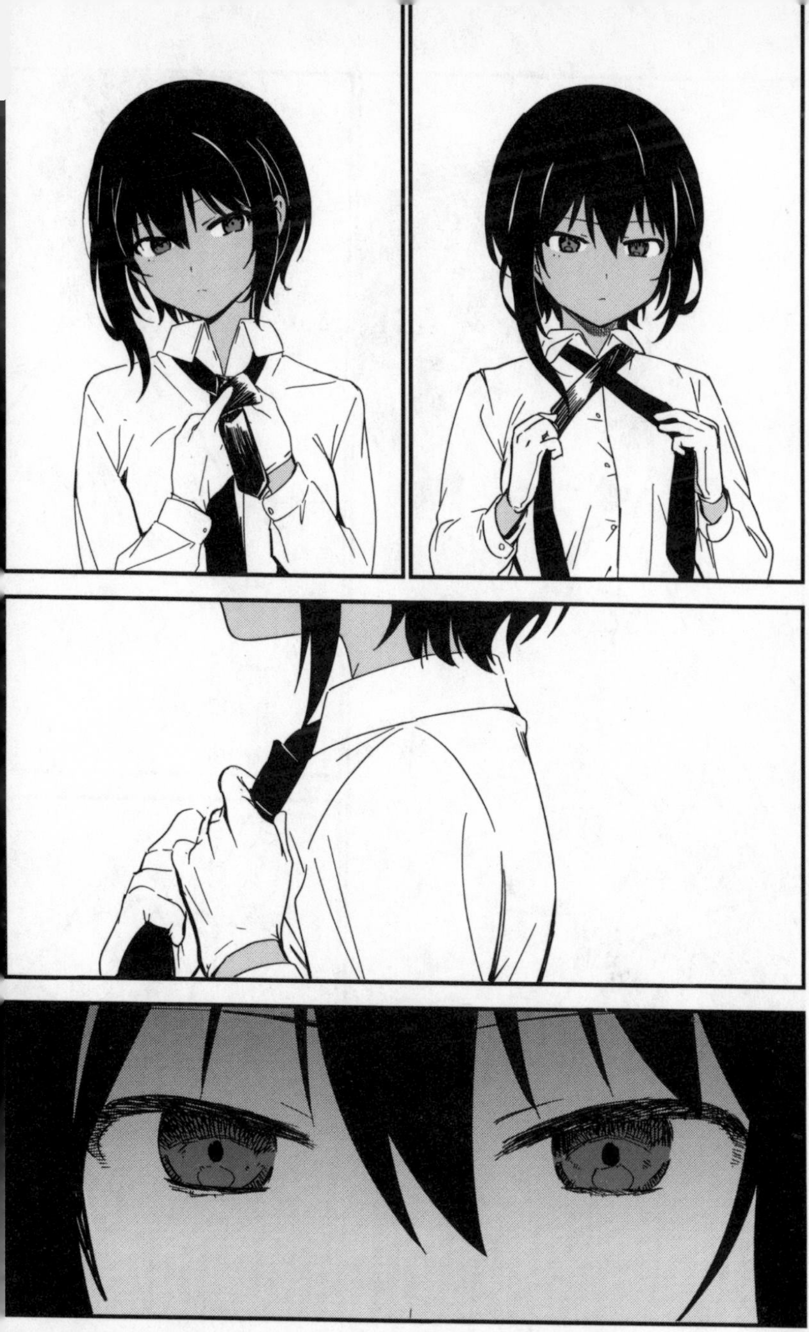

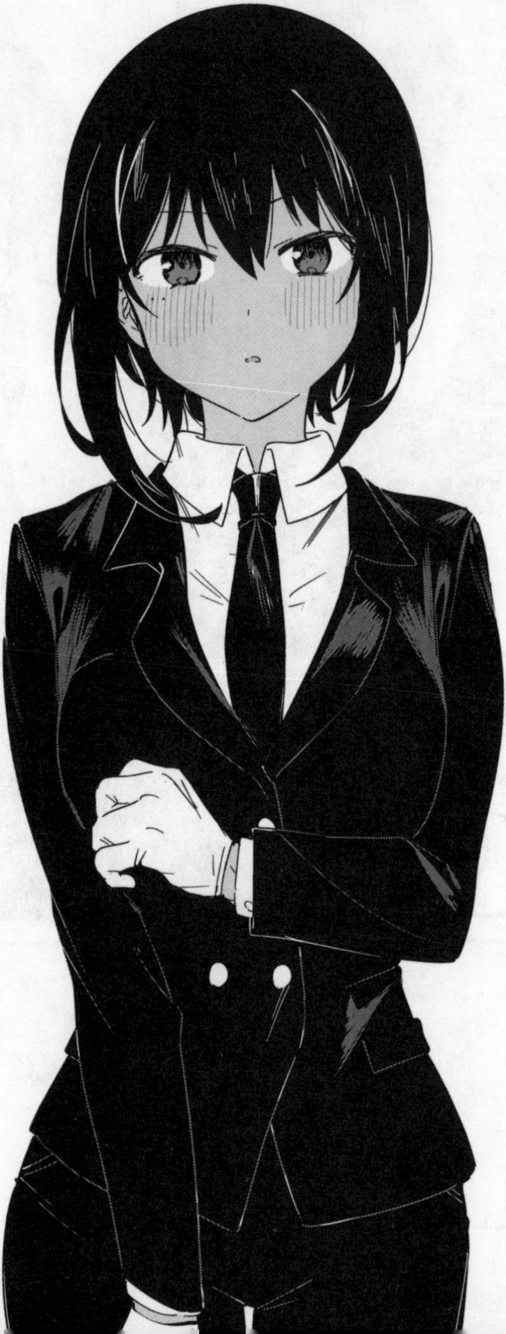

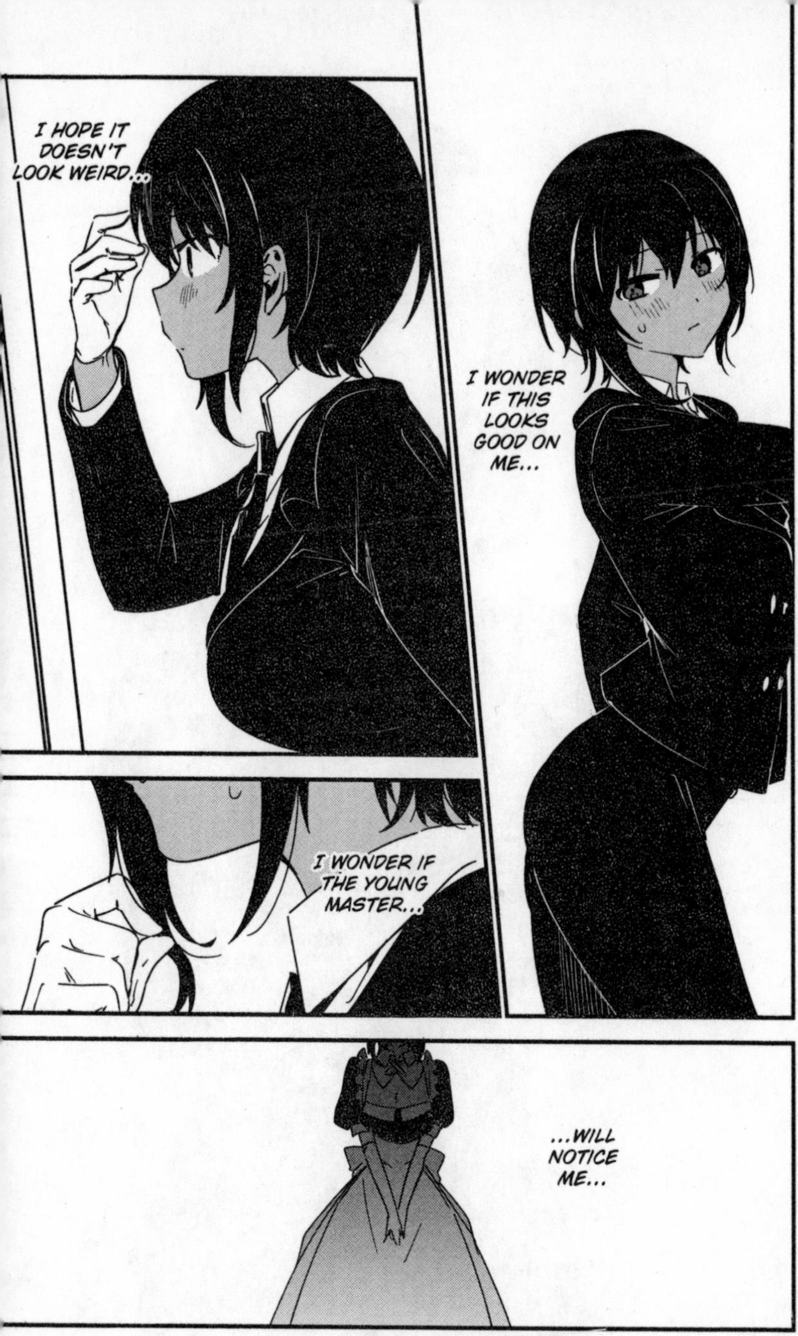
I WONDER IF THIS LOOKS GOOD ON ME...
I HOPE IT DOESN'T LOOK WEIRD...
I WONDER IF THE YOUNG MASTER...
...WILL NOTICE ME...

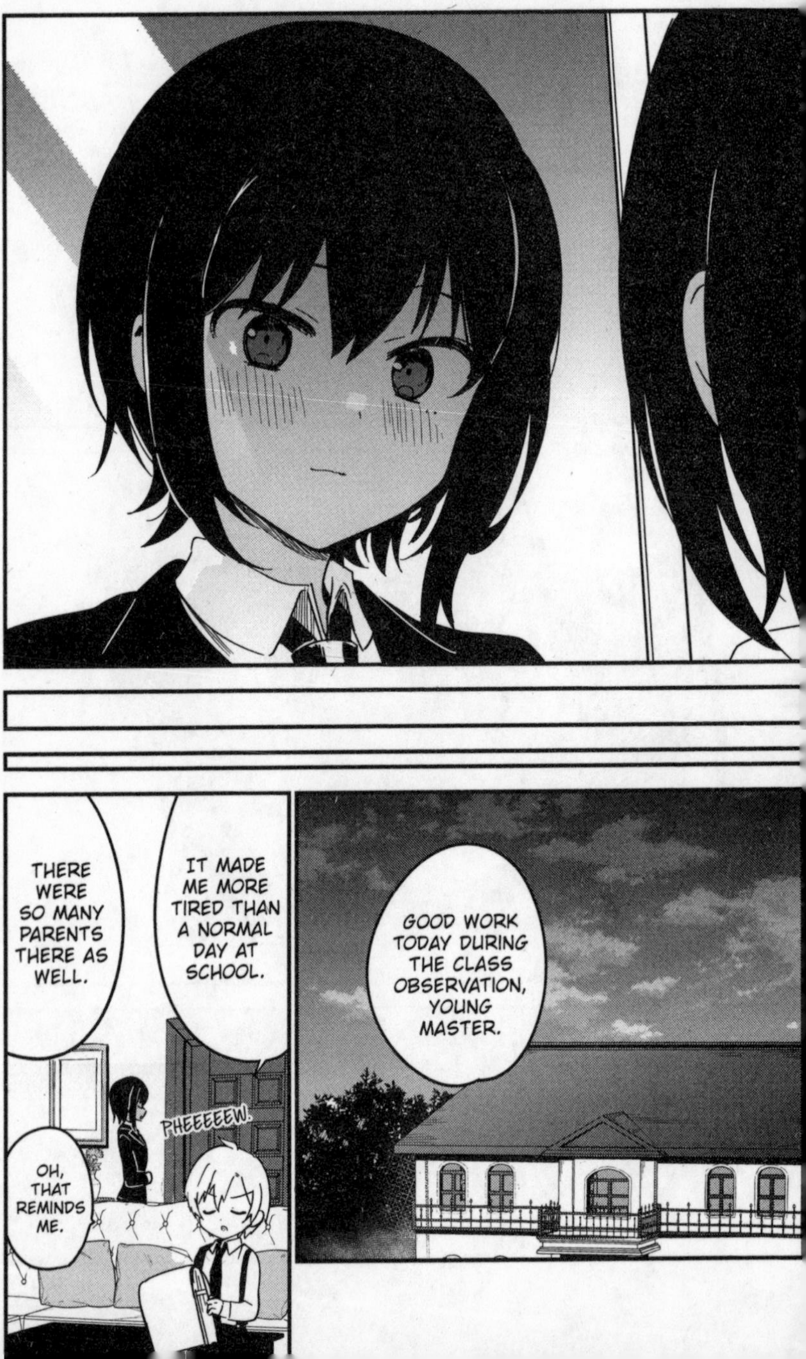
GOOD WORK TODAY DURING THE CLASS OBSERVATION, YOUNG MASTER.
IT MADE ME MORE TIRED THAN A NORMAL DAY AT SCHOOL.
THERE WERE SO MANY PARENTS THERE AS WELL.
PHEEEEEW.
OH, THAT REMINDS ME.

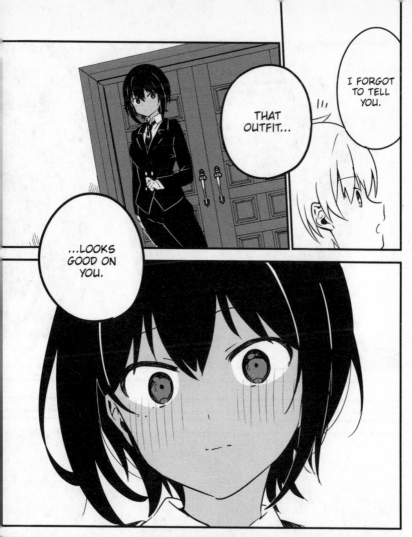

I FORGOT TO TELL YOU.

THAT OUTFIT...

...LOOKS GOOD ON YOU.

I REALLY AM NO MATCH FOR YOU... YOUNG MASTER...

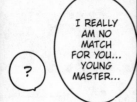

?

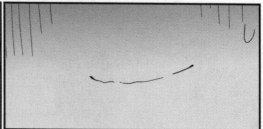

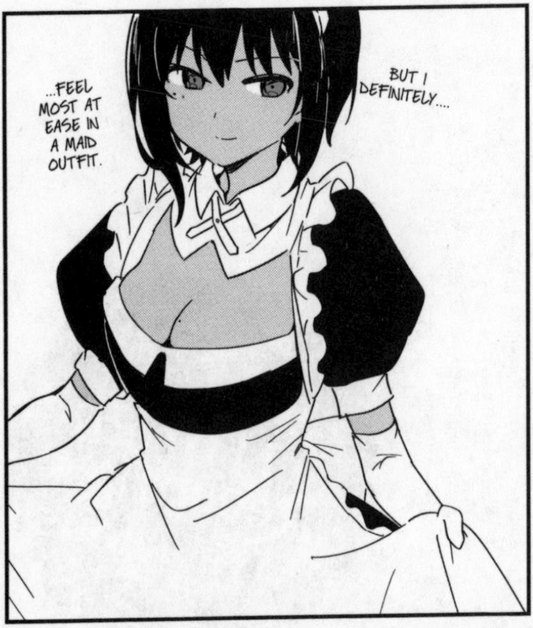
BUT I DEFINITELY....
...FEEL MOST AT EASE IN A MAID OUTFIT.

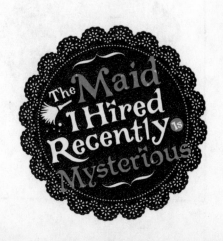

The Maid I Hired Recently is Mysterious

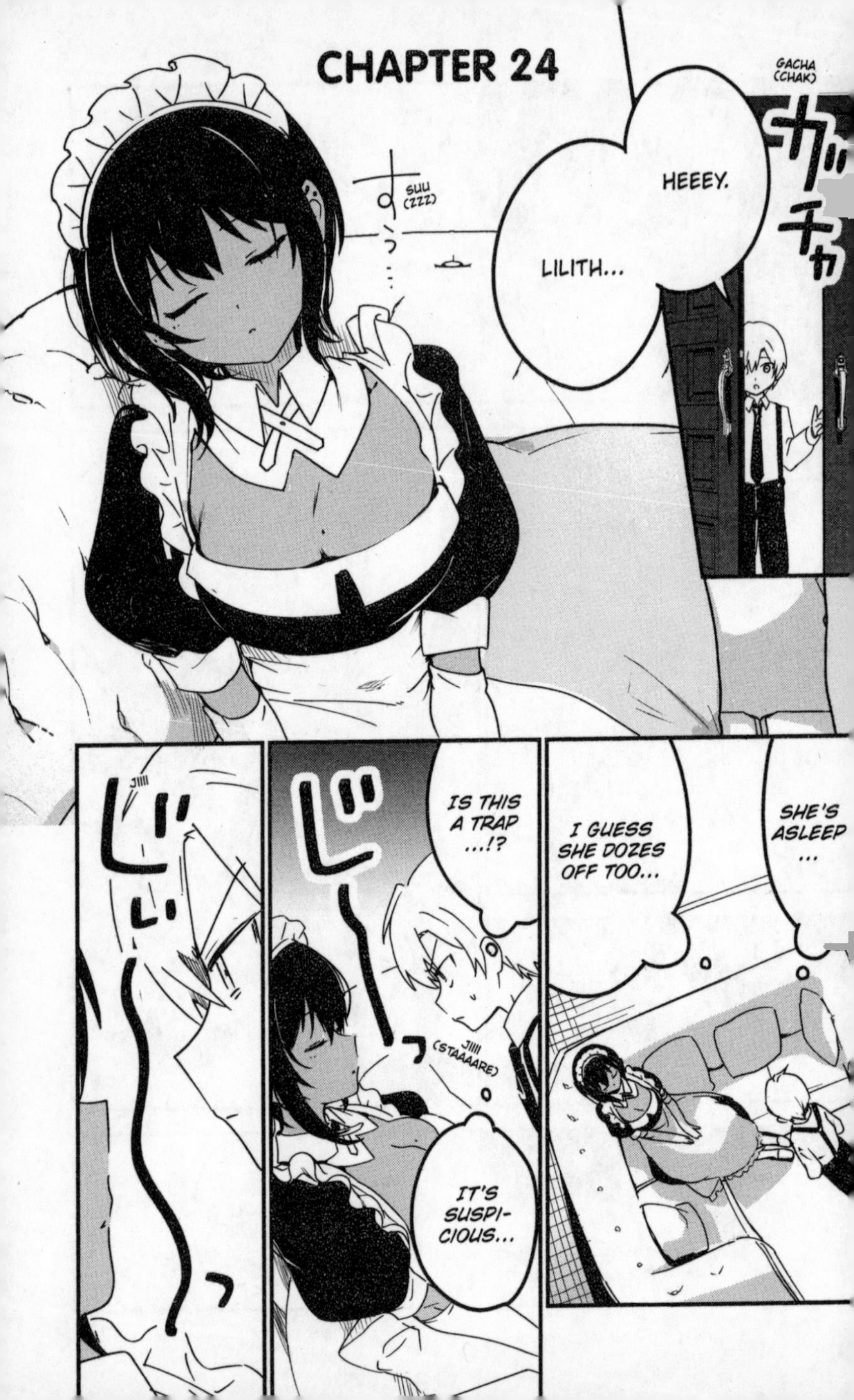
CHAPTER 24
ガチャ
GACHA (CHAK)
HEEEY.
LILITH...
すぅ…
SUU (ZZZ)
SHE'S ASLEEP...
I GUESS SHE DOZES OFF TOO...
IS THIS A TRAP ...!?
JIIII (STAAAARE)
IT'S SUSPICIOUS...
JIIII

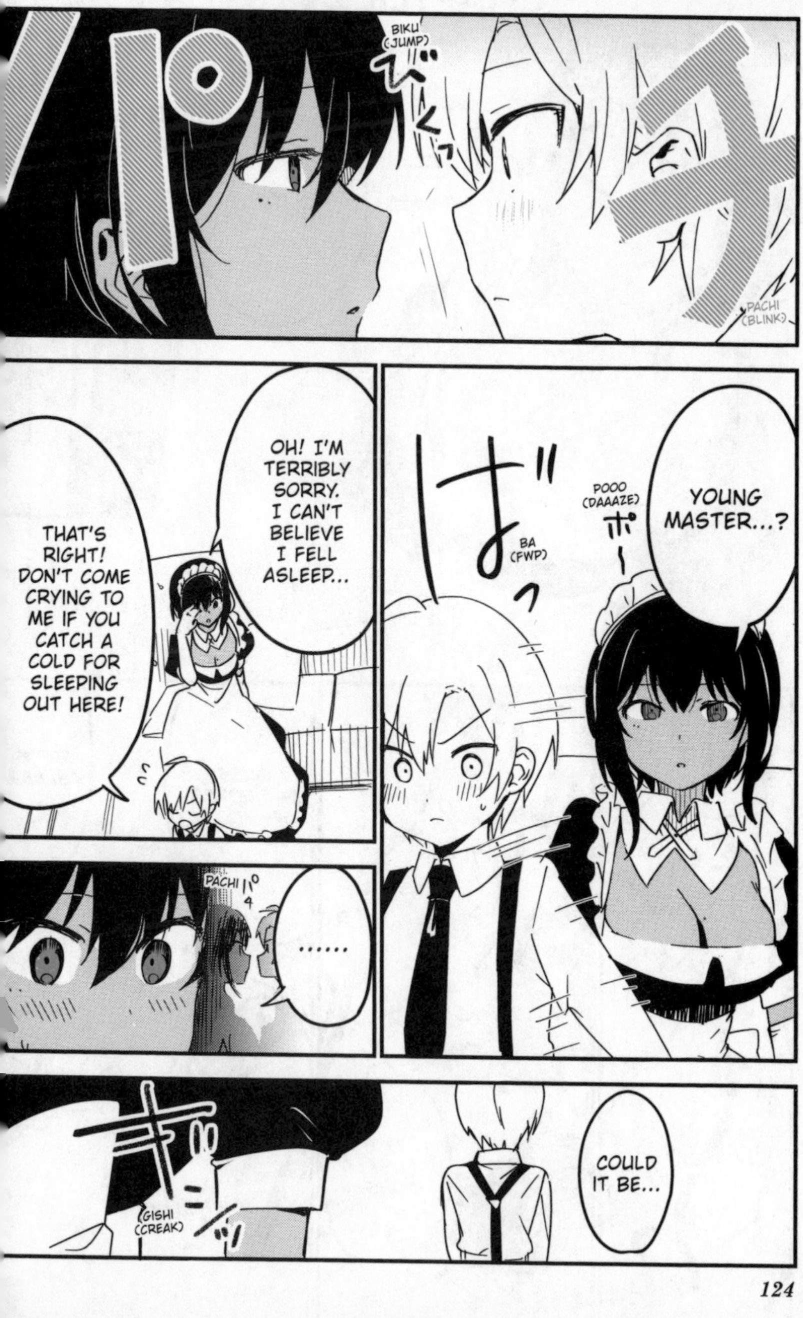
BIKU (JUMP)
PACHI (BLINK)
YOUNG MASTER...?
POOO (DAAAZE)
BA (FWP)
OH! I'M TERRIBLY SORRY. I CAN'T BELIEVE I FELL ASLEEP...
THAT'S RIGHT! DON'T COME CRYING TO ME IF YOU CATCH A COLD FOR SLEEPING OUT HERE!
PACHI
......
COULD IT BE...
GISHI (CREAK)

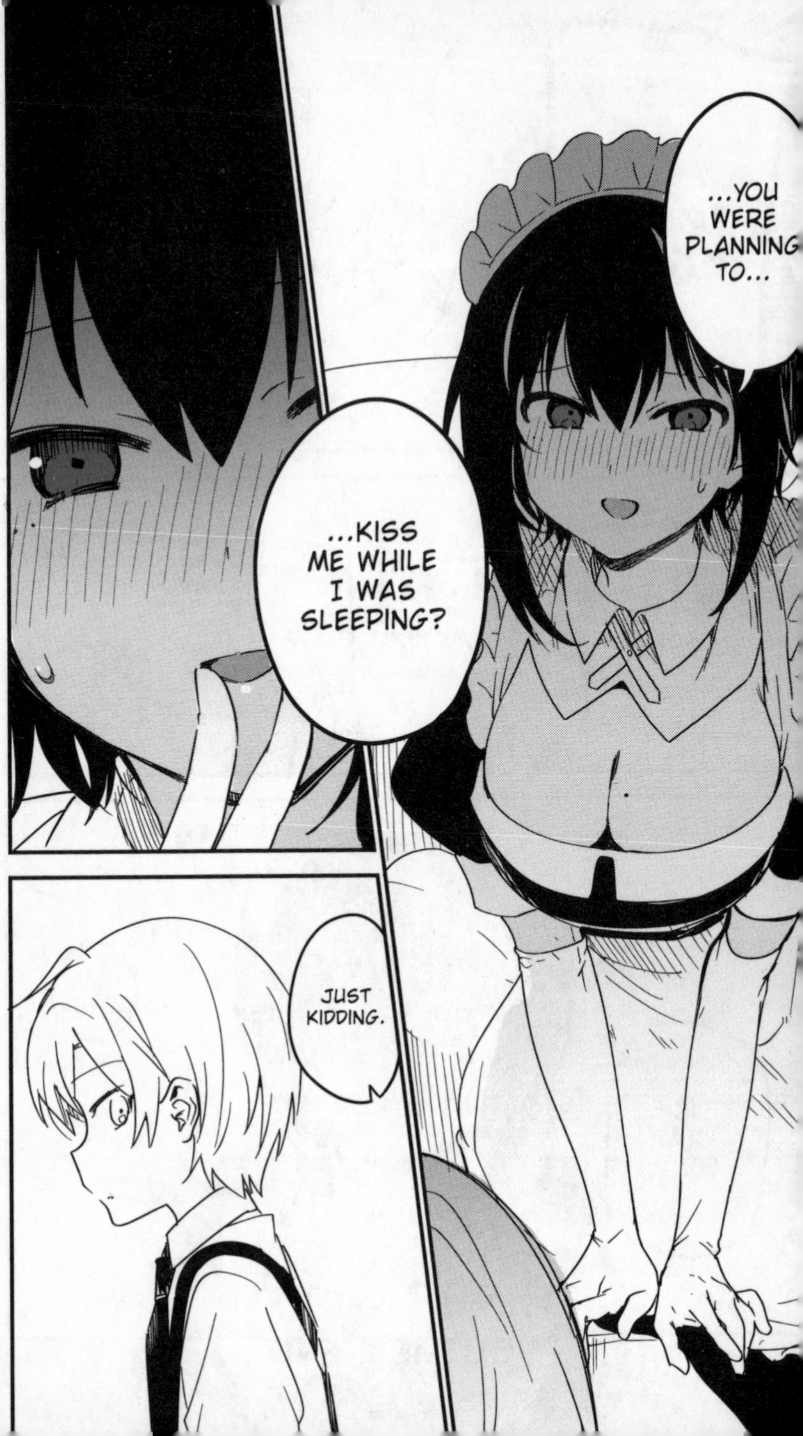
...YOU WERE PLANNING TO...
...KISS ME WHILE I WAS SLEEPING?
JUST KIDDING.

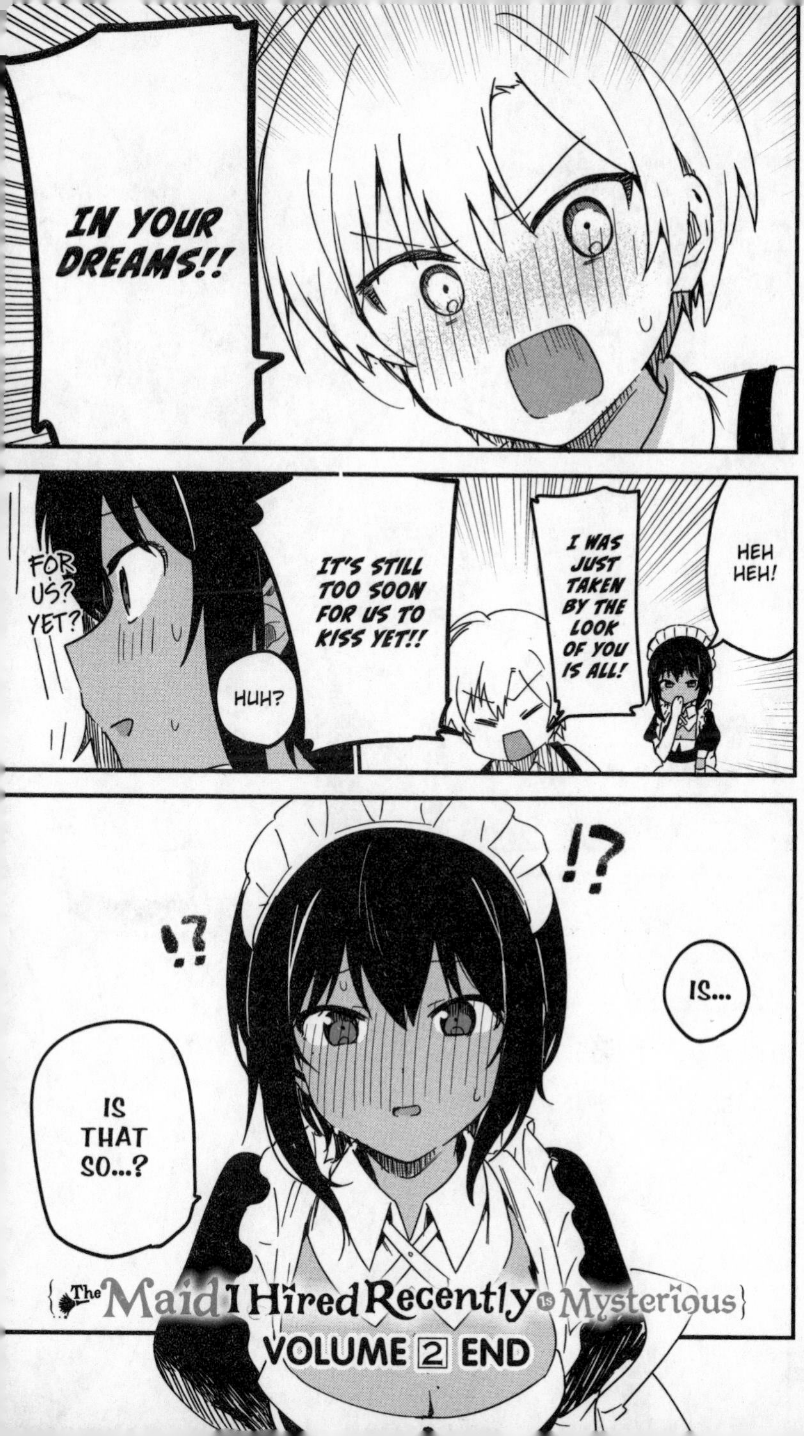
IN YOUR DREAMS!!
HEH HEH!
I WAS JUST TAKEN BY THE LOOK OF YOU IS ALL!
IT'S STILL TOO SOON FOR US TO KISS YET!!
HUH?
FOR US? YET?
!?
!?
IS...
IS THAT SO...?
The Maid I Hired Recently Is Mysterious
VOLUME 2 END

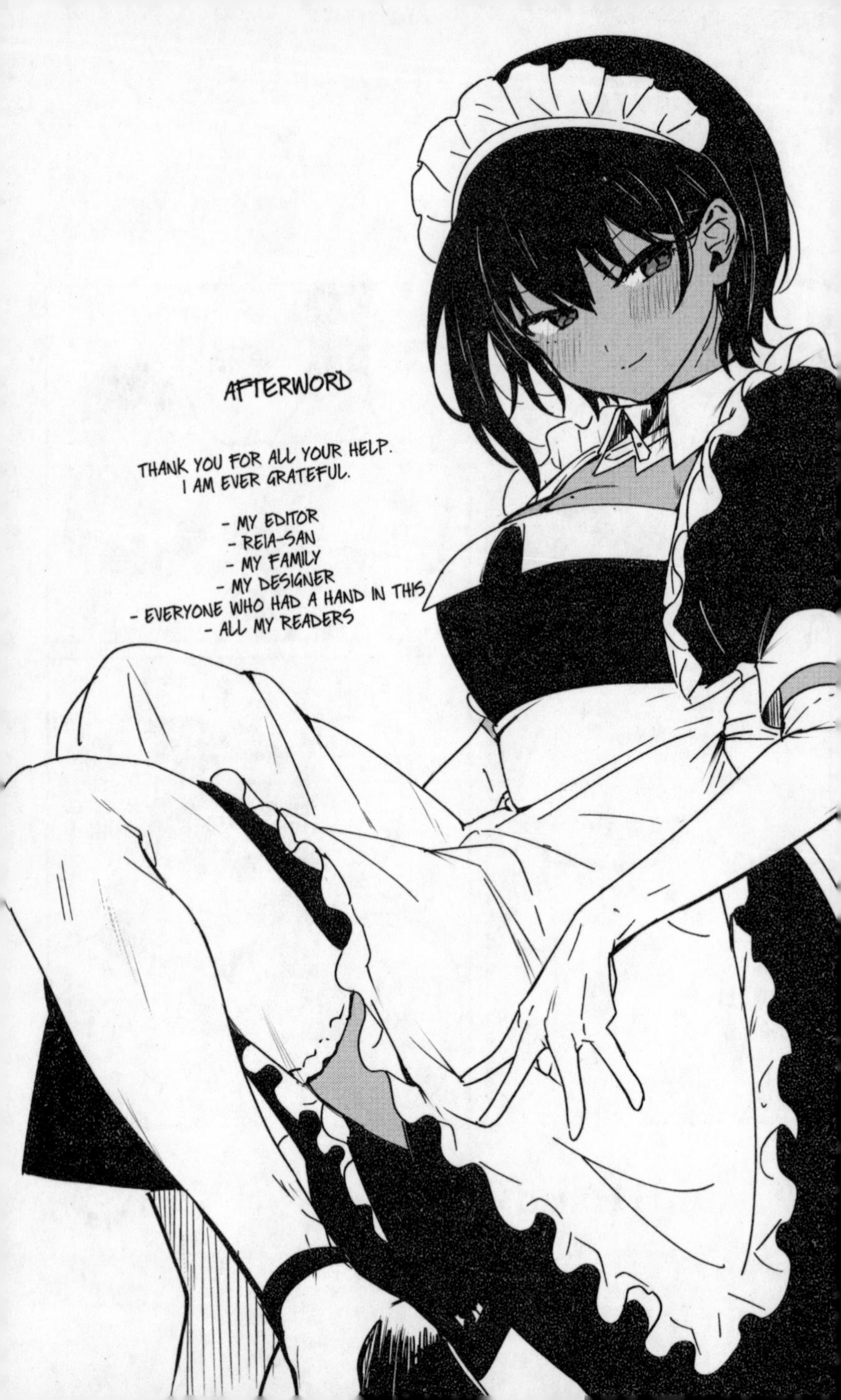
AFTERWORD
THANK YOU FOR ALL YOUR HELP.
I AM EVER GRATEFUL.
- MY EDITOR
- REIA-SAN
- MY FAMILY
- MY DESIGNER
- EVERYONE WHO HAD A HAND IN THIS
- ALL MY READERS

A REQUEST FROM THE YOUNG MASTER ≠ COMMUNICATION?

NEXT VOLUME PREVIEW

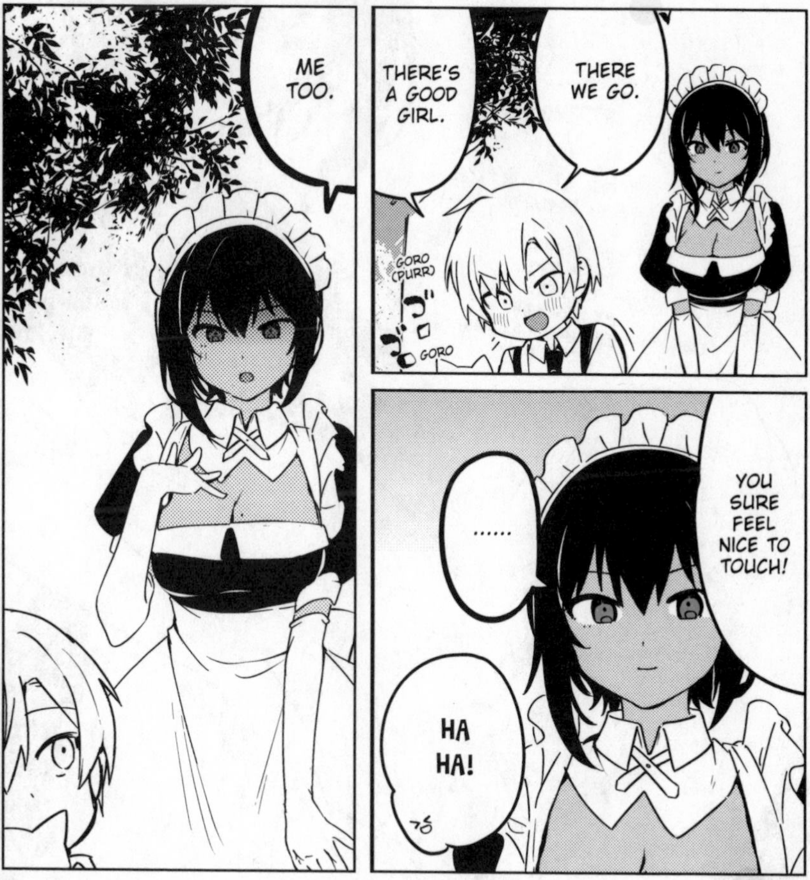
THERE WE GO.
THERE'S A GOOD GIRL.
GORO (PURR)
GORO
YOU SURE FEEL NICE TO TOUCH!
......
HA HA!
ME TOO.

The Maid I Hired Recently is Mysterious 3

ON SALE IN SUMMER 2022!

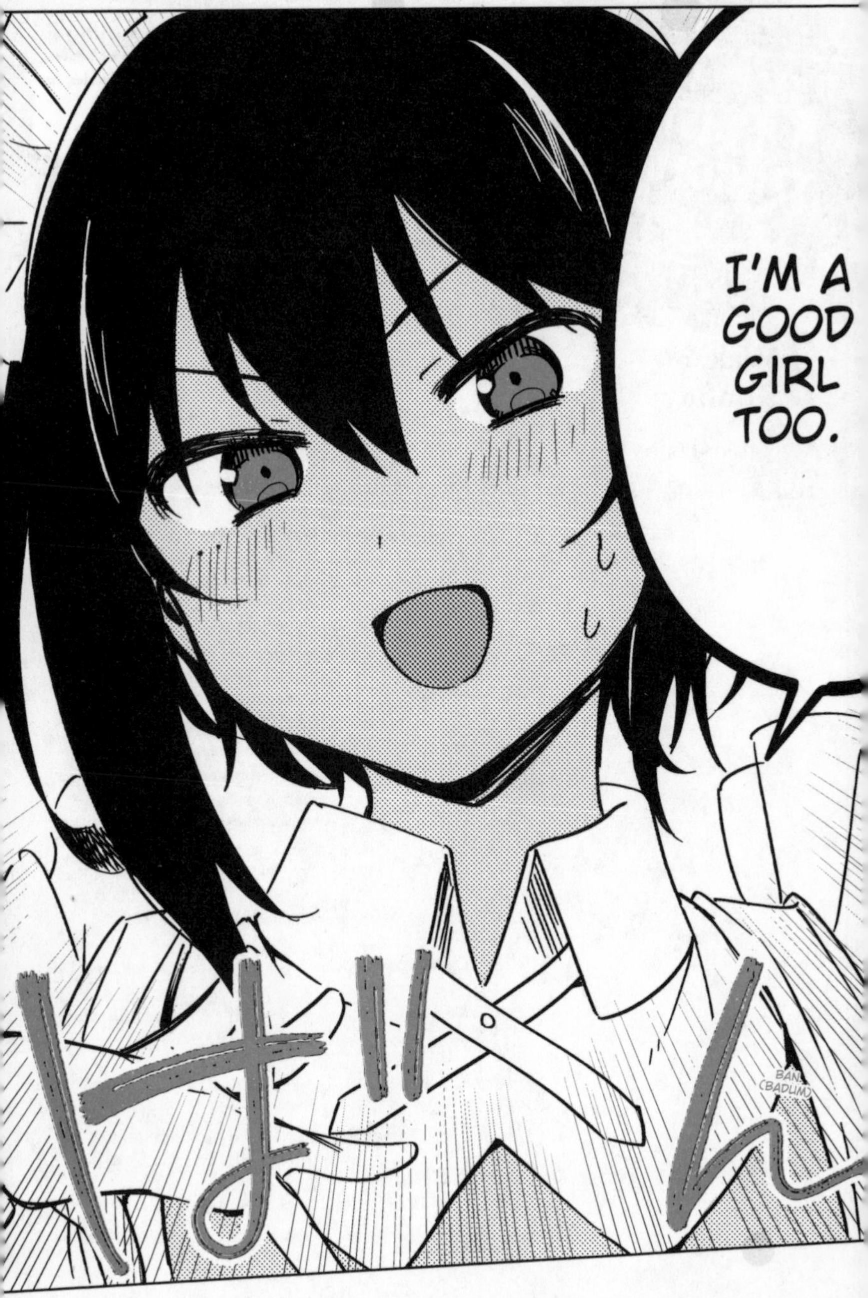
I'M A GOOD GIRL TOO.
ばーん
BAN (BADUM)

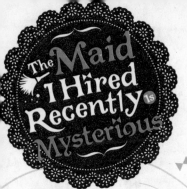

The Maid I Hired Recently Is Mysterious

2 Wakame Konbu

Translation: Christine Dashiell

Lettering: Brandon Bovia

SA...

©2020 wakame Konbu/SQUARE ENIX CO., LTD.

First published in Japan in 2020 by SQUARE ENIX CO., LTD. English translation rights arranged with SQUARE ENIX CO., LTD. and Yen Press, LLC through Tuttle-Mori Agency, Inc.

English translation ©2022 by SQUARE ENIX CO., LTD.

Yen Press
150 West 30th Street, 19th Floor
New York, NY 10001

Visit us at yenpress.com
facebook.com/yenpress
twitter.com/yenpress
yenpress.tumblr.com
instagram.com/yenpress

First Yen Press Edition: January 2022

Yen Press is an imprint of Yen Press, LLC.

The Yen Press name and logo are trademarks of Yen Press, LLC.

The publisher is not responsible for websites (or their content) that are not owned by the publisher.

Library of Congress Control Number: 2021935580

ISBNs: 978-1-9753-2478-0 (paperback)
978-1-9753-2479-7 (ebook)

10 9 8 7 6 5 4 3 2 1

WOR

Printed in the United States of America